THE
NOTATION
OF
MEDIEVAL
MUSIC

Books by Carl Parrish

THE NOTATION OF MEDIEVAL MUSIC

MASTERPIECES OF MUSIC BEFORE 1750
(with John F. Ohl)

CARL PARRISH

THE
NOTATION
OF
MEDIEVAL
MUSIC

Bill Bowen

Toronto.

9.9.74

W · W · NORTON & COMPANY · INC · *New York*

Library of Congress Catalog Card No. 59-10939

PRINTED IN THE UNITED STATES OF AMERICA
FOR THE PUBLISHERS BY THE VAIL-BALLOU PRESS
56789

TO

Catherine and David

CONTENTS

PLATES

Between pages 124 and 125

▄▄

ix

FOREWORD

IT IS gratifying to those concerned with the study of music in American colleges and universities to note the increasing recognition of the values attached to the study of early notation. There are several important reasons why this discipline should be pursued. Perhaps the most obvious one is the added dimension it gives to the understanding of and feeling for the music of the Middle Ages and by extension to that of the Renaissance. Broadly speaking, the present system of notation has not changed essentially since the early seventeenth century, but in the span of some seven centuries before that many thoroughgoing changes took place, presenting many aspects of notation which are faithfully reflected in the manuscripts of successive periods. The manuscripts often suggest through their graphic designs something of the character of the music itself that cannot possibly be transmitted by a transcription in modern notation. The subtle rhythmic nuances conveyed by the Gregorian neumes of the tenth and eleventh centuries, the sense of phrasing communicated by the ligatures, plicas, and conjuncturas of the modal period, the Gothic structural character inherent in the iso-rhythmic motets of the French Ars Nova—all these are reflected in the notational symbols of the periods in which they were written. Even such vital matters as tempo can be derived from a study of the sources, once a fuller understanding of them has been acquired. In brief, the study of the manuscripts leads to knowledgeable performance, the ultimate aim of all work in this field.

A knowledge of notation also gives the study of early music an independence from others who have transcribed it, perhaps incorrectly and with lack of understanding. It is unhappily not rare to see transcriptions published today which betray an ignorance of certain fundamental principles of early notation. In this era of the microfilm it is usually possible to secure pictures of almost any manuscript in a European library, and to check the transcription of compositions in which one has an interest.

The study of notation will also reveal the fact that there remain problems in every aspect of early music that are yet unsolved (some perhaps unsolvable), so that in many cases a transcription is merely a personal interpretation, and other interpretations may also be possible, at least in the light of our present knowledge. An understanding of the evolution of notation can often aid in forming a reasonable presumption on which to work, pending a final solution.

There remains to be mentioned an additional increment connected with this study—the undeniable aesthetic pleasure offered by the manuscripts themselves. They are usually the products of great skill and craftsmanship, and are sometimes very beautifully illuminated; they are truly representative of the artistic sensibilities of the age in which they originated.

It is the aim of this book to present the development of notation from the late ninth century, when the first written musical notation of Western Europe appeared, to the beginning of the fifteenth century; that is, from the several varieties of monophonic notation through the Ars Antiqua, up to and including the Ars Nova. The heart of the book is the series of facsimiles from important manuscripts in this time span, arranged in general chronological order, which are given in the central part of the book. The text is based on a discussion of these facsimiles, divided into periods more or less unified by certain common practices, each period being introduced by a summary of the principles governing the notation of the period. An effort has been made to include the results of the most recent studies in the discussion of each phase, and to present the essential facts and principles in such a way that students can transcribe each of the facsimile examples with some confidence that his results will be in line with the views held by specialists in the field today. To that end, the general plan of each chapter is to present:

1) An exposition of the basic principles that formed the notational thinking of the period based on contemporary theoretical explanation,

and of the present interpretation of these where there is ambiguity in
the old treatises.
2) Comments on the particular problems of each facsimile. This varies
in extent with the individual examples, but the general approach is to
offer the minimum of comment and musical illustration necessary to
make clear the special problems involved.
3) Suggestions at the end of each chapter for the transcription of the
facsimile examples discussed in that chapter; these sometime include
recommendations for alternate versions when different views about
interpretation are held. The transcribed examples will form an an-
thology of the various characteristic forms and styles of medieval
music.

Any author attempting to treat a subject as vast and complex as
that of early notation is faced with the dangers of over-simplifica-
tion as well as of entanglement in a maze of details. I have tried hard
to avoid both, particularly the former. Nevertheless, certain necessary limits placed upon the scope of the study made it advisable to
curtail exhaustive consideration of some problems, and even though
all important phases of notation in the Middle Ages have been included, a certain few side-currents in the main stream of development have not been represented. In such cases, however, reference
has been made to detailed studies, and the student who has mastered
the material will be able to proceed on his own.

Since there is only one other work of similar content published in
English, in fact, the only other modern manual of notation in any
language—*The Notation of Polyphonic Music,* by the distinguished
specialist in the field, Willi Apel—it is to be expected that there will
be some curiosity about the differences or similarities between that
book and this. Dr. Apel's book is more detailed and treats certain aspects of the subject more exhaustively than this book pre-
tends to do; aside from these considerations, the two books
differ in both material and arrangement. This one, for example,
devotes a sizeable section at the beginning to monophonic notation,
a subject not touched upon in Apel's book; on the other hand, the
Apel study is devoted in large part to the notation of the music of
the Renaissance, a period that is not covered in this work for reasons
explained below. Also, the arrangement of materials in this book is
chronological, whereas the other is arranged on the principle of
proceeding from the known to the unknown, a plan that has obvious

advantages. Advantages may also be claimed for chronological presentation, however; the expansion and development of resources of notation are observed in historical succession, and the changes in technique from one period to the next are seen as a matter of logical growth. Not only does this approach appear to be educationally sound, but it is of practical value as well, for it avoids the necessity of anticipating many a problem which arises as the result of elaboration or extension of a previously used process. In the sections of both books where similar material is dealt with, there is no duplication, so that the two may be considered as complementary insofar as the presentation of facsimile examples for study is concerned.

The scope of the present volume has been purposely restricted to the notation of the Middle Ages for several reasons. First of all, there is the practical one of keeping the size of the volume within convenient limits, for this is a book which because of its very nature must be handled a good deal, especially in transcribing the facsimiles. Also, the book is intended as a practical guide through the thorniest stages of notation, and not as a complete history of the subject, even though it is historically directed. Its emphasis upon the earlier periods of written language of music is justified by the fact that a full understanding of Renaissance notation depends upon a thorough familiarity with the notation of the Middle Ages. A student who has worked through the examples of this book should be able to transcribe most of the Renaissance vocal music that he is likely to encounter, for there are not many differences between the notation of the fifteenth and sixteenth centuries and that of the period of Machaut, even though the introduction of white (outlined) notation in the middle of the fifteenth century gave a considerably different visual aspect to the music. There is, of course, a large and important category of instrumental music written in a system of "touch" notation called *tablature*, which is almost entirely a product of the Renaissance; and it is my intention to deal with this, as well as with other phases of Renaissance notation, in a future volume similar in plan and general character to this one. The example of organ tablature from the early fourteenth century that is discussed in the last chapter of the present volume is exceptional, and probably more than a century earlier than the actual period of tablature notation;

it is included here partly for reasons of chronology and partly as an illustration of "things to come."

Acknowledgments and thanks are due to many for valuable assistance in the preparation of this study. To my government I owe the privilege, under the Fulbright Act, of spending a period of studying and gathering material in France, where the priceless collection of the Département des Manuscripts of the Bibliothèque Nationale in Paris was made available to me. To the unfailing courtesy and patience of the officials of this institution, as well as to those in charge of the magnificent collections in the British Museum and the Bodleian Library at Oxford University, many warm thanks are due. To the extraordinary kindness and hospitality as well as to the vast erudition of the Gregorian specialists among the monks of Solesmes Abbey I have a very special obligation, and it is to them that credit is largely due for whatever merit may be attached to the chapter on Gregorian notation. It is my hope that all these, as well as the many others who have assisted in various ways in the compilation of this book, may share my pleasure should it prove that the work may have some usefulness for those who are curious about the ways of early notation.

Carl Parrish

The second printing of this book includes a number of corrections, typographical and otherwise, of errors that occurred in the first edition. I am indebted to several colleagues in American colleges and universities who have made valuable suggestions along these lines, suggestions which are incorporated in an appendix in the back of the book entitled *Corrigenda and Addenda*. In this respect I should like especially to acknowledge the kindness of Edward R. Lerner of Columbia University, and Lincoln B. Spiess of Washington University. The Index has been thoroughly revised, and now includes subjects and titles, authors, books, and periodical articles of special pertinence. One Plate (XVII) has been replaced by a better facsimile of the same composition.

C. P.

THE
NOTATION
OF
MEDIEVAL
MUSIC

1

GREGORIAN NOTATION

GREGORIAN chant and its notation occupy a very special place in the development of Western music. Despite many vicissitudes, the chant itself has remained a living tradition over an incomparably longer period of time than any other style of Occidental music, and its present notation has remained practically unchanged in appearance for about seven centuries. The notes used in modern non-Gregorian notation can be traced back in a direct line to the earliest symbols (neumes) in which plainchant was written. In the general history of notation, the character of notated plainsong became fixed when the neumes evolved to the stage of square notation on a staff, while the notation of polyphonic music continued to develop from the symbols of square notation into the elaborate mensural system of the late Middle Ages, and ultimately to modern notation.

The notation and interpretation of Gregorian chant have been the object of an enormous amount of research within the past hundred years, the bulk of which has been carried on by the monks of the celebrated Benedictine Abbey of St. Pierre at Solesmes, France, although certain independent investigators, such as Peter Wagner, have also contributed important studies. The matter of Gregorian rhythm has been the focal point of much lively controversy; certain opposing theories regarding its interpretation have been supported by an impressive amount of historical, philological, and paleographic evidence on each side.

This chapter will present a description of the neumes and other signs used in chant notation, an account of the most important medieval schools of neumatic notation, and a résumé of the present-day theories of Gregorian rhythm. Concerning present-day theories, emphasis will be placed on the method of Solesmes, the most influential of those currently advocated. This emphasis is justified not only because of the many valuable studies that have issued from the Solesmes scriptorium, and because this method is the only one in actual widespread use today, but also because of the supremely beautiful artistic results that have ensued from its practice. It should be added that in spite of its wide renown, many musicologists do not by any means regard the case for the Solesmes interpretation as closed.

The Neumes

The origin of the neumes (from the Greek word *neuma*, meaning "nod" or "sign") has been a matter of speculation, some scholars believing them to be derived from the Byzantine *ekphonetic* ("pronunciation") notation—the recitation marks used in the musical reading of Scripture lessons—first brought to the West in the eighth century. Many of the signs in this notation are strikingly similar to the western European neume figures; but they are prosodic rather than musical, and indicate melodic formulae rather than independent melodies such as those expressed by the individual notes and ligatures of Gregorian notation. Other mnemonic systems such as the psalmodic signs in Hebrew texts have been studied as possible sources of neumes; but it is generally held today that the direct origins of the neumes lay in the accentuation signs of Greek and Roman literature, ascribed to Aristophanes of Byzantium (*ca.* 180 B.C.), which were used to indicate important points of declamation by marking the rise and fall of the voice.

The two basic signs of the classical grammarians were the *acutus*, /, indicating a raising of the voice, and the *gravis*, \, indicating a lowering. These could be combined to represent graphically vocal inflections on a syllable—   ∧ ∨ ∧   etc. These two signs became the basic figures of Gregorian neume notation. The acutus retained its original shape, and was called the *virga* ("rod"); the gravis was modified to the shape of a dot, called the *punctum* ("dot"). In the period of neumatic notation between the time of the earliest extant manuscripts (late ninth century) and the time when nearly all the styles of neume writing had evolved into square notation on a staff (late twelfth century), the virga and punctum remained the symbols for single notes. All other neumes—those of two notes or more joined together, called *ligatures*—are essentially combinations of these two signs.

A comparative table of the neumes of certain important schools of neume writing is given in Fig. 1; the neumes are arranged from left to right in a roughly chronological order. The last vertical column to the right represents the equivalents of the neumes in modern non-Gregorian notation. The neumes in the other columns are those of the schools represented in most of the facsimile examples discussed in this chapter, and are arranged systematically from simple neumes at the top to compound neumes in the fourth horizontal block of columns, below which are the "expressive" neumes that convey certain effects of interpretation to the singer.[1] The names of the neumes are derived from Greek, and in most cases refer to their fancied resemblance to certain objects or movements.[2] The table represents a basic vocabulary of the most frequently used neumes found in chant notations; it should be referred to continually in considering the following paragraphs, particularly that column of it containing the neumes of square notation.

In the earliest neume writing, which was staffless, the virga represented a relatively higher pitch than the note preceding it, and the punctum indicated a relatively lower pitch; however, these signs did not generally indicate the degree of highness or lowness. (Later, when the neumes were placed on the staff, these distinctions of note shape were retained for a while, even though the staff rendered them unnecessary. In mensural music, however, the distinction between virga and punctum was put to use to indicate differences of time value. In modern Gregorian notation, single notes are indicated by the punctum only.)

The two-note neumes are the *podatus* ("foot"), also called the *pes*, which represents a lower note followed by a higher, and the *clivis* ("bend"), indicating the opposite pitch movement.

[1] For more complete tables of neumes see Bannister, *Monumenti vaticani di paleografia musicale*, and *IPM*.

[2] See the valuable study on this subject by Dom Huglo, "Les noms des neumes et leur origine," in *Études grégoriennes*, I, 53.

FIG. I

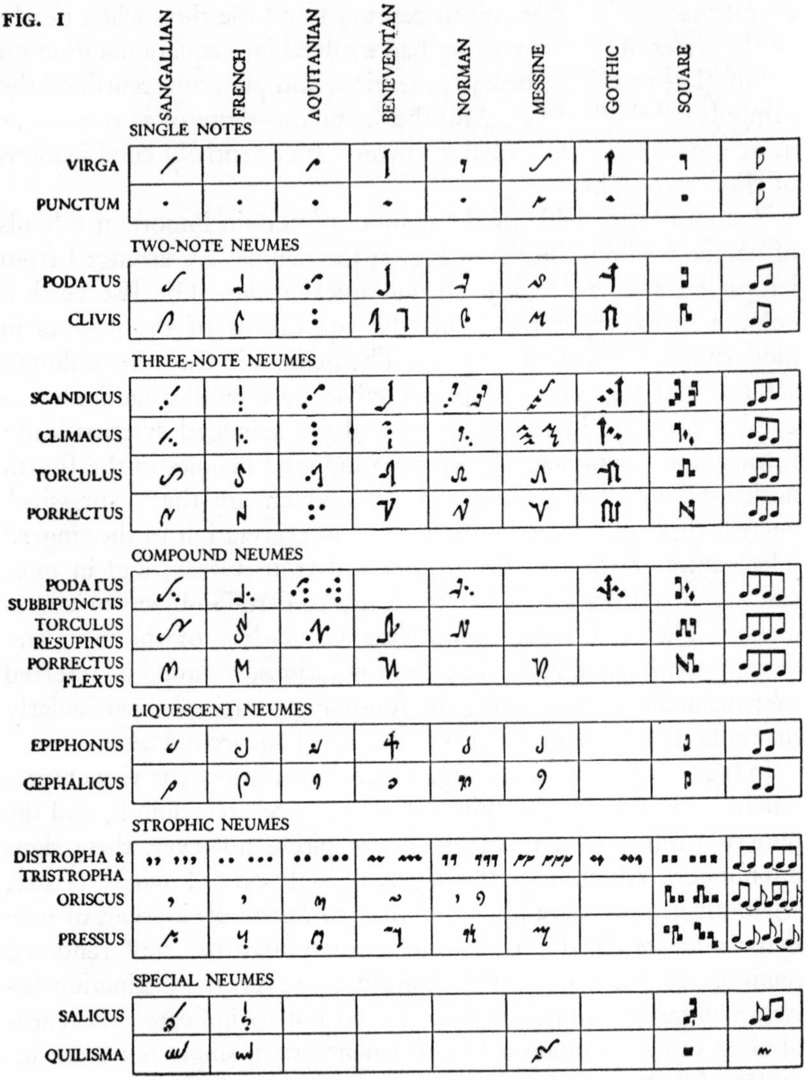

	SANGALLIAN	FRENCH	AQUITANIAN	BENEVENTAN	NORMAN	MESSINE	GOTHIC	SQUARE
SINGLE NOTES								
VIRGA	/	I	⌐	⌐	⌐	⌐	↑	⌐
PUNCTUM	.	.	.	.	.	⌐	.	.
TWO-NOTE NEUMES								
PODATUS	⌐	⌐	⌐	J	⌐	⌐	⌐	♫
CLIVIS	⌐	⌐	:	⌐⌐	⌐	⌐	⌐	♫
THREE-NOTE NEUMES								
SCANDICUS	⌐	!	⌐	J	⌐ ⌐	⌐	⌐	⌐⌐	♫♫
CLIMACUS	⌐	⌐	:	⌐	⌐	⌐⌐	⌐	⌐	♫♫
TORCULUS	⌐	⌐	⌐	⌐	⌐	⌐	⌐	⌐	♫♫
PORRECTUS	⌐	⌐	::	⌐	⌐	⌐	⌐	⌐	♫♫
COMPOUND NEUMES								
PODATUS SUBBIPUNCTIS	⌐	⌐	⌐		⌐		⌐	⌐	♫♫♫
TORCULUS RESUPINUS	⌐	⌐	⌐	⌐	⌐			⌐	♫♫♫
PORRECTUS FLEXUS	⌐	⌐		⌐		⌐		⌐	♫♫♫
LIQUESCENT NEUMES								
EPIPHONUS	⌐	⌐	⌐	⌐	⌐	⌐	⌐	♫
CEPHALICUS	⌐	⌐	⌐	⌐	⌐	⌐	⌐	♫
STROPHIC NEUMES								
DISTROPHA & TRISTROPHA	⌐⌐ ⌐⌐⌐	.. ...	.. ...	⌐⌐ ⌐⌐⌐	⌐⌐ ⌐⌐⌐	⌐⌐ ⌐⌐⌐	⌐⌐ ⌐⌐⌐	♫♫ ♫♫♫
ORISCUS	⌐	⌐	⌐	⌐	⌐ ⌐		⌐ ⌐	♫♫
PRESSUS	⌐	⌐	⌐	⌐	⌐	⌐	⌐ ⌐	♫♫♫
SPECIAL NEUMES								
SALICUS	⌐	⌐					⌐	♫♫
QUILISMA	⌐	⌐				⌐	.	⌐

Three-note neumes which indicate motion in a straight line are the *scandicus* ("climb"), which consists of three ascending notes, and the *climacus* ("ladder"), which consists of three descending notes. In square notation the scale-wise descending second and third notes of the climacus are diamond-shaped. Three-note neumes which indicate motion other than in a straight line are the *torculus* ("twist"), made up of a lower, a higher, and a lower note, and the *porrectus* ("stretch"), a higher, lower, and a higher note. In square notation the porrectus takes the shape of an oblique descending line which stands for the first two notes of the ligature.

Neumes of more than three notes are called *compound neumes;* they are essentially combinations of the neume ligatures and single notes described above. Their names are derived from the addition of certain qualifying terms to the name of the neume with which the compound figure begins; the additional term conveys both the position and the number of the added notes. Three of the most commonly used of the compound neumes are in the neume table. They are:

1) the *podatus subbipunctis*—a podatus with "two puncta below"; if followed by three descending puncta, the ligature is called a *podatus subtripunctis;*
2) the *torculus resupinus*—a torculus "turned back," that is, a torculus followed by an ascending note;
3) the *porrectus flexus*—a porrectus "bent," that is, a porrectus followed by a descending note.

Some special neumes, which occur very frequently in the manuscripts and to a lesser extent in modern Gregorian notation, are so written as to indicate a certain manner of execution as well as of pitch motion. Most important among these are the *liquescent* neumes, which have to do with the pronunciation of the text, and are a warning to the singer that the neume is over a diphthong (*AllelUIa, Elus*), or over the first of two adjacent consonants (*AeteRNum, PraeseNTet*), so that the voice is to flow—that is, become "liquescent"—in going from one to the other.[3] These neumes appear as two-note ligatures which are modified forms of the podatus and clivis, and are called the *epiphonus* ("upon the voice") or liquescent podatus, and the *cephalicus* ("head") or liquescent clivis. The special character of these notes is indicated in square notation by their shape; the second note of the ligature is smaller than the first.

Another special class of neumes, the *apostrophic neumes,* are used

---

[3] Guido of Arezzo describes the liquescents in his *Micrologus* (*GS*, II, 17) and *Regulae musicae* (*ibid.*, 37). *PM*, II, 38, offers an exhaustive treatment of these notes.

to indicate rhythmic accentuation, especially the lengthening of a note. This is done by placing the note to be lengthened "in apposition," that is, by following it with one or two other notes of the same pitch. These following notes are not sounded separately, but prolong the value of the first note. The most important of the apostrophic neumes are:

1) the *distropha*, which doubles the value of the first note;
2) the *tristropha*, which triples the value of the first note. When the same principle is applied to the virga, the neumes are called *bivirga* and *trivirga;*
3) the *oriscus* ("limit"), a single note following in apposition to a two- or three-note neume, giving it something of the effect of a syncopation;
4) the *pressus* ("closed"), a two-note neume following in apposition to a single note. The pressus may follow appositely another two-note neume.

A note similar in effect to the strophic neumes is the *salicus* ("leaper"), a special form of the scandicus in which the second note of the group receives a rhythmical accent.

The list of special neumes is complete with the *quilisma* ("roll"), described in the Preface to the *Liber Usualis* (vii) as "a note with a trill and gradually ascending." It always occurs as a kind of passing tone between two notes lying a third apart. The quilisma also has the effect of retarding the note immediately preceding it.

Oratorical and Diastematic Neumes

Even though the golden age of chant composition is considered to have occurred from the fifth to the eighth centuries, the earliest neumes are later additions to the text over which they appear, and are not found in any manuscript before the ninth century. The remarkable basic similarity in neumatic figures of codices from widely scattered regions indicates the possible existence of a common prototype, of which nothing is known at the present time. In spite of many common features, however, very pronounced regional differences appear even in the earliest examples of neume writing.

A good many of the oldest manuscripts are written in neumes called *oratorical* or *chironomic* (after the Greek word for "hand," referring to the gestures of a choir leader); that is, neumes used only as a general reminder to the singer of the course of a melody. They are *in campo aperto* ("in an open field"; that is, written without staff lines), and give no idea of the actual intervals of the melody. At a time when trained singers knew the Gregorian repertory by heart, a system of melodic reminders such as this filled practical needs satisfactorily. The St. Gall and French examples of neume notation on Plates II and III are oratorical neumes. These pieces would obviously be impossible to interpret accurately today if they did not exist in later versions in which the notation is definite in pitch.

Another kind of neume writing is called *diastematic*, from the Greek word for "interval." In this writing neumes are carefully "heighted," that is, placed at various distances from an imaginary line representing a given pitch, according to their relationship to that line. Certain schools of neume notation display this feature even in their earliest manuscripts. The facsimile of Aquitanian neumes on Plate IV illustrates diastematy of a very precise kind, while a lesser degree is seen in the Paleofrankish neumes of Plate I. Diastematy is implicit even in the oratorical neumes, but not in the purposeful way in which it is seen in the Aquitanian example.

About the end of the tenth century the imaginary line about which diastematic neumes were placed became a real one. At first it was a dry line scratched on the parchment, an idea probably suggested by the use of the guidelines on which the text was written. The addition of another line, and the use of color to indicate the pitch of the lines (begun by Guido of Arezzo) are illustrated in the facsimile of Norman notation on Plate VII; in the original, the upper of the two lines is F and is colored red; the lower is C, colored green. The selection of these pitches was probably due to the fact that they both had the half-step below. The letters F and C, designating their pitch, were also added to the left of the lines; when the four-line staff (the *Tetragram*) was introduced, these letters became the clef signs, and the practice of coloring was abandoned. This evolutionary process did not by any means proceed uniformly; some manuscripts were still being written *in campo aperto* at St. Gall in the fourteenth century. Also, certain styles of notation, notably the Messine (Plate XVI), and its late offshoot, the Gothic (Plate IX), survived after the introduction of the staff, and their

characters were used on the staff even after the use of square notation became general.

Neume Elements

Another characteristic in which neume notations differ is the
manner in which the component elements of neumes of two or
more notes are associated. Three styles may be distinguished:

1) Point neumes, characterized by a predominant, though not exclusive, use of separate points or dots, each representing a note. The dots
are grouped in conventional ways to represent compound neume
figures, but these figures sometimes include strokes to represent two
notes. The expressive French term for this style is "*notation à points
superposés,*" and the only true point neume notation is the Aquitanian
(Plate IV).
2) Accent neumes, characterized by a predominant use of "accents" or
strokes representing notes. Most of the compound neume figures are
bound together in ligatures. The accent neume style may be seen in the
St. Gall, French, Beneventan, and Norman notations (Plates II, III, VI,
and VII).
3) Mixed point and accent neumes, in which the separate points and
connected accents are employed to a more or less equal degree, and the
neume components are not separated to the extent that point neumes
are. These features are seen in the examples of Paleofrankish and Messine notation (Plates I and XVI).

With the thickening and squaring of the neume figures due to
the introduction of the quill pen used in Gothic script, which replaced the reed pen of Carolingian writing, Gregorian notation
acquired in the thirteenth century the square appearance that it
has maintained ever since.[4] A striking instance of this later writing
is seen in the facsimile of the Introit, *Puer natus* (Plate VIII), from
a thirteenth-century Missal of the Abbey of St. Denis, near Paris;
a comparison of this with the same piece in the *LU*, printed in 1950
(reproduced in Fig. 8), will reveal remarkably few essential differences.

The evolution of neume writing toward the precision of that of
Puer natus was not without losses in subtleties of performance indications, such as the liquescents, quilisma, and other interpretative

[4] See pictures of quills and writing tools used by scribes in Winternitz, *Musical
Autographs*, I, 19.

nuances indicated by modifications of the neume shapes, to say nothing of the rhythmic signs, which disappeared during the twelfth century. One of the achievements of the Solesmes monks is to have restored certain of these details to modern editions of the chant, and ecclesiastical legislation authorizes the chant to be used "with the addition of the Solesmes rhythmic signs" (*LU*, vii).

The Rhythmic Signs

A great many of the manuscripts of the ninth through the eleventh centuries contain in addition to the neume figures certain other signs in the form of single letters; also some of the common neume forms are at times modified in one way or another in appearance. These additional signs and modifications are indications to the singer to make certain rhythmical or expressive inflections of the melodic line at those places. Some of the letters also have a melodic significance, indicating pitch direction in case of doubt, or possibly correcting a scribal error of a note written too high or too low. These letters and signs become less frequent and finally disappear in the course of the twelfth century.

Such signs appear with the greatest frequency in the manuscripts written at St. Gall, and are often referred to as "Romanian letters," after Romanus, a papal emissary to St. Gall at the end of the eighth century to whom the invention of the letters is legendarily attributed. They are also called *litterae significativae*, and are explained in the famous letter of Notker Balbulus (ninth century), who was himself a monk of St. Gall.[5] Concerning the other neume schools, it is an interesting fact that the further they were from St. Gall, the fewer letters appear in their notations.

The rhythmic letters used most frequently are *t* (*trahere*—retard) and *c* (*cito* or *celeriter*—lightness, swiftness, possibly a warning against a retard). Melodic signs include *a* (*altius*), *l* (*levare*), and *s* (*sursum*)—all indicating a rise in pitch; *d* (*deprimatur*) and *i* (*inferius*) for a lowering in pitch; and *e* (*equaliter*) for the same pitch. Other schools also employed the letters *a* (*augete*—a broadening), *n* (*naturaliter*—the usual value), and *h* (*humiliter*—a pitch

---

[5] *GS*, I, 95. See also *PM*, IV, pl. B. The most extensive modern study of these letters is in J. Smits van Waesberghe's *Muziekgeschiedenis der Middeleeuwen II.*

lowering). Other letters, less frequently used, have to do with the manner of using the voice in singing.

The neume modifications most frequently seen are the addition of an *episema*, a stroke attached to a neume figure, ⫨ , the enlargement of part of a figure, ⁄ , and the horizontal prolongation of a punctum (sometimes called the *virga jacens* or *tractulus*), — ; all of these indicate a retard or lengthening of the note modified in this way. In some schools a retard was indicated by the separation of neumatic elements that would ordinarily be joined in ligature. Many such subtleties of neumatic writing exist, especially in the earliest manuscripts; their meaning is not always clearly known, but they must have been intended as rhythmic inflections coloring the melodic line.[6] Many instances of the rhythmic letters occur in the facsimile on Plate II, and this and various of the other plates have examples of neume modifications. The presence of these signs has been variously interpreted by scholars to justify one or another theory of Gregorian rhythm.

The Schools of Neume Notation

The various schools of neume notation have been identified and classified by Gregorian scholars as comprising about a dozen general types, each with distinctive but related features. They are found in Italy, France, Switzerland, Germany, England, and Spain, and they correspond roughly to the groups of ecclesiastical provinces of the early Middle Ages. It is assumed that the schools originated during the course of the ninth century, and it has also been considered—without any recorded evidence—that a possible prototype of these neumatic "dialects" may have been in use at the time of Saint Gregory (*ca.* 540–604); however that may be, singers trained in his Schola Cantorum were sent out to disseminate the chant in the various parts of Western Europe toward the end of the sixth century. Saint Augustine, for example, who later became the first Archbishop of Canterbury, was sent to England by Gregory in 598, and Canterbury had a Gregorian school as early as 630. Missionary monks from England and Ireland in turn had great in-

---

[6] See the study of the Abbé L. Agustoni, "Notation neumatique et interprelation," *RG*, 1951, 173 and 219.

fluence upon the development of Gregorian notation on the continent, notably at their foundation of St. Gall. Similar interrelationships and reciprocal influences were carried on in other regions, to which the use of the same styles in widely separated areas is striking witness.[7]

In this connection, a good deal of present Gregorian research is directed at the question of whether the chant diffused by Gregory's missionaries was the same as what is now known as Gregorian chant. It is a remarkable fact that there is no existent chant manuscript originating from Rome earlier than the thirteenth century, while there are four Roman manuscripts of that century which contain a melodic repertory quite different from Gregorian chant.[8] This repertory is called "Old Roman" chant; compared to Gregorian, it is more primitive and sombre, with frequently-repeated little motives and small intervallic leaps, and its modality is less pronounced. It has been suggested that Old Roman chant is much older than Gregorian chant, and was the original chant sent out by Gregory to the ecclesiastical provinces, where it became transformed into "Gregorian" chant and was then retransmitted to Rome in this form.[9]

The pages which follow are devoted to an analysis of the facsimiles of Gregorian notation that appear in this volume, Plates I–XII. They illustrate the most important schools of neume notation, and are arranged in a more or less chronological order. The majority of them are chants still in use today; the modern version of each chant, as it appears in the Vatican Edition of the *Liber Usualis*, is reproduced in the text at the end of the section devoted to it. There are some cases where the medieval version does not correspond note for note to the modern edition; this is explained by the fact that the latter is based on the collation of all the known early man-

---

[7] Anglès summarizes the diffusion of the chant in *NOHM*, II, 99*ff.*; his essay also has a map of the "Families of Neumatic Notations" facing p. 109.

[8] Vat. lat. 5319, V. S. Pietro B. 79, Pietro F. 22, and London, Br. Mus. Add. 29.988. An example of this chant is in *PM*, II, 4, No. 1.

[9] Another theory is that both Old Roman and Gregorian chant sprang from a common source; Gregorian became the *cantus romanae ecclesiae* that was used all over Europe, while the other—the *cantus curiae pontificale*—was reserved as a special music for Papal services. Several studies dealing with this problem have appeared in the last five years, one of the most interesting being that of J. Smits van Waesberghe, "The Two Versions of the Gregorian Chant," IMS, 6th Congress. See also W. Apel, "The Central Problem of Gregorian Chant," *JAMS*, 1956, 118.

uscripts of the chant melodies, and the version in the Solesmes liturgical books is that with which the majority of the best manuscripts agree.

PLATE I. Hymn: *Gloria in excelsis* (Paris, Bibl. nat. lat. 2291, fol. 16; ninth century)

Plate I is a facsimile of what is considered to be possibly the oldest melody known to us that is written in neumes. It is in a style of notation which may be the earliest of all neumatic writing, one which has been called, in recent studies, "Paleofrankish" notation. The late J. Handschin thought that this may have been the original style of neumatic notation from which all other styles derived.[10] Examples of this notation exist in only about a dozen manuscripts, and in only a few pages in most of these. Because of this, and because details of the characteristics of this writing are still under investigation by scholars, Paleofrankish neumes have not been included in the neume table, Fig. 1.

The text is written in Greek, but with Latin characters; the Latin translation appears in the column to the right, representing a vestige of the ancient practice of chanting the Gloria in both Greek and Latin on major festivals. Both text and melody (found in about twenty manuscripts of the tenth, eleventh, and twelfth centuries) are undoubtedly of Byzantine origin; the melody corresponds closely to Gloria XIV of the Vatican Edition (*LU*, 54), but is earlier than the Roman version of the melody.*

The neumes of this manuscript, which were added to a text not originally planned for neumes, are diastematic, showing that diastematy occurred at an early stage in the evolution of neume writing. Unlike other notations, Paleofrankish has no symbol for the virga; the upward stroke which seems to be this sign, as at the beginning of the second line and elsewhere, is actually a podatus, according to other early manuscripts containing this hymn. The very light vertical stroke seen in the first few lines is to divide syllables. The punctum has two forms—the usual dot, and the elongated form (tractulus); the latter is used when a single note is sung to a syllable.

---

[10] "Zu 'Eine alte Neumenschrift'," *AM*, 1953, 87. See also E. Jammers, "Die paleofrankische Neumenschrift," *Scriptorium*, 1953, 235.
* Translations of the texts from all Plates appear in the Appendix, p. 207.

Most of the two- and three-note symbols have more than one form. In addition to the virga-like form mentioned above, the podatus is also seen in an angular shape, as at the end of the first line and in the middle of the second. The clivis has two corresponding forms, the first of which is the obliquely descending stroke, slightly curved, which is seen twice in the seventh line, and the angular shape seen twice in the third line. It has been noted in later manuscripts of the hymn that the simpler of the two forms in both podatus and clivis represents a step-wise interval, while the angular form stands for a melodic skip. The scandicus, in a three-note ascent, consists of ordinary puncta, as at the very beginning; when four ascending notes occur the tractulus is employed, as in line three. The climacus appears in the last line with three descending puncta, the last of which is lengthened.

There are several different torculus forms, of which the most frequently occurring are the rounded shape (similar to the St. Gall clivis) seen at the beginning of lines ten and eleven, and the shape consisting of a podatus to which a descending stroke is attached, as in lines one, three, and ten. The porrectus is the V-shaped sign seen in lines two and five, and in several subsequent lines. An instance of a compound neume—the podatus subbipunctis—is near the end of line eleven; it is formed by a podatus joined to a clivis. There do not appear to be signs of liquescence or of ornamentation in this manuscript, although such signs are said to exist in other manuscripts in Paleofrankish notation. Their absence in this manuscript has caused some scholars to suppose that this notation may already have been in use in France before the arrival of Roman missionaries and choirmasters in that country.

The hymn is seen in Fig. 2 in a transcription by J. Handschin which is noncommittal in rhythm, that is, which suggests no definite rhythm. The ligatures are indicated by phrase marks below the notes, and the melismas on individual syllables by similar marks above them.[11]

[11] J. Handschin, "Eine alte Neumenschrift," *AM*, 1950, 74. Another transcription of the Gloria is in Dom Huglo's "La mélodie grecque du 'Gloria in excelsis'," *RG*, 1950, 35. The latter (in Gregorian notation) is a collation of all the early manuscripts, and includes the Solesmes rhythmical signs.

FIG. 2

Do- xa en yp-sis- tis the-o ke

e- pi gis i- ri- ni en an-thro-

pis eu- do-ki- as. Eu-nu- men

se, eu-lo-gu- men se,

pro-sky-nu- men se, do-xo-lo-

gu- men se, eu-cha-ri-stu-

men si di- a tin me-ga- lin

su do- xan. Ky- ri- e ba-sil-

eu e- pu- ra- ni- e

PLATE II. Gradual: *Liberasti nos*, and Verse: *Deo laudabimur* (St.
Gall, Cod. 359, fol. 125; late ninth century) for the Mass of
the twenty-third Sunday after Pentecost (*LU*, 1075)

The facsimile of Sangallian notation on Plate II is from the oldest
extant codex written especially to receive neume notation—the
celebrated *Cantatorium of St. Gall*. (The whole manuscript is reproduced in *Paléographie musicale*, Series II, No. 2.) The notation
is oratorical, and includes many rhythmical letters and neume modifications, reflecting a great deal of rhythmical nuance.

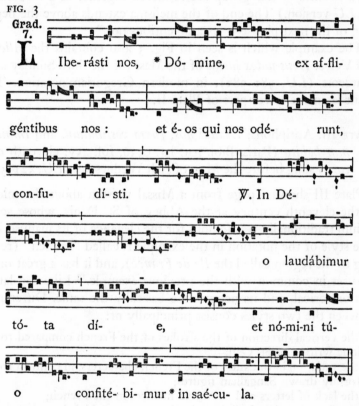

FIG. 3

In the phrase "Liberasti nos," the first neume is the punctum
that looks as if it were the dot over the *i* (this letter is never dotted
in medieval manuscripts). The next sign, over the letter *b*, is not
a neume, but the letter *c*, for *celeriter*. The neume above the syllable "-be-" is a bivirga that is epismatic—that is, at the end of each
virga stroke a small dash is drawn, indicating emphasis. The next

syllable, "-ra-," bears a podatus, the beginning of which is thickened for emphasis, followed by a salicus over "-sti." The neume over "nos" varies from the *LU* version; instead of a porrectus, the manuscript has a salicus with the letter *i*, for *inferior*, above the beginning of the neume, probably as a pitch reminder.

In "Domine," the small sign above the porrectus flexus is the letter *c*. The melisma on "-ne" consists of the following series of neumes: clivis with rhythmical letter *t* above, episematic virga, clivis with *c* above, torculus, and episematic clivis. (The second and third neumes of this group are rendered together as a torculus in the *LU* version.) The end of the melisma extends above the beginning of the next phrase—"ex affligentibus nos."

The example which is seen in Fig. 3 also contains the *Alleluia* and Verse: *Deus judex justus* of the Mass for the third Sunday after Pentecost (*LU*, 982–983), in modern Gregorian notation. This chant is on the lower part of Plate II.

PLATE III. Antiphons: *Exaudi nos, Juxta vestibulum*, and *Immutemur habitu* (Paris, Bibl. nat. lat. 9436, fol. 45v; eleventh century) sung before the Mass of Ash Wednesday (*LU*, 521–524)

Plate III shows a page from a Missal written about the middle of the eleventh century at the Abbey of St. Denis, whose scriptorium traditionally was famous for the elegance of its manuscripts. The style of the notation in the example is called "French" (referring to the region called the *Ile de France*), and it has a great many features in common with the previous example.[12] Like the latter, it is oratorical, and its neumes are basically the same. Differences between the two styles consist principally of:

1) the vertical direction of the strokes of the French compared to the oblique writing of St. Gall;
2) the variation in thickness of the French characters, in contrast to the uniformly drawn Sangallian figures;
3) the lack of letters and rhythmic nuances in the French;
4) the French pointed clivis and other neumes which have a rounded shape in St. Gall writing.

[12] This style is sometimes called the "primitive notation of Northern France," referring to its early appearance and its regional location. There are other "French" notations, of course, such as Aquitanian, Norman, Messine, and Chartrain.

The first line of the antiphon *Exaudi nos* is interrupted about two-thirds through by the end of the text, in larger letters, that belongs to the prayer above; the antiphon continues at the beginning of the next line. The incipit of the Psalm verse *Salvum me* is then given. The antiphons *Juxta vestibulum* and *Immutemur habitu* occur in the opposite order to their position in the *LU;* the former begins on the fourth line of music, and the initial letter of *Immutemur* is lacking.

The versions of these chants in the facsimile and the *LU* are closely similar, as a neume by neume comparison will reveal, although the version in the manuscript is slightly more elaborate. For example, in *Exaudi nos* the middle syllable of "quoniam" is set to a podatus rather than a single note; the middle syllable of "tuarum" contains a quilisma which is lacking in the *LU;* and the final syllable of this same word is set more elaborately.

Signs indicating liquescence are occasionally seen. In addition to the cephalicus, there are signs for the *ancus,* a neume indicating a more pronounced degree of liquescence, as in line four— ⌒ and

𝄐. Probably liquescence is also meant by the use of the oblique virga, which occurs in a few places in lines three and five.

Fig. 4 also contains the Introit of this Mass (*LU,* 525–526).

FIG. 4

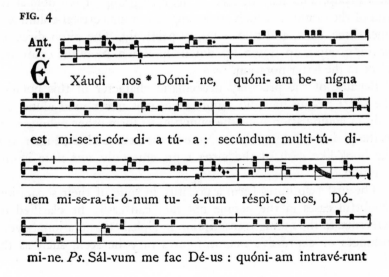

Ant. 7.

ⅇ Xáudi nos * Dómi- ne, quóni- am be- nígna

est mi-se-ri-cór- di- a tú- a : secúndum multi-tú- di-

nem mi-se-ra-ti- ó-num tu- á-rum réspi-ce nos, Dó-

mi-ne. *Ps.* Sál-vum me fac Dé-us : quóni- am intravé-runt

PLATES IV AND V. Tonarium: *Ecce modus primus* (Paris, Bibl. nat. lat. 7211, fol. 127v and 128; late eleventh century)

This example is not a Gregorian chant, but a *Tonarium*, or vocal exercise for learning the modes. It is a characteristic illustration of the distinctive and very important Aquitanian school of neumatic notation, however, and is included because it also contains certain additional features of considerable interest. It is from a late eleventh-century collection of musical treatises from Hucbald to Guido. Each page is arranged in two columns, and each of the two facing pages contains the same piece—the left one in Aquitanian neumes, the right in alphabet notation.

The Aquitanian style originated in the celebrated Abbey of St. Martial in Limoges, and had a widespread influence in the south and west of France. The style presents a wholly different graphic picture from those of the two previous examples because of its point neume character and its precise diastematy. It makes no use of rhythmical letters or signs, but has some expressive neume modifications. A basic principle of this notation is that when the points are superimposed vertically over one another, the melodic direction is always downward; the melodic movement is always from the last note of such a group in vertical alignment to the top note of the next group. This may be seen in the final group of ten dots at the end of the example, which are arranged in four vertical columns of one, three, four, and two notes, respectively. The pitch direction of this group is up–down–up–down–up–down. Note the equivalent place in the letter notation.

Because of the precisely diastematic character of this notation the virga has no melodic significance; it is never used alone, but only in combination with the punctum to form other neumes such as the podatus and scandicus. Note in the neume chart, Fig. 1, that the hook-like dash of the virga represents only *one* note in this notation.

The first two notes form a podatus, in spite of their separation. Doubtful cases in the neume notation can easily be clarified by reference to the facing transcription in alphabetic notation. Several instances of expressive neume figures may be seen, such as the pressus—which occurs on almost every line—and the epiphonus and cephalicus, both of which appear on the second line over "atque" and "secundus" respectively. The figure at the end of the next-to-last line on the column to the right is a torculus resupinus. A *custos* ("guard," which indicates the first note of the subsequent line of music), in the form of a punctum with a diagonal dash through it, is used except for the last two lines of the column to the left.

In the alphabetically-notated version the system used is that of the so-called "Guidonian letters," in which only the letters from *A* to *G* are employed (compare the alphabet notation in Plate X). The diastematic placing of the letters is unnecessary; the octave positions are indicated by the use of capital and small letters. B-flat and B-natural are distinguished by the use of square and round letters. Letter notation is not naturally adapted to the use of expressive neume modifications; but the scribe has used double letters for the pressus (not to be confused with repeated notes, as in "primus"), and in one instance has indicated a liquescence (the F at the end of the melisma on "ar-" in the second column, line four). Neumes of two or more notes are usually, though not always, separated by a dot.[13]

The text reads as follows:

> Ecce modus primus sic noscitur atque secundus.
> Accipitur tritus sic. Quartus adest iste probatur.
> Quintus adest iste. Sextus sic noscitur esse.
> Septimus armoniam tenetur hanc. Octavus adest istam.

Fig. 5 shows the beginning of the Tonarium.

FIG. 5

Ec - ce   mo -   dus   pri - mus

---

[13] An account of similar didactic methods used in the Middle Ages is given in J. Smits van Waesberghe's *Guido Aretino*, 86. See also *GMB*, No. 7.

PLATE VI. *Alleluia* and Verse: *Confitemini domino* (Monte Cassino, Cod. 339, fol. 61; eleventh century) for Holy Saturday
(*LU*, 759)

The example of Beneventan notation on Plate VI is from a Missal of the famed Abbey of Monte Cassino, the center of this school.
The writing differs greatly from the previous examples in its thickness and angularity; it already suggests the Gothic style. Beneventan
scribes did not employ rhythmical letters, but conveyed much rich-
ness of nuance through subtle modifications of neume shapes. The
writing is carefully diastematic. The manuscripts of this school are
unique in employing a style of lettering in the text that goes back
to the pre-Carolingian epoch.

FIG. 6

The first neume lies between the first two letters of "Alleluia";
it is a punctum with a characteristic hook-like addition to indicate
liquescence, calling attention to the two adjacent *l's* in "Alleluia."
The short melisma on "-le-" consists of a punctum joined in apposition to a virga, then a podatus, tristropha, and clivis. The next syllable carries a distropha and podatus. The final syllable has a melisma
including punctum, liquescent podatus, torculus resupinus, punctum, and clivis pressus—the arrangement, but not the actual notes,
differing slightly from the *LU* version.

"Confitemini" begins with a liquescent punctum, then a lengthened punctum, podatus, punctum on "-mi-" (a degree lower than

the corresponding note in the *LU* version), distropha, and a union of two clives (compare the climacus in the *LU* at this point).

The remainder of the chant includes some nuances, such as the liquescent sign on the tristropha in the middle of the second line, and the two instances of the liquescent scandicus on the third line, over "*in saeculum*" and "misericor*d*ia," the second of which obviously implies a greater degree of liquescence than the first.

PLATE VII. Trope of the Gloria (Paris, Bibl. nat. lat. 1107, fol. 32v; twelfth century) Mass XI, *Orbis factor* (*LU*, 46)

The Gloria trope of Plate VII is an example of Norman notation from a Gradual of St. Evroult. Troped passages (interpolated amplifying phrases) are inserted between each sentence of the liturgical chant; for some reason, the phrase "hominibus bonae voluntatis" has been omitted.

Norman notation belongs to the general group of accent neumes, but has a special character of its own in that the two- and three-note neumes consist essentially of thickened dots connected by thin strokes (whence the French "*notation à points liés*"). A noteworthy feature is that the virga is the same as in square notation. This piece is the first of the illustrations employing actual rather than imaginary lines, the upper (red) line representing F, the lower (green), C. The singer is further guided by the letters *e* and *a* at the beginning of each "staff," with lightly-drawn lines after them.

The neumes need no special explanation; they correspond to the *LU* version, with one curious discrepancy: the phrase "Gratias agimus tibi" is one tone higher in the manuscript (see Fig. 7, the chant without the interpolated passages). The troped insertions include several neumes which do not occur in the Gloria itself; these will be found illustrated in Fig. 1. Rhythmic and expressive nuances are not lacking in this example; the pressus occurs in almost every line, liquescents are fairly frequent, and the oriscus also occurs. B-flat and B-natural are used at several places.

An interesting feature of the notation is the retention of the distinction between punctum and virga to represent relatively lower and higher pitches. With a system as clear in its pitch representation as this, there is no need for such a distinction; yet it occurs throughout, except for notes given emphasis (like the pressus on "Deo" in the first line and elsewhere), and in the little descending melodic formula that occurs in most of the troped passages. These exceptional uses of the virga for notes of lower pitch appear to have been traditional.

Another example of Norman notation is seen in the facsimile of letter and neume notation in Plate X, which is an earlier stage of Norman notation than the Gloria trope; it is without lines, and only slightly diastematic. A similar example of Norman notation is seen in the organa of Plate XXIII.

The first part of the Gloria of Mass XI is shown in the *LU* version in Fig. 7.

FIG. 7

2.

G Ló-ri- a in excélsis Dé- o.   Et in térra pax ho-

mí-ni-bus bónae voluntá- tis. Laudámus te   Benedí- cimus

te.   Ado-rámus te. Glo-ri-ficámus te.   Grá-ti- as ági-

mus tí-bi   propter mágnam gló-ri- am tú- am. Dómi-ne /

A very important neumatic notation in which many Gregorian manuscripts were written was the so-called Messine, which appears in the neume table, Fig. 1.[14] While this notation is not represented by a chant example, it does appear in Plate XVI, the trouvère chanson *Par quel forfait*, and also in the Minnesong of Plate XVII. The most distinctive feature of this notation is the shape of the punctum, which was used exclusively for single notes; the virga, as in Aquitanian notation, was used only in combination to form other neumes.

<hr />

[14] This notation derives its name from the city of Metz, in northeastern France; but recent studies have shown that the number of extant manuscripts actually written at that city are relatively few. Mme. Solange Corbin has suggested that the name "Lorraine" is more suitable: "Les notations neumatiques en France à l'époque carolingienne," *Revue d'histoire de l'église de France*, 1952. See also Dom Hourlier, "Le domaine de la notation messine," *RG*, 1951, 96 and 150.

The particular character of the punctum has caused a page of this notation to be likened to a "flight of swallows"; it has also been called the *Fliegenfuss* ("fly-foot") notation. Further details of this neumatic style are considered in the section of Chapter 2 devoted to the trouvère chanson of Plate XVI.

PLATE VIII. Introit: *Puer natus* (Paris, Bibl. nat. lat. 1107, fol. 19v; thirteenth century) from the Mass of the Day for the Nativity (*LU*, 408)

This example comes from the Abbey of St. Denis, like the antiphons of Plate III. It is a very early example of the square notation in which all Gregorian chant came to be written.

FIG. 8

The vestigial distinction between virga and punctum seen in the previous example has completely disappeared in this notation. Only the virga is used for single notes, and this represents the principal difference between the manuscript version and that in the *LU;* in the latter only the punctum is used for single notes, and the virga appears only in combination, as in several older neumatic styles. Other differences, relatively inconsequential, consist of the use of the custos at the end of each line in the modern version, and the slightly different arrangement of certain ligature groupings.

In square notation the use of expressive neumes all but disappears. Certain traces of the liquescents remain, however, in the *plica*, which was widely used in the mensural polyphonic music from the late twelfth through the entire thirteenth century. The plica occurs in *Puer natus* on the first note of the third line (represented by an epiphonus in the *LU*), which is an ascending plica, and also on the word "ejus" in both the fifth and sixth lines. In the last two cases the descending plica is represented by an additional note with two descending tails; in the *LU* a climacus is used at these places. Another descending plica is seen over the word "et" in the fifth line; in the equivalent place in the *LU* this is a simple clivis. In the polyphonic music of the time this manuscript was written, the plica represented an actual note with a definite time value; in plainchant, the single-note form may have represented only a sign of liquescence.

The *LU* version of *Puer natus* is given in Fig. 8.

PLATE IX. Introit: *Requiem*, and Verse: *Te decet hymnus* (Brussels, Bibl. roy. 4767, fol. 83; sixteenth century) from the Mass for the Dead (*LU*, 1807)

Gothic notation is the latest of the distinctive neumatic styles. It originated in the fourteenth century as a derivative of Messine notation, the *Hufnagel* ("horseshoe nail") shape of the virga being a German version of the Messine "swallow." The example shown on Plate IX, from a Missal dated 1542, illustrates both melismatic and syllabic writing in this notation. The late date of the manuscript is significant, as this style of notation persisted concurrently for a long time with square notation and after all other neumatic styles had disappeared.[15] Gothic notation is entirely lacking in expressive nuances. Another example of this style is seen in Plate XVIII.

The neumes in the example will be readily identified by reference to Fig. 1. It will be noted that in Plate IX the punctum is used only in combination with other neumes, never alone. There are several

---

[15] Wolf's *Musikalische Schrifttafeln* has an example of Gothic notation in a manuscript of the eighteenth century (No. 40).

minor differences in this version of the Requiem chant from that in the *LU*, as a comparison will reveal.

FIG. 9

PLATE X. Hymn: *O quam magnifice* (Paris, Bibl. nat. lat. 13.765, fol. 5; tenth-eleventh century) from the Office of St. Turian

This is a combined letter-and-neume notation called *digraphic*, from St. Germain-des-Prés, of the tenth or eleventh century, and is a Hymn to St. Turian, a bishop of Dol in Brittany. The use of letters to denote melodies occurs in some manuscripts of the ninth, tenth, and eleventh centuries, probably for pedagogical reasons, although they may have had a practical use as well. An example of letter notation has already been seen in the Tonarium of Plate V; in the system used there, capital letters from *A* to *G* stand for the lower octave, small letters for the higher. In the complete letter system another *G* was added below *A*, and was represented by the Greek letter Γ (hence the name *gamma* for the scale; English *gamut*).

An important feature of letter notation was the use of two different note shapes for the letter B—a square shape, representing B-natural; and a round shape, representing B-flat. These shapes still exist as the natural and flat signs of modern notation. The reasons for using these two signs were 1) to allow for the proper intervals in each of the three hexachords on C, F, and G (called "natural," "soft," and "hard"); and 2) to be able to change over when necessary from one to another of the three hexachords, a process called *mutation*. Guido of Arezzo used double letters for notes going beyond the second octave (aa, bb, etc.). Letter notations do not appear in any Gregorian manuscript after the eleventh century.[16]

In the system of letter notation used in the hymn, *O quam magnifice*, only small letters are employed, going alphabetically from *a* through *o;* this system is called (though unjustifiably, it seems) "Boethian notation." Dots are used between letters to set off groups of neumes, corresponding to the notation in neumes above the letters.

FIG. 10

a b c d e f g h i k l m n o

The neumes of Plate X are Norman, of a much earlier stage than those seen in the Gloria trope of Plate VII, and are slightly diastematic. For some reason, possibly forgetfulness on the part of the scribe, a part of the neumatic notation over the melisma in the lowest line has been omitted. Liquescents are indicated in the neumes at appropriate places. The first line of the hymn shows two—the first is on the virga at the end of the neume group over "quam," the other at the end of the scandicus over "mag-." An interesting detail is that the liquescent signs are also present at the same places in the letter notation.

The text (beginning at the fourth line) is as follows:

O quam magnifice coelum petis, O Turiane,
Ad cenam regis tamquam conviva fidelis invitatis
Ades resonant coelestia laudes.

[16] For Guido's description of letter notation, see *SR*, 119. Alphabet notation appears to have been used principally in Normandy, and the earliest examples are of Norman provenance. For other examples of combined neume-and-letter notation see *PM*, VII and VIII.

PLATE XI. Sequence: *Rex coeli domine* (Paris, Bibl. nat. lat. 7369; fifteenth century?) from an anonymous *Tractatus de musica*

Some examples of chant exist in the notation called *Daseia*, the invention of which was attributed by Guido to Odo of Cluny. This system was also used in the ninth-century treatise, *Musica enchiriadis*, to illustrate the earliest known examples of polyphonic writing. Unlike any other system in which the chant was notated, this was based on the tetrachord principle of Greek musical theory, and Greek symbols were employed in it.

The Daseia system covers the usual two-octave range of notes used in the early medieval period by employing a series of successive tetrachords, each of which consists of a set of four signs. These signs, as used in the tetrachord from D to G, are 𝄆 𝄇 𝄈 𝄉 . The first, second, and fourth of these signs are like different shapes of the letter *F*, while the third sign is like the acutus accent sign of the Greek grammarians. The difference in shape of the third sign signifies the half step between it and the sign below it.

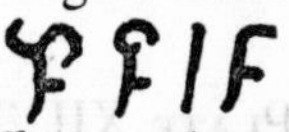

These signs are used to represent the other tetrachords as well by placing them in various positions. For example, in the tetrachord immediately above that of D to G—the one from A to *d*—the signs are inverted, in the lowest they are turned backwards, and in the highest they are both inverted and backwards. Also, a different accent sign is used in each of the four tetrachords— *N* , *I* , *η* , and ✠ —from lowest to highest, and this sign always occurs as the upper note of the half step in each tetrachord. The accent signs stand for *N inclinum*, *Iota*, *N versum*, and *Iota transfixum*.

The example, *Rex coeli*, is from a codex containing a collection of nine medieval treatises that appear to have been copied down and bound together in the latter fifteenth century, perhaps by an antiquarian of that period. The key to the system is written just below the sequence; it follows the plan described above, except that the lowest tetrachord is incomplete, and the highest appears to use a set of symbols that differ somewhat in appearance from those of the other tetrachords. The third tetrachord has a symbol for both B-flat and B-natural.

The text is as follows:

> Rex coeli domine squalidi que soli
> Titanis nitidi maris undisoni
> Te humiles famuli modulis venerando piis
> Se iubeas flagitant variis liberare malis.
> Ego sum via veritas et vita, Alleluia, alleluia,
> Vacat hoc tempore potentibus
> Opprimere privatis perdere miseris flere.

The first phrase of the piece is transcribed as in Fig. 11.[17]

FIG. 11

Rex coe - li   Do - mi - ne   squa - li - di   que   so - li

PLATE XII. Tonarium: *Ter tria iunctorum*, Hermannus Contractus
(Vienna, nat.-bibl. Hs. 2502, fol. 27v; twelfth century)

Another empirical notation in which at least one manuscript of
Gregorian chant of the twelfth century is written is that of Hermannus Contractus (d. 1054). The system is explained by Hermannus in his *Opuscula musica* (*GS*, II, 149) in the form of a Tonarium.
According to this system, letters representing melodic intervals
were placed above the text, as follows:

e	*(equaliter)*	= unison
s	*(semitonium)*	= half step
t	*(tonus)*	= whole step
ts	*(tonus cum semitonus)*	= minor third
tt	*(ditonus)*	= major third
d	*(diatesseron)*	= perfect fourth
δ	*(diapente)*	= perfect fifth
δs	*(diapente cum semitonus)*	= minor sixth
δt	*(diapente cum tonus)*	= major sixth

The explanation further states that notes with a dot underneath
are lowered (*remissas*), while those without a dot are raised (*in-
tensas*). As an illustration, Hermannus included in his treatise the
piece on Plate XII, which is apparently a different manuscript from

---

[17] The first half of this sequence, treated in organum, appears in the *Musica enchiriadis* (see Plate XX), according to which the note over the first syllable of
"titanis" is *C* rather than *A*.

that on which Gerbert's edition is based. The key to the system is in the nine large capital letters in the second half of the top line. There are no indications of rhythm in this notation, which is offered as one of the interesting curiosities in the history of notation.

The didactic melody beginning on the third line from the bottom is devised to teach the intervals. The letter *G* above the first word indicates the note on which to start. Following Hermannus' explanations, the opening phrase is transcribed as in Fig. 12.[18]

FIG. 12

Ter tri - a iunc - to- rum sunt in - ter - val - la so - no - rum

The foregoing account of neumatic and other notations of Gregorian chant has included only certain of the styles employed in the period up to the advent of square notation. Other distinct families of neume writing existed contemporaneously with those described—Novalesan, Nonantolan, Chartrain, and Anglo-Saxon— and a style was used in Spain for the Mozarabic rite that has thus far defied any attempt to unravel the special manner of its notation or of the music it represents.[19] Research in Gregorian paleography continues to shed light on existent manuscripts, of which the recent identification of Paleofrankish notation is a striking example; and it is not unreasonable to suppose that further discoveries will continue to be made that will throw more light on the origins of our written musical language.

Gregorian Rhythm

The rhythm of Gregorian chant is a subject that has been and continues to be a matter of controversy ever since scholars of our era began their plainchant researches. The chief problem confronting those who undertake the study of the chant is its rhythmic delivery, for the neumatic notation in which it exists in the earliest manuscripts offers nothing in the way of a clue to the nature of

[18] See *IPM*, 397, and Mocquereau, "De la transcription sur lignes . . . ," *Riemann-Festschrift*, 137.

[19] An impressive monument of this notation in facsimile is the *Antifonario visigotico mozarabe de la Catedral de Leon*, Madrid, 1953.

Gregorian rhythm; the rhythmic signs that have been referred to merely indicate that certain notes are to be treated differently from others, but they tell nothing about the essential underlying character of the rhythm itself. Basically, the question is whether the original rhythmic tradition of the chant was measured or free, and it is about this fundamental problem that most studies have centered. The writings of the same medieval theorists have been interpreted by various scholars as evidence supporting opposing viewpoints, and the same is true of paleographic evidence. The bibliography on the subject is immense.[20] There are two different main methods of rhythmic interpretation which have become known as the "mensuralist" and the Solesmes "free rhythm" theories. A third interpretation is sometimes made using the "accentualist" theory, but this is very closely related to that of the Solesmes school; in fact, it was Dom Pothier's accentual theory of "oratorical" or free rhythm—with accentuation of naturally-stressed text syllables—that gave rise to the modern Solesmes method.

The conflict of viewpoints concerning plainchant rhythm is significant for the student of notation, for if he wishes to transcribe a piece written in medieval neumes (or even in modern Gregorian notation) into regular notation he will have to adopt one or another concept of what the neumes convey rhythmically. Most students do not have the opportunity of examining the evidence of the sources and must therefore depend on the interpretation of these sources by scholars equipped to form judgments about them. If a judgment were to be formed on the basis of subjective evidence alone—by the aesthetic impact of the chant as actually sung in the different ways that have been advocated—there would hardly be any doubt of the "rightness" of the Solesmes manner.

As a background to the understanding of this problem, it should be realized that during the twelfth and thirteenth centuries the decline in the traditions of the chant which had begun a century or two earlier was considerably advanced. It has commonly been supposed that this was due to the growth of polyphonic music, but this assumption is not supported by studies that have been made of con-

[20] See lists of books, articles, etc. in *MMA*, 437–445, *IPM*, 511–565, and Ursprung's *Die katholische Kirchenmusik*, 43–98.

ditions in centers of musical activity. Whatever the reason, a low point was reached in 1614, when an edition of the liturgical chants appeared in which the chant melodies were maimed and distorted by many incorrect notes and by the ruthless deletion of many of their expressive melismas. Furthermore, the neumatic signs of plainsong were interpreted as mensural notes and ligatures, with the same rhythmical meaning that they had in medieval polyphonic music. This was the *Editio Medicea* prepared by Anerio and Soriano and authorized by Pope Paul V. About the middle of the nineteenth century, under the influence of the so-called "Liturgical Movement," a general surge of interest in restoring the purity of the liturgy, scholarly studies were undertaken at various centers, notably at Solesmes and Ratisbon; the latter study resulted in F. Haberl's re-edition in 1893 of the Medicean Edition, now known as the Ratisbon Edition. This edition was authorized by Pope Leo XIII as the official ecclesiastical version. Meanwhile, the work of the Solesmes Benedictines in restoring the ancient form of the melodies by a comparative study of all the available manuscripts, and in formulating a method for their interpretation, had gained recognition to the extent that in 1904 Pope Pius X appointed the monks of Solesmes to prepare a Vatican Edition of the various liturgical chant books. The monks also published for their own use a special edition containing the rhythmic signs devised by Dom Mocquereau to represent the rhythmical letters and signs found in the oldest manuscripts, and the use of these signs is now officially authorized for universal use by the Congregation of Rites.

The Free Rhythm of the Solesmes School

The Solesmes method is based on what has come to be called "additive" rhythm—using the concept of a single individual pulse as the basic time unit, usually rendered in regular notation by the eighth-note. These indivisible time units are grouped into compound elements of either two or three notes in which each note is equal in value, whether occurring in a binary or a ternary group. Larger units are in turn formed by a succession of the binary and ternary groups, freely and irregularly following each other. Thus the rhythm is "free" from the regular recurrence of metrical accents, but is nevertheless controlled by the steady pulse of the indivisible single beat.

The beginning of each two- or three-note component is marked by the *ictus*, a point in the movement of beats that is conceived of as the completion of one rhythmical impulse and at the same time the commencement of another; it is "that which ends and that which begins," like the bounce of a ball. The ictus is dissociated from the idea of intensity or stress, and is independent of the tonic accent of the text; this is illustrated in Fig. 13, the beginning of the Communion, *Memento verbi tui* (*LU*, 1065), in which the tonic accent and the ictus coincide only once in the course of the phrase.

FIG. 13

Me-mén - to   vér-bi   tú - i   sér- vo   tú- o, Dó- mi -   ne,

Text rhythm is subordinate to musical rhythm, and generally it is the ends of words rather than their accented syllables that are made ictic, in order to create a light, soaring quality. Certain notes are given quantitative or retarding rhythmic nuances, following the rhythmic signs in the manuscripts; but the prevailing movement is uniform, in keeping with the uniform length of syllables in the Latin of Pope Gregory's time.[21]

One of the most interesting results of the Solesmes researches has been the discovery of an astonishing uniformity of rhythmical signs in the various manuscripts of the same melodies, even among different schools of neume notation.[22] The rhythmical signs in the Solesmes liturgical books represent a restoration of these markings to the chant. Figs. 14a and 14b show the Antiphon, *Asperges me* (*LU*, 11), in both Gregorian and regular notation.

The Solesmes rhythmical signs that appear in these examples are:

1) the *dot*, which doubles the value of the note it follows;
2) the *horizontal episema*, which indicates a slight retard of a single note

[21] The most authentic summaries of the Solesmes rhythmical theories are Dom Gajard's monographs, *La méthode de Solesmes*, and *The Rhythm of Plainsong*.
[22] See the monograph, *The Rhythmic Tradition in the Manuscripts*, by Mocquereau-Gajard, trans. Dom Bevenot, Paris, 1952. Plate C of that study shows a single melody collated from ten different manuscripts.

(like the first note of the clivis over "-so-" of "hyssopo") or of a group
of notes (like the torculus over "-da-" of "mundabor" and "-ba-" of
"dealbabor");

3) the *vertical episema*, which marks the ictus (like the last note of the
climacus on "et" of the first line, the punctum on "-per" of "super," and
the last note of the climacus on "de-" of "dealbabor").

FIG. 14A

-SPERGES me,* Dómi-ne, hyssópo, et mundá-

bor : lavá- bis me,   et   super nívem de- albá-bor.)

FIG. 14B

A - spér - ges me, Dó - mi - ne, hyssó - po   et

mun- dá - bor: la - vá -   bis me, et   su -

per ní - vem   de -   al- bá -   bor.

One other sign is employed, which does not occur in these examples:

4) the *comma*, which is the usual breath mark. The small vertical bar
lines placed on the top line of the staff, marking off the "incises" or sections, also function in this way.

The ictus occurs at many places that are not marked by the vertical episema, which is only used in case of doubt. These places are:

1) the first note of each two- or three-note neume, unless this note is
immediately preceded or followed by another note with the ictus;
2) the notes that are lengthened by the dot;
3) the first note of a pressus;
4) the note preceding a quilisma.

The trill sign that occurs in the version in regular notation is a rendering of the quilisma of Gregorian notation.

From the paleographic standpoint, a crucial area of difference between the advocates of mensuralism and of free rhythm is concerned with the virga and punctum. The mensuralists consider these signs as indicating long and short values; whereas the Solesmes school regards them as vestigial traces of pitch direction used in oratorical neumes which remained after the neumes were placed on a staff. Dom Mocquereau compiled impressive evidence to support this view, one of the most telling proofs being a two-voiced setting of the *Alleluia* and Verse, *Dies sanctificatus* in an eleventh-century manuscript of Chartres. In this composition (a facsimile of which is seen on Plate XX) the virga in one voice occurs consistently against the punctum in the other, just as the clivis occurs against the podatus, the torculus against the porrectus, and the scandicus against the climacus. An ensemble of the two voices is possible only if there is an equivalence of duration between the neumes; therefore virga and punctum must be the same in value. (See also Mocquereau's *Le nombre musicale*, I, 228.) [23]

The Measured Rhythm of the Mensuralists

The Solesmes theory and practice of plainchant have been disputed by a number of scholars, including Dechevrens, Jeannin, Houdard, Riemann, and P. Wagner; they regard the principle of uniform note-values as a relatively late development occurring when plainchant was used as cantus firmus material in polyphony, and which was then retained even when the chant was not sung polyphonically. They regard the real Gregorian tradition as one in which long and short values, represented by virga and punctum, were used in a strictly measured proportion of two to one; and they consider the note groupings that arose as falling naturally into measures of the usual kind. They quote certain medieval theorists in support of their views, and defend the Medicean Edition for preserving the difference in note values which they believe char-

---

[23] A corroborative example has been noted by the author in a Guidonian Hand in a fourteenth-century manuscript of Erfurt (reproduced in J. Smits van Waesberghe's *Guido Aretino*, Pl. 18) in which a "gamut" on the Hand shows tails on the ascending scale notes, but not on those of the descending scale. On the same page a brief melody is written similarly.

acterized the rhythm of the chant before its decadence. They regard the ictus as a "mysterious invention" of Dom Mocquereau, and
favor strong and weak beats with regularly recurring metrical accents, although they admit the possibility of measures with varying
numbers of beats. The rhythmical letters and the episemas of the
manuscripts they regard as auxiliary means of changing note values
proportionately, not as rhythmic nuances of undetermined values.[24]

Unlike the Solesmes monks, who have made the neumatic manuscripts the central point of their researches, the mensuralists have
tended to place much dependence upon certain passages from medieval writers on music, and some statements found in the treatises
do appear to support the mensuralist viewpoint. The evidence from
these sources is not convincing, however, because of the ambiguous
manner in which they are written; also, the treatises are often con-
tradictory. Even such eminent medieval theorists as Guido of
Arezzo and Franco of Cologne, both of whom touch briefly on
Gregorian rhythm, have conflicting views about it—Guido com-
pares it to the poetic meters, while Franco says that it is "not precisely measured." [25]

The mensuralists apply mensuration to the chant in differing
ways. The *Asperges* melody quoted in Fig. 14, for example, is
given in Fig. 15 in a transcription by the Jesuit priest, Père
Dechevrens.

FIG. 15

A - spér - ges me, Dó - mi - ne, hys- só -
po et mun-dá - bor; la - vá - bis me
et su - per ní- vem de - al - bá - bor.

[24] The mensuralist point of view is well stated in L. Bonvin's "The 'Measure' in
Gregorian Music," *MQ*, 1929, 16.
[25] For a summary of medieval references to Gregorian rhythm see Sachs,
Rhythm and Tempo, 151, and *IPM*, 432.

The same melody is treated by G. Houdard in a different kind of mensuralism, called *neume-temps* ("neume beat"), in which all the notes of a neume are treated as the equivalent of one pulse or beat, and each beat is the equivalent of one syllable of the text, regardless of how many notes there are in the neume. His treatment appears in Fig. 16.[26]

FIG. 16

The eminent scholar Peter Wagner, who actually disclaimed allegiance to either the mensuralist or free rhythm schools, arrived at an interpretation of the neumes which is based on the assumption that each neume unmistakably conveys its rhythmical character through its graphic shape.[27] He considers that neumes consist of three basic figures—the stroke, the dot, and the hook. The hook is used only in combination to form neumes of two or more notes. The stroke is the virga and is always a long, represented in modern notation by a quarter note. The dot is the punctum and is always a breve of half the value of the long. The hook is also a breve. Since the podatus is a hook combined with a stroke, he transcribes it as ♭Γ ; the clivis, being a combination of a stroke and a hook,

[26] This and the previous example are quoted in Dom Gajard's *La méthode de Solesmes*, 11.

[27] Wagner's theory is based on his study of two eleventh-century neume tables, one from Southern Germany, the other from Monte Cassino, both of which have detailed explanations for the use of choir directors. See Adler, *HdN*, I, 90ff. A penetrating study of Wagner's ideas appears in Sister Marion Geraghty's *The Genesis of Peter Wagner's Theories of Gregorian Chant Rhythm*.

is ⌐⌐ . The torculus, being a stroke with a hook at either end, is
ᗡᒋᗡ ; the porrectus is the opposite: ⌐ᗡᒋ . The scandicus consists of two dots and a stroke: ᒋᒋᒋ ; the climacus is the opposite:
⌐ᒋᒋ .

The normal rhythmical meaning of the neumes may be altered
by rhythmical letters and signs. For example, a clivis with a horizontal dash above it becomes two longs; with the letter *c* above it,
it becomes two breves. A podatus that begins with a straight line
instead of a hook becomes two longs. A torculus is changed from
breve-long-breve to three breves when the letter *c* is above it. The
virga, if episematic, is lengthened by half its value, ⌐· ; a bivirga in
which both strokes are episematic is twice as long, ⌐·⌐· .

Wagner considered the second element of the salicus to represent
a short note followed immediately by another note just below it
before proceeding to the note represented by the virga: ᗡᒋᒋ .

Fig. 17 shows how the first phrase of the Gradual, *Liberasti nos*
(Plate II), would read, using Wagner's principles.[28]

FIG. 17

Li- be - ra - sti, nos, Do -, mi -
ne,

Wagner held that it was impossible to re-establish the original
rhythm of plainchant, and in his own writings there are only a
handful of examples to illustrate his theories of neumatic writing.
He believed that free rhythm applied only to syllabic pieces, and
that melismatic chants were measured according to the interpretation of the neumes in the manner outlined above.

---

[28] The staccato mark over the first note is suggested by the letter *c* in the manuscript, indicating lightness. The porrectus flexus with *c* over "Dom-" is rendered
like Wagner's version of the same figure in Adler, *HdN*, I, 104.

The Transcription of the Facsimiles

The following suggestions are to be regarded as exercises in gaining a familiarity with neumes, rather than as a guide to definitive transcriptions. For, as the preceding discussion has indicated, the transcription of Gregorian into regular notation is in many ways more controversial than that of any other style of medieval music. Actually, the square notation used in chant books today is a more satisfactory vehicle than modern notation for conveying chant melodies; but a good deal may be learned by transcribing the neumes into terms of the common written language of music.

Write in the neumes of the Sangallian, French, and Beneventan facsimiles (Plates II, III, and VI) above the neumes in the corresponding versions of these pieces from the *LU*, reproduced above. Then transcribe the *LU* versions into regular notation, using the Solesmes principles of free rhythm.

Complete the transcription of the Gradual *Liberasti nos* (Plate II), according to Peter Wagner's principles of mensural rhythm. Follow Fig. 17.

Complete the transcription of the Aquitanian Tonarium (Plates IV and V) in the manner begun in Fig. 5.

Transcribe the *Gloria* of Plate VII, including the troped sections, into regular notation, using the Solesmes method.

Transcribe the Gothic *Requiem* (Plate IX) according to Houdard's *neume-temps* method. Consider the beat as the quarter note, and put all the notes of a neume figure into one beat.

Transcribe the hymn *O quam magnifice* (Plate X) into regular notation, using Fig. 10 as a guide in determining the correct pitches; write it in the noncommittal rhythm of Fig. 2.

Complete the transcription of *Rex coeli domine* as begun in Fig. 11.

2

SECULAR MONOPHONIC
NOTATION

▪▪

THE MONOPHONIC secular music of the Middle Ages has also been a subject of controversy among scholars. As in Gregorian chant the main point of disagreement centers on the problem of its rhythm. The matter is complicated by the fact that a large part of this music is extant in manuscripts that were written down in the thirteenth century, a time when the notation of polyphonic music was undergoing a rapid development in the direction of precise mensuration. The mensural character of polyphonic notation is reflected in some of the latter thirteenth-century collections of troubadour and trouvère chansons, some of which are fairly definite in their rhythmical notation. However, the puzzling fact remains that such pieces are relatively few in number, even within those collections of songs (*chansonniers*) which are in the same hand throughout, and were written throughout at the same time. Moreover, in some chansons there are only certain passages that are notated mensurally, the rest being in a rhythmically noncommittal notation like plainchant. Also, some chansons exist both in earlier nonmensural versions and in later versions which convey a definite rhythmic meaning; an example is the chanson *De bone amour*, which is seen in Plates XIV and XV in facsimiles from two different manuscripts. Some scholars have assumed that in such cases the rhythm expressed in the later version must have existed in the earlier one also, although not expressed by notation; but this assumption has not gone unchallenged.

It is not surprising, therefore, that different conclusions have been reached about the great body of secular monophonic song written in unmeasured notation. Some scholars consider that by implication all such music must have been performed in a measured manner regardless of the way in which it is notated; others hold that metrical rhythm should not be applied to pieces written in a "free" notation at a time when measured notation was well-known and available for the use of composers and scribes. The question of the use of duple meter in some pieces has also been raised.

The Modal Theory of Troubadour-Trouvère Music

The opinion most generally held today about the rhythm of troubadour-trouvère music is the "modal" theory, formulated in the early years of this century by Pierre Aubry and Jean Beck.[1] The modal theory is based on the assumption that sets of rhythmic patterns, known in the Middle Ages as the *rhythmic modes*, formed the rhythmic basis of the entire chanson repertory. Of the six rhythmic patterns or modes employed in the music of the twelfth and thirteenth centuries, the courtly singers used only the first, second, and third; the alternating tonic and atonic accents of the poetry corresponded to the long and short values of the modes. This is the way the chansons are written when they are in a notation with mensural values, and Aubry and Beck believed that the same principles applied to the nonmensurally notated chansons as well.

In support of this thesis, Aubry quotes Johannes de Grocheo (*ca.* 1300), one of the few theorists of the period who refer to secular music, to the effect that all music is divided into either plainsong or measured music.[2] However, primary importance is placed by

---

[1] P. Aubry, "L'oeuvre mélodique des troubadours et des trouvères," *La revue musicale*, 1907, 317, 347, and 389; J. Beck, "Die modale Interpretation der mittelalterlichen Melodien," *Caecelia*, 1907, 97. It should be understood that the words "mode" and "modal" as used in this and the next chapter do not have the usual reference to music based on those melodic patterns called the "church modes," but to the rhythmical character of the music which was based on the patterns of the rhythmic modes.

[2] J. Wolf, ed., "Die musiklehre des Johannes de Grocheo," *SIMG*, 1899, 65. This passage has been interpreted quite differently by others. J. Westrup, for ex-

Aubry upon the evidence of the notation in the chansonniers. The scribes were obviously familiar with mensural rhythm, for some collections contain both chansons and polyphonic motets in the same hand, and the notation is the same for both kinds of music. Since it is certain that the polyphonic pieces must have been performed in a measured manner, he assumes that the chansons must have been also. Furthermore, Aubry shows that on the grounds of paleographic evidence a long time cannot have elapsed between the writing of certain pieces in earlier, unmeasured notation, and later versions of those same pieces in mensural writing—perhaps not more than twenty or thirty years at most—and he regards this as far too short a time within which a great change of rhythmical style could have taken place.

Some Mensural Principles of the Thirteenth Century

The notation employed in the mensurally-written chansons was borrowed from polyphonic music, which in the late twelfth and early thirteenth centuries was written in the system of modal notation described in detail in Chapter 4. This system was based on the rhythmic modes, whose time values were conveyed by certain conventional arrangements of the ligatures; single longs and breves were not distinguished in appearance, but were determined by context. Shortly after the middle of the thirteenth century, modal notation took on more precise indications of mensuration. That most pertinent to the chansons was the adoption of the virga of square notation to represent the long, and the punctum to represent the breve (referred to hereafter as L and B). The L had a time relationship to the B of either two to one, which was called *imperfect*, or three to one, called *perfect*. Perfection and imperfection were not expressed by the appearance of the L itself, but by its position —that is, by the value of the note or notes that preceded or followed it. The underlying reason for these rules was to insure the

ample, has called attention to another statement in this treatise which objects to calling "immeasurable" music that is "not precisely measured." Westrup considers Grocheo's meaning to be that secular song had a regular rhythmic foundation, but that it was not necessarily sung in strict time (*NOHM*, II, 227).

flow of the music in a series of "perfections," each comprising a total value of three B's.

The three modal patterns used in the French chansons may be expressed through the use of L and B in the following manner:

1st mode: ♩ ♩ ♩ ♩ = ▪ ▪ ▪ ▪
2nd mode: ♩ ♩ ♩ ♩ = ▪ ▪ ▪ ▪
3rd mode: ♩· ♩ ♩ ♩· ♩ ♩ = ▪ ▪ ▪ ▪ ▪ ▪

The underlying principles that bring about the above rhythms are:

1) L followed by B is imperfect: that is, ▪ ▪ = ♩ ♩ .

2) L followed by L is perfect: that is, ▪ ▪ = ♩· ♩· .

3) L followed by two B's is also perfect; but the second of the two B's becomes an "altered" B (*brevis altera*) which is equal in value to two normal B's, or to an imperfect L: that is, ▪ ▪ ▪ ▪ = ♩· ♩ ♩ ♩· .

4) L followed by three B's is perfect, as the combined value of the latter is equal to a (perfect) L.

Ligatures of two or three notes—the podatus, clivis, scandicus, and climacus of square notation—are frequently used on single text syllables, thus breaking up the succession of L's and B's. Each ligature, whether two-note (*binaria*) or three-note (*ternaria*), re-places the value of a single note, whether this note falls as a B or L in the modal pattern. This is the principle of *equipollentia,* or the equivalence of a group of two or more notes to a single note. Thus, in the first and second modes:

1) A binaria replacing an imperfect L = ♩ ♩ .
2) A ternaria replacing an imperfect L = ♩♩♩ .
3) A binaria replacing a B = ♩♩ .
4) A ternaria replacing a B = ♩♩♩ .

In the third mode, the equivalence of ligatures involves the per-fect L and the altered B, so that:

1) A binaria replacing a perfect L = ♩ ♩ .
2) A ternaria replacing a perfect L = ♩♩♩ .
3) A binaria replacing an altered B = ♩ ♩ .
4) A ternaria replacing an altered B = ♩♩♩ .

Concerning the above tables of equivalence, the rhythmical ar-rangement of the smaller notes in the various time values is another controversial matter, and one that will arise frequently in subsequent chapters. The question is basically whether the division of the B is binary or ternary; that is, whether a two-note ligature should have the rhythm ♩♪ or ♩♪ , and a three-note ligature ♩♪♪ or ♩♪♪ . Historically, binary division (into literal *semibreves*) was the first used, but in the late thirteenth century it was replaced by ternary.[3]

The plica, which occurs frequently in the chansons, has already been noted in the chant *Puer natus* (Plate VIII). In the discussion of that example it was suggested that the plica in its single-note form might still have been merely a sign of liquescence in plainchant. In mensural music, however, it evolved into an actual note with a definite time value, which is half that of the note to which it is attached if that note is imperfect, and a third the value if the note is perfect. The chanson facsimiles contain the following instances of plica forms:

ascending: ♩ ♩ ♩

descending: ♩ ♩ ♩ ♩ ♩

As these examples show, the plica may be attached either to single notes or to ligatures, and may be either a stroke or an added note closely adjacent to the main note; both forms appear to be used indifferently in the chansonniers. It usually occurs as a passing tone between two notes lying a third apart, although it also appears as a neighboring note which returns to a note of the same pitch as that to which it is attached. If the note to which it leads is a step from the note to which it is attached, the plica may either skip a third and then return to the next note, or move a step in the manner of an anticipation, as in the last two notes over "os-" of "oster" in Fig. 19.[4]

The examples selected to illustrate the monophonic secular notation of the Middle Ages in this chapter are from manuscripts of trouvère, Minnesinger, and English song, and include both mensurally and nonmensurally notated illustrations. In the commen-

[3] Medieval treatises before Franco of Cologne's *Ars cantus mensurabilis* (*ca.* 1260) are ambiguous concerning this matter; they merely state that the last note of a ligature is long, a statement which can be interpreted in different ways.

[4] It is customary to transcribe the plica as a note of smaller size than the others, but exceptions to the practice will be seen.

taries on each of the following examples the problems of modal interpretation are considered further in relation to the individual illustrations, as well as to questions of free rhythm and of duple meter in medieval monophonic song.

PLATE XIII. Chanson: *De touz max*, Thibaut, Roy de Navarre (Paris, Bibl. nat. fr. 846, fol. 35; thirteenth century)

The beginning of the mensurally-notated ballade, *De touz max*, indicates that it is in the first mode because of the alternating succession of L and B. Following the principles of equipollentia for the ligatures, the first phrase is transcribed as in Fig. 18.

De   touz max   n'est nuns plai -   sanz

The plica occurs twice in the last line of the manuscript, and in two different forms—as a separate added note over "ne," and as a descending tail from the next-to-last binaria. The last note of all is a sort of large-scale custos, a reminder to the singer of the note on which the melody began, so that the subsequent verses of the poem, which follow immediately after the notated melody, will be started on the correct pitch. The last phrase is transcribed in Fig. 19.

Que nuns ne   s'en doit   os -   ter.

In the phrase quoted in Fig. 19, it will be noted that in the facsimile the main note of the first plica lacks a tail, although it is actually a L. In this form of the plica, that is, as an added note, a tail is never attached to the main note, whose value must be inferred from its context. The second plica is a tail attached to the last note of a binaria which replaces a B; the binaria is therefore equal to two eighth notes, and the plica shares the value of the second.

Ligatures are employed at two cadence points—the end of the bottom line of the column to the left, on "-ter" of "conforter," and at the final cadence. The rhythm of the former (a *quaternaria*) is probably ♫♫♩ 𝄽 ; the latter, according to equipollentia, is B-L. Since it is a final ending, it is likely that in actual performance a natural relaxation of the movement would occur here, and the ending might be transcribed as ♩♩ , or even ♩'|♩ .

The ends of phrases are marked in the manuscript by Gregorian marks of musical punctuation, vertical dashes called incise marks, which later became the rests of mensural notation. The rest in the third line is longer than the others, probably indicating a L rest, in which case the L preceding it would be perfect, following the mensural principle that L before L is perfect.

The text of the chanson is:

> De touz max n'est nuns plaisanz
> Fors soulement cil d'amer,
> Mais cil est douz et poignanz
> Et de li tous a panser.
> Et tant set biau conforter,
> Et de granz biens i a tant
> Que nuns ne s'en doit oster.

PLATE XIV. Chanson: *Bone amor*, Gaces Brulles (Paris, Bibl. nat. n. a. fr. 1050, fol. 29; thirteenth century)

PLATE XV. Chanson: *De bone amour*, Gaces Brulles (Paris, Bibl. nat. fr. 846, fol. 41; thirteenth century)

The *chanson courtoise* ("courtly chanson") on Plate XV, *De bone amour*, is from the same manuscript as *De touz max*, and is also in ballade form. An earlier form of the chanson (*Bone amor*, Plate XIV) has no indications of mensurality; but the later version unmistakably conveys the third mode pattern through its continual use of the note pattern L-B-B, L-B-B, etc.[5] Fig. 20 shows the first phrase of Plate XV transcribed.

FIG. 20

De bone a - mour et de le - aul a - mi - e

[5] There are a few melodic differences in the two versions, and also some slight variations in the text, as at the beginning and in line six of each facsimile.

The *nota plicata* in the third line falls on an altered B, hence is transcribed as two quarters, and the same is true of the two notes with ascending plicas in lines seven and eight. The descending plica in line eight is attached to a perfect L, so that the rhythm here is a half note followed by a quarter.

The vertical dashes that indicate rests are of various lengths in this example. The context indicates that the rest at the cadence near the beginning of the sixth line has the value of a perfect L, and this is also true of the cadence in the middle of line eight.

The text is as follows:

> De bone amour et de leaul amie
> Me vient sovant pitiez et remembrance.
> Si que iamais, a nul ior de ma vie
> N'oblierai son vis ne sa semblance.
> Por ce, s'amors ne se puet plus soffrir,
> Qu'ele de touz ne face son plaisir
> Et de toutes mais ne puet avenir
> Que de la moie aie bone esperance.

The Modal Theory Applied to Pieces in Nonmensural Notation

The transcription of mensurally notated chansons such as *De touz max* and *De bone amour* in the manner described above is relatively clear and simple, except for some question about the rhythm of third mode pieces (to be discussed further on in this chapter). In the very much larger number of pieces whose notation gives no clue to the nature of their rhythm, however, such as those in the facsimiles of Plate XIV (*Bone amor*) and Plate XVI (*Par quel forfait*), the rhythm must be sought through the text. Aubry and Beck assumed that the modal principles applied to all troubadour-trouvère melodies that were written for rhymed metrical poetry. They based their assumption on the generally held belief that Old French and Old Provençal had emphatic stress accents, unlike the modern languages, and that the scansion of each poem would determine in which mode the melody to which it was set should be cast. The principles upon which they proceeded may be summarized as follows:

1) The rhyming syllable at the end of each line is the keystone of the rhythmic framework; the note or ligature above it must without exception coincide with the first note of the modal pattern.

2) The mode will be either first or second if the syllables of the verse preceding the rhyming syllable fall into groups of two, with the tonic accent falling alternately on every other syllable; if the accentual grouping is by three syllables, the third mode is used.

3) The choice between first and second mode is made by noting whether the accents coming before the rhyming syllable fall predominantly on the odd- or even-numbered syllables; if the former receive most of the accents, the first mode is indicated, as in the following:

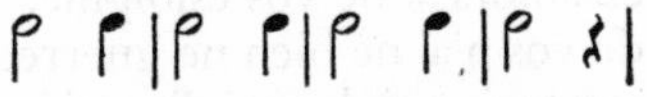

Vo - lez vos que je vous chant

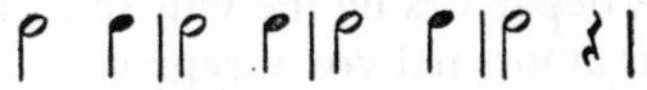

Un son d'a-mour a - ve - nant?

If, however, the accents fall predominantly on even-numbered syllables, the second mode is used:

En ces - te no - te di - rai

D'une a - mor-e - te que j'ai.

4) Should feminine endings occur in the poem, they are considered to fall on the second note of the modal pattern. An anacrusis may be used in the first mode to obtain the proper coincidence of tonic and melodic accents.

PLATE XVI. Chanson: *Par quel forfait*, Le Chastelain de Coucy
    (Paris, Bibl. nat. fr. 20.050, fol. 41v; early thirteenth century)

The chanson *Par quel forfait* is from the oldest of all trouvère manuscripts, the St. Germain-des-Prés chansonnier of the early thirteenth century. It is written in Messine neumes on a staff, and is completely lacking in mensural indications.

The predominating neume figure used is the Messine punctum, occasionally varied by ligatures which include the clivis, podatus, climacus, and pressus. Two rather unusual ligatures occur; that in the third line over the second syllable of the word "pitié" (called by French paleographers a *climacus lié*, a climacus "tied" or "connected" to another neume) which is indistinguishable in effect from the more usual form of climacus that occurs elsewhere in the piece; and the ligature near the beginning of the bottom line, which represents a porrectus to which a virga has been attached.

The words of the verse are as follows:

>Par quel forfait ne per quel mesprison
>M'avez amors si de vos esloignié.
>Que de vos n'ai ne bien ne guerredon
>Ne je ne truis qui de moi dit pitié.
>Malement ai mon servise emploié
>Cainz depar vos ne me vint se mals non.
>Encor amors nel vos ai reproié
>Mon servise mais ore men plaig gié,
>Et di que mort m'avez senz oquison.

Scansion of the first line shows that the word accents divide the syllables naturally into a dactylic pattern; hence the mode of the melody is the third. Thus the first two phrases would read as in Fig. 21.

FIG. 21

The last (rhyming) syllables of each line are doubtless to be held, as is indicated in Fig. 21, so that the third mode pattern starts again at the beginning of the next line. The beginning of the sixth line ("Cainz") varies the pattern, as it starts with a ligature. To be consistent with the usual meaning of the pressus, the one over "mals" should be transcribed as a dotted quarter note followed by an eighth.

The manner of treating trouvère rhythm outlined above has been followed by many distinguished scholars who have worked in the field of medieval secular song, such as Ludwig, Gennrich, and others. There are two major questions, however, which continue to be raised by some writers: one concerns the possibility that duple rhythm may have been used in melodies that have been transcribed in the third mode; the other whether the melodies written in non-mensural notation may not have been sung in a free rhythm according to the taste of the singer.

Concerning the first question, Hugo Riemann set up a system, now discredited, which he called *Vierhebigkeit* ("fourfold stressing"); in this system, all monophonic melodies of the Middle Ages were considered to fit into a four-beat, four-measure pattern, and any mensuration indications which did not fit his theory were disregarded. (*HdN*, I, Ch. 15, Sec. 46, 5a.) Beck, in his edition of the Cangé chansonnier (1927), changed his original approach to the problem of chanson rhythm to admit the likelihood of duple rhythm in some chansons, basing his new viewpoint on a rather obscure statement in Grocheo's treatise.[6] For example, his transcription of the chanson *De bone amour* begins as in Fig. 22 (*Le chansonnier Cangé*, II, No. 99; Beck's note values have been doubled).

FIG. 22

De   bone a - mour et de   le - aul a - mi -/   e

Other scholars who follow the modal principle in general agree to the use of binary rhythm where ternary produces an awkward movement. Some make a distinction between chansons and non-Gregorian songs with Latin texts, allowing binary movement in the former but only modal rhythm in the latter. Still others make exactly the opposite distinction, while others admit both rhythms in any monophonic, nonliturgical song. The question really hinges on whether the modal system of the twelfth and thirteenth centuries was so all-pervading as to exclude the possibility of the use of duple

[6] The passage refers to a special type of song that Grocheo calls the "*cantus coronatus*," made up of long notes, which Beck took to be the spondiac mode, consisting of two long syllables; hence his justification for the use of duple meter.

meter. This hardly seems likely; but it should be noted that no mention is made of duple meter in medieval theoretical treatises until the early fourteenth century.

The question of free rhythm in medieval secular song will be taken up after a consideration of the rhythmical problems presented by the Minnelieder repertory.

Minnelieder

The matter of Minnesong rhythm is obscured by the fact that German scribes continued to write down these melodies in neumatic notation long after other countries adopted mensural notation for all music other than the chant. The facsimiles of Minnelieder on Plates XVII and XVIII, for example, are from two of the most important sources of these songs; the first was written in the fourteenth century, the second in the fifteenth century. (The latter source also includes some Meistersinger pieces that were added to the manuscript in the sixteenth century.)

Since the notation itself offers little in the way of a clue to the rhythmical interpretation of this music, scholars have depended upon the rhythm of the poetry in transcribing Minnelied melodies. This has not been as easy in the German songs as in their French counterparts, because the French poetry is measured by syllables and the German is measured by the number of strong accents, the number of unaccented syllables not being constant. Consequently, modal rhythms are not always applicable to Minnelieder, although some transcribers have used them consistently. Rietsch, the editor of the Vienna manuscript (*DTÖ*, XX2), for instance, takes the position that since the Minnelieder are modelled after the trouvère chansons, and since the chansons are founded on the modes, it follows that the Minnelieder are also. He also thinks that the tunes fall naturally into triple time, and has transcribed the entire Vienna codex in modal meter. Ludwig (Adler *HAM*, I, 204) believes that many of the German melodies, especially those of the thirteenth century, lend themselves well to modal rhythm; but that some, such as the famous Crusader's Song of Walther von der Vogelweide, are as well in either duple or triple time. German melodies of the fourteenth or fifteenth centuries, however, he considers unsuitable for modal rhythm, which had generally gone out of use in music by 1300.

PLATE XVII. Spruch: *In der grünen wyse*, Frauenlob (Vienna, Nat.-bibl. Hs. 2701, fol. 17; fourteenth century)

Das ist vrouwinlobis in der grünen wyse is the title at the head of this composition by the famed Minnesinger, Frauenlob (Heinrich von Meissen, d. 1318). Like *Par quel forfait*, the piece is notated in Messine neumes, to which certain Gothic elements have been added. It has one figure that is not in the neume table of Fig. 1—the punctum with plica, which occurs several times on the page. An example is the third neume of the first line, over "ist"; another, better shaped, is the tenth neume of the second line, over "-gan-" of "begangyn." The neume above "tage" is a Gothic form of the distropha.

The beginning of this Lied is seen in Fig. 23a as transcribed by Rietsch (*DTÖ*, XX2, 67).

FIG. 23A

Myn vroud ist gar czu-gan-gyn, nu ho-rit ia-mir-li-che clag, mich

rü-wit my-ne sün-de, di ich be-gan-gyn han myn tage:

Fig. 23b shows the same passage as it appears in Schering (*GMB*, No. 21).

FIG. 23B

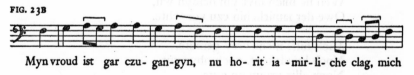

Myn vroud ist gar czu-gan-gyn, nu ho-rit ia-mir-li-che clag, mich

rü-wit my-ne sün-de, di ich be-gan-gyn han myn tage;

The most striking difference between the two versions is that of meter, of course; but the following points should also be noted:

1) The treatment of the plica in each.

2) The fact that equipollentia is not always applied literally, because of the meter of the verse. See the clivis on "-gyn" of both versions; note, however, the difference in treatment of the podatus on "clag." It is not clear why Rietsch did not use the rhythm ♪ ♫ in the thirteenth measure.

3) The lengthening of the second syllable of "sünde" because it is the end of a verse line.

The composition is called a *Spruch* ("proverb"), and is in a rounded Barform, a three-section form—*a a b*—with the final phrase of *a* repeated at the end of *b*. The beginning of each of the three main sections is marked in the manuscript by an ornamental capital. There are a few slight differences between the two *a* sections (called the *Stollen*); the final phrase, which all three sections have in common, begins in the *b* section (called the *Abgesang*) at the second neume on the bottom line, over "das."

The words of the text follow:

> Myn vroud ist gar czugangyn,
> Nu horit iamirliche clag,
> Mich rüwit myne sünde
> Di ich begangin han myn tage;
> Der ist leydir also vil
> Nu wil der tot mich breng der werld czu nichte.
>
> Myn lebyn wert nicht lange,
> Der tot myn ende hot gesworn,
> Waz ich an yn gesende
> Das ist allis gar vorlorn,
> Wen he mich myt ym nemyn wil,
> Owe der iamirlichin czu vorsichte.
>
> Mich hilft nicht vrey gemute,
> Noch kundekeyt, noch obyrmüt,
> Noch allir vrouwyn gute.
> Myn tognt, myn kraft, myn synnyn,
> Das ist allis gar vorlorn;
> Der mich czu gesellin hot dyr korn
> Das ist der tot myt dem mus ich von hynnyn.

PLATE XVIII. Two *Lieder: Ey ich sach in dem trone* and *Nu merkent wie sie truge,* from the Leich, *Unser frawen,* Frauenlob (Munich, Staats-bibl. germ. 4997, fol. 19; fifteenth century)

The facsimile on Plate XVIII contains the first two melodies, or *Töne,* and the beginning of the third, from Frauenlob's Leich, *Unser frawen,* in the famous Colmar manuscript.[7] The Leich was the German equivalent of the trouvère *lai,* a sequence-like design in which a number of sections are strung together. Each section is more or less independent, and consists of a melody and its repetition; two stanzas are set to each section. The entire Leich, *Unser frawen,* contains twenty-two melodies and forty-four stanzas. It is in Gothic notation, in which the predominating sign is the virga. Ligatures used in the first melody include the porrectus, climacus, and torculus; the second has the podatus, clivis, climacus, and scandicus. The pitch of *F* is always indicated by the use of a red line in the staff, the others being black. The red line is the second line from the top in staff one, the third line in staves two, three, five, and six, and the fourth line in staves four and seven. At the end of line four, after "witzen," it changes from the fourth to the third line.

Runge, the editor of the published volume containing the Colmar manuscript, made his transcriptions, which were actually transliterations into a special kind of nonmensural square notation, before the modal theory had been formulated.[8] He advocated the execution of the Lieder in either triple or duple meter, according to the suggestion of the meter of the poem, although he admits that it is not always easy to determine what the poem suggests. He lengthens the end of each line, and both the last and the penultimate syllables in feminine endings.

The punctum occurs occasionally in the manuscript; Runge considered the punctum to be a plica, a theory no longer held. There

---

[7] The title and rubric at the top of the page read: "Carmina magistralia. Hie folget gesang der meister geticht, zum ersten: in meister Heinrich Frauwenlobes tönen, die nach einander gent und die ersten genotiert, et sic de aliis. Diss ist unser frawen leich oder der guldin flügel zu Latin Cantica Canticorum. Stent je zwey lied in eym tone und in eym gemesse und sint der töne XXII der lieder XLIII."

[8] *Die Sangsweisen der Colmarer Handschrift.*

seems to be no rational explanation for the use of this symbol in the manuscript, however.

Transcribing the beginning of the tune in both triple and duple meters, as in Figs. 24a and 24b, seems to indicate clearly the preferability of duple meter from the standpoint of sheer musicality.

FIG. 24A

Ey ich sach in dem tro -   ne ein jung-fraw die   was swan-ger,

FIG. 24B

Ey ich sach in dem tro -   ne ein jung-fraw die   was swan- ger,

A comparison of the facsimile of *Ey ich sach* with the transcription shows how the meter of the poem affects the equivalence of ligatures. The verse lines are each four feet in length, with anacrusis at the beginning; there is one syllable in each of the last two feet. Therefore, the porrectus over "tro-" of "trone" must occupy a whole foot, while that over "die" takes up only half a foot.

The remainder of the first verse and the whole of the second verse follow:

> Sie trug ein wundercrone
> In myner augen anger.
>
> Sie wolte sin enbunden
> Suss gie die allerbeste,
> Zwolff steine zu der stunden
> Kosz in der kronen veste.

The second *Ton* of the *Leich* poses a different problem as its verses are quite irregular in length. The basic line is four feet in length, but lines one and four each have an additional ending that is like an echo of the preceding syllables. The last line of all appears to have six feet ($\smile / - / - \smile / - / - \smile / - / -$).

The text of the poem follows:

> Nu merkent wie sie truge die gefüge
> Der naturen zu genüge;
> Von dem sie was geburdet

Den sach sie vor ir sitzen mit witzen
In siben luchteren;
Und sach in doch gesundert
In eynes lammes wyse
Uff syon dem berge gehuren.

Sie tet auch waz sie solde ja die holde
Sie trug den blumen ein tolde fraw (?)
Meit ob ir muter würdet
Des lammes und der tuben den truben
Ir liessent uver sweren
Davon mich nit en wundert
Daz uch dyselb spyse
Kan zu der früchte gesturen.

Free Rhythm

The questions raised by the secular repertory of France and Germany apply to most of the twelfth- and thirteenth-century secular monophonic song in the other countries of Europe as well. This large body of music includes Spanish songs in praise of the Virgin —the *cantigas;* German penitential songs of the flagellants—the *Geisslerlieder;* Italian devotional hymns—the *laudi;* the melodies of the wandering scholars—the goliardic songs, Latin counterparts of the French chanson; the monophonic conductus; and a few English songs. The greater part of this repertory is written in nonmensural notation; whether a given nonmensurally notated piece is transcribed modally or in free rhythm, or whether duple or triple time is used, depends in most cases on the viewpoint of the individual transcriber rather than on any definite and reliable information.

The possibility of free rhythm in medieval song has been raised by some scholars in recent years. Curt Sachs, for example, has recently affirmed his view that the existence of mensurally-notated passages within a chanson indicates that these were exceptional rhythms that applied only to those particular passages, which, he thinks, a singer could probably not perform without special guidance. French verse, he says, is numerical rather than metrical or accentual, and patterns of meter or accent should not be imposed on the chansons, which are not subject to the modes but "had the privilege of free rhythm." In general, Sachs considers that "the use of a rhythmically noncommittal notation in times when a metrical script was available indicates a free or optional rhythm." [9] Like other investigators, he draws upon Grocheo for support, interpreting him as stating that the modes applied only to polyphonic music.

PLATE XIX. Song: *Worldes blis* (Oxford, Bodl. Lib. Rawl. G18, fol. 105v and 106; thirteenth century)

An interesting example of the difference between modal and free rhythmical versions of the same piece is seen in two recent transcriptions of one of the relatively few English secular pieces of the thirteenth century—*Worldes blis*—a facsimile of which is seen on Plate XIX. It is in nonmeasured notation, which J. Westrup has transcribed in the second mode (*NOHM*, 251). Fig. 25a shows the beginning of his version.

FIG. 25A

Willi Apel, on the other hand, prefers "a free rhythmic rendition over one in modal rhythm," and transcribes it as in Fig. 25b; in his transcriptions each separate L is made a quarter note, and each ligature is in equipollentia (*HAM*, I, No. 23b). [10]

FIG. 25B

[9] *Rhythm and Tempo*, 178.
[10] Italian musicologists employ the term "*isosillabalismo*" for this kind of transcription of monophonic secular songs. See E. Paganuzzi's "Sulla notazione neumatica della monodia trobodorica," *Rivista musicale italiana*, 1955, 23.

The Transcription of the Facsimiles

The facsimiles of Plates XIII through XIX offer an opportunity for practice in transcribing in the various manners that have been discussed in this chapter. In those that are mensurally written there is no choice of rhythm, of course (with the possible exception of the third mode pattern, which might be rendered in duple time); but in the others the use of either modal, free, or duple rhythm would be justified. Suggestions for transcriptions are indicated below.

Transcribe modally:
Plate XIII, *De touz max*, as begun in Fig. 18.
Plate XV, *De bone amour*, as begun in Fig. 20.
Plate XVI, *Par quel forfait*, as begun in Fig. 21.
Plate XVII, *In der grünen wyse*, as begun in Fig. 23a.

Transcribe in duple meter:
Plate XIV, *Bone amor*.
Plate XVIII, *Ey ich sach* and *Nu merkent*.

Transcribe in free rhythm, in the manner of Fig. 25b:
Plate XVI, *Par quel forfait*.
Plate XIX, *Worldes blis*.

3

EARLY POLYPHONIC
NOTATION

▀▄▀

T HE EARLIEST period of polyphonic music—from the
first actual records in the treatises of the late ninth century to the St. Martial organa of the early twelfth century
—is represented by a relatively small number of examples.
With the notable exception of the Winchester Troper, they consist
of only a page or two from manuscript sources of various kinds.[1]
These isolated examples are written in various kinds of notation—
Daseia signs, letters, and oratorical and diastematic neumes—and no
summary of basic principles can be drawn up as an introduction
to them; rather, each example must be considered as an individual
problem. By far the larger number of them are written in oratorical
neumes, and hence are not transcribable into accurate pitch symbols; and the rhythmic character of all of them is entirely a matter
of speculation. It is only from the carefully diastematic organa in
Aquitanian neumes of the St. Martial school that polyphonic music
can be consistently transcribed with accuracy of pitch, but the
rhythm of these works is still problematical. The first body of polyphony in a notation that enables both pitch and rhythm to be
determined is the repertory of the Notre Dame school of the late
twelfth and early thirteenth centuries, and even here the modal
notation in which it is written does not allow for certainty in all

---

[1] L. Spiess has listed fourteen such sources in "An introduction to the pre-St.
Martial practical sources of early polyphony," *Speculum*, 1947, 16. See also the
list in J. Wolf, *HdN*, I, 214, fn. 3.

60

respects. It will be the purpose of this chapter to consider the problems connected with the notation in which the earliest body of polyphonic music is written, from the simple examples in the treatise entitled *Musica enchiriadis* to the great works of the Notre Dame school; in other words, polyphonic notation up to the advent of modal notation.

Polyphony in Neumatic Notation

PLATES XXa AND XXb. Organa: *Rex coeli domine* (Paris, Bibl. nat. lat. 7211, fol. 9v; eleventh century), and *Miserere mei deus* (Paris, Bibl. nat. lat. 10.509, fol. 89; tenth century)

Facsimiles *a* and *b* of Plate XX illustrate two styles of notation in which the earliest specimens of polyphony exist. They are notations that were intended for didactic purposes, and were not widely used in medieval music generally; they are included here principally for their historical interest.[2] The first, *Rex coeli domine*, is from an eleventh-century copy of the epoch-making anonymous ninth-century *Musica enchiriadis*, and is in a curious kind of notation that may have been the invention of the author of the famous treatise. It is in a sort of diastematy of the text itself, whose syllables are heighted according to pitch. In order to insure the proper pitch, Daseia symbols are placed vertically at the beginning, functioning thus as "clef signs."[3] The *vox principalis* is in the upper voice; it is the same as the monophonic version of this melody which is in Daseia notation on Plate XI. It is likely that the scribe who made this copy of the *Musica enchiriadis* intended to put horizontal lines between the lines and to the right of the Daseia symbols, as they appear this way in other existing copies of the treatise.

An example of polyphonic letter notation is seen in the second facsimile of Plate XX—an illustration by Guido of Arezzo of three-

[2] The only example of polyphony in letter notation not found in a treatise is the two-voiced *Ut tuo propitiatus* (Oxford, Bodl. Lib. 572), from the twelfth century, which is given in facsimile in *EEH*, I, Pl. i, and in Apel, *NPM*, 205, with a transcription on 208.

[3] Only the first part of the composition is shown in the facsimile; the rest follows on the succeeding page of the manuscript. The whole piece is in *GS*, I, 169, and is transcribed in Parrish-Ohl, *Masterpieces of Music*, 17. In the copy of the *Musica enchiriadis* from which the facsimile has been taken, the lines of the text somehow became transposed.

voiced parallel organum in his *Epistola ad Teodal* where he discusses
"Diaphonia." The copy of the letter from which this facsimile was
made is in a tenth-century Gradual written for the Abbey of St.
Wandrille. What Guido is illustrating here is a method that can be
used to "improvise" in parts, so that the example is not an actual
specimen of polyphonic composition. A curious detail occurs in
the final melisma, where C is twice repeated in the lower voice but
only once in the upper, probably a scribal error.

More significant than the preceding examples are the sources in
neumatic notation, headed by the imposing collection of the early
eleventh-century Winchester Troper which contains 164 two-part
organa. The contents of this monument have remained a mystery,
as it is written in Anglo-Saxon oratorical neumes which are closely
similar in appearance to St. Gall neumes, and no later manuscript
exists that contains these pieces in pitch notation. In spite of the
apparent hopelessness of the task, Marius Schneider has attempted
to transcribe some items from the Troper.[4]

PLATE XXc. Organum: Alleluia and Verse, *Dies sanctificatus*
(Chartres, Bibl. de la ville 130, fol. 50; eleventh century) for
the Mass of the Day of the Nativity

The two-part organum reproduced on Plate XXc is characteristic
of the isolated examples of polyphony in neume notation which occur in various eleventh-century manuscripts. In these examples the
added counterpoint proceeds in note-against-note style against the
liturgical cantus firmus, and in predominantly contrary motion to
it. The folio page of the Chartres manuscript containing this example includes five *Alleluias* with their verses for Christmas and
Easter, four of which still remain in the liturgy, as does this one.
(See *PM*, I, Pl. xxiii.) They are written in Norman neumes that
are slightly diastematic. There is a complete correspondence in the
use of neume figures in the vox organalis against those of the same
number of notes in the cantus firmus—as punctum against virga,
podatus against clivis, torculus against porrectus, etc. (This is the
example referred to in Chapter 1 as evidence offered by Dom
Mocquereau to refute the mensuralists' interpretation of virga and

---

[4] *Geschichte der Mehrstimmigkeit*, II, Beisp. 5–11. This volume also contains
facsimiles of two pages from the Winchester Troper, Anhang II, 54–55.

punctum as long and breve.) Unlike the Winchester Troper, in which each of the two parts is on a separate page with the text beneath each part, the example shown here is "in score," and the same line of text presumably serves for each of the voice-parts.

While any attempt to transcribe a manuscript like this is largely conjectural, certain known factors make it possible to arrive at results that can be assumed to come close to the composer's intentions. The lower part presents no problem, as it is a Gregorian melody still in use (*LU*, 409–410); and the upper added part can be realized with a fair chance of approaching the correct notes by following the pitch directions indicated by the neumes, and by limiting the choice of harmonic intervals to those employed by musicians of the period. These intervals are determined by the analysis and comparison of existing eleventh-century polyphonic examples in definite pitch notation, and by statements in early medieval treatises concerning "symphoniae," or harmonic intervals. Even the practice of the twelfth century—when actual examples are far more extensive—can be a guide, as it may be presumed to have been not strikingly different from the period of the Chartres manuscript. Such considerations show that the octave and unison occur with the greatest frequency of any intervals, that the order of frequency after that is of the fifth, third, and fourth (although the third was technically a dissonance and the fourth a consonance), and that the dissonance of the second occurs frequently, and those of the sixth and seventh seldom.[5]

With the foregoing as guiding principles, a transcription of the first line of the Chartres organum would read as in Fig. 26. The organal voice is partly after Schneider's transcription (*GM*, II, Anh. II, Beisp. 7), which was collated with organa from the Winchester Troper and from Br. Mus. Add. 27.630, both of which use the same cantus firmus. The transcription is noncommittal in rhythm, and in actual execution the most likely rendition would be that of the free rhythm of plainsong.[6]

In the early twelfth century a significant expansion of contrapuntal technique took place with the introduction of independent,

---

[5] See the discussion of interval frequency in Dom Hughes, *NOHM*, II, 296ff.
[6] Other examples of eleventh-century organa notated in neumes may be seen in facsimile in H. Bannister, "Un fragment inédit de discantus," *RG*, 1911, 29; and in *PM*, IV, Pl. 416.

freer movement in the added organal voice, or *duplum*, which was often melismatic in character, sometimes highly so. This new art first made its appearance at the Abbey of St. Martial in Limoges, and is represented by about eighty organa in the four different

FIG. 26

Al - le-lu - ia

Di -   es

san - cti - fi -   ca -   tur il - lux - it

manuscripts which contain the repertory of this school.[7] The notation of these compositions is in precisely diastematic Aquitanian neumes; this notation tells nothing of the rhythm of the organa, however, and any transcription is tentative in this regard.

Historically, this repertory is important in having established two distinct and basic styles of polyphonic writing, both of which are represented in the two St. Martial facsimiles of Plates XXI and

[7] Paris, Bibl. Nat. lat. 1139, 3719, and 3549, and London, Br. Mus. Add. 36.881.

XXII. These styles are the *melismatic* style—in which the duplum consists of a chain of melismas over a tenor of single sustained notes like a series of pedal-points; and the *note-against-note* style—a continuation of the older style of organum which was now used for the new sacred strophic songs, and also for occasional passages within a melismatic organum.

PLATE XXI. Organum: *Jubilemus, exultemus* (Paris, Bibl. nat. lat. 1130, fol. 14; early twelfth century)

This is a Benedicamus Trope for the Nativity, from the oldest of the St. Martial sources, which may have been written as early as 1100. Its two lines of music are separated by a heavily-drawn line, and a dry line representing G is scratched into the parchment in each voice part. Another pitch aid is used in the fifth line of the lower voice, where an additional heavy line is employed to indicate the pitch F. There are also several letters in the upper parts serving as further pitch-guides, as in the third line (G), fifth line (G and C), and bottom line (G, A, and F). Several notes have descending plicas attached to them.

The probable rhythm in which this and other St. Martial pieces of similar style were performed has been an intriguing subject of speculation. The number of notes in the upper part to those in the lower varies considerably—from one to fifteen, actually—so that an effort to keep the lower part uniform in pace would cause a great variety of speeds in the upper note groups. On the other hand, a uniform pace in the upper part would cause as much variety in the notes of the slower-moving tenor. The first possibility was favored by J. Handschin, who believed that the interpretation of *Jubilemus* should be free and nonmensural, with a slight lingering on the last note of each group in the upper part whenever it seems appropriate. When a single note of the upper part occurs against a note of the lower it should be sung more broadly; the notes of a duplum group should be accelerated (*zusammengedrängt*). In general, up to about six notes might be included in the value of one broad syllabic note; beyond that the prevailing movement should be relaxed.[8] F. Ludwig, on the other hand, has transcribed another St. Martial trope similar to this one by evening out the gait of the notes of

[8] "Die mittelalterlichen Aufführungen in Zürich . . . ," *ZfM*, Oct. 1927, 8.

the duplum, thus giving indefinite and variable length to the tenor notes (Adler *HMG*, I, 179).

Both interpretations produce satisfactory musical results, although there is no way of knowing which, if either, corresponds to the manner originally intended. The beginning of the organum is transcribed in Fig. 27, partly after Handschin, who pointed out that the first and fifth notes of the tenor are probably incorrectly written in the manuscript, as they would be A and E-flat, respectively, if literally transcribed.

The complete text is as follows:

Jubilemus, exultemus, intonemus canticum.
Redemptori, plasmatori, salvatori omnium.
Hoc nathali, salutari, omnis nostra turmula.
Deum laudet, sibi plaudat, per eterna secula.
Qui hodie de Marie utero progrediens.
Homo verus, rex atque, herus in terris apparuit.
Tam beatum, ergo natum, cum ingenti gaudio.
Conlaudantes, exultantes, benedicamus Domino.

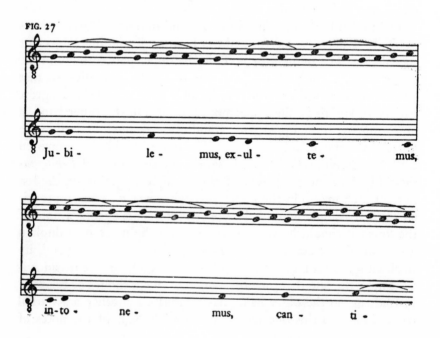

FIG. 27

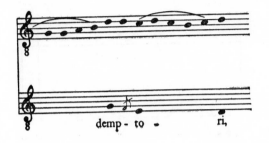

PLATE XXII. Organum: *Lux descendit* (London, Br. Mus., Add. 36.881, fol. 2 and 2v; twelfth century)

The examples on Plate XXII are representative of the note-against-note style of many hymns of the St. Martial repertory. The first of the three hymns in the facsimile is transcribed in Fig. 28. The character of the piece and of its notation suggests that it proceeds in straightforward movement, and one might be justified in transcribing it in a more frankly metrical manner than that in which it is here rendered—that is, a transcription in which stems and flags would be attached to the note heads, representing definite time values.

The other two hymns in the facsimile are similar in character to this one. The texts read as follows:

> Per hanc matrem victa fraude
> Laudet patrem dignum laude
> Chorus choro timpano.
>
> Omnis curet homo pro iure cantica
> Sunt completa modo dicta prophetica.

FIG. 28

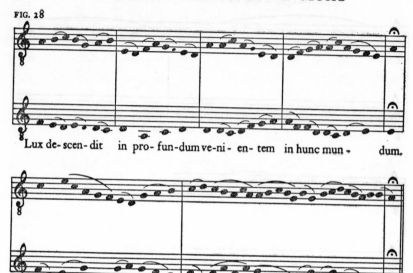

Lux de- scen- dit   in pro- fun-dum ve-ni- en- tem   in hunc mun ‑   dum.

Lux il ‑   lus ‑ trant   ho ‑   ‑   ‑   ‑ mi- nem.

PLATE XXIII. Organum: *Congaudeant catholici* (Santiago de Compostela, Cod. Calixtinus, fol. 185; early twelfth century)

Another source of early polyphony related in style to the St. Martial organa is the Codex Calixtinus, which was inscribed in 1137, according to Anglès (*CMH*, I, 59), at the famed medieval shrine of pilgrimage, Santiago de Compostela, in Galicia. The manuscript contains twenty-two pieces in two parts, and one in three parts—the celebrated *Congaudeant catholici*—which is seen in the lower part of Plate XXIII.[9]

The codex is written in Norman neumes on a four-line staff, so that problems of pitch are practically nonexistent. The notation tells nothing about the rhythm, though, and an examination of the page indicates that, as in the example from the Chartres manuscript on Plate XX, virga and punctum can have no mensural meaning whatever; they are used only in their original significance of denoting pitch relationships.

[9] The contents of the manuscript are published, with facsimiles, in the *Liber Sancti Jacobi. Congaudeant* is in Vol. III, facing p. lvi. A curious feature of the manuscript is the attribution of many of the songs to certain ecclesiastical dignitaries, apocryphally, it is believed.

Congaudeant is considered to be the oldest extant composition in three parts; it is thought that the third (middle) part was a later addition, although scholars have not agreed on just which notes were added. It is a Benedicamus Trope, or, rather, a free paraphrase on the words "Benedicamus Domino," which occur at the end of the sixth strophe of the text (third line from the bottom of the page, beginning with "be-" at the end of the line). This piece has been a particular subject of study, and has been transcribed by scholars in a number of ways. A comparison of these transcriptions will give an instructive insight into the different approaches which have been used by modern scholars in attempting to solve the riddle posed by medieval polyphonic music written in nonmensural notation.

W. Apel and H. Anglès have made transcriptions of the Calixtinus pieces which purposely avoid an outright mensural rendering, and in which the predominantly single notes of the tenor proceed at a uniform pace, and all ligatures are in equipollentia. Fig. 29a is a transcription of *Congaudeant* made in this manner.

FIG. 29A

Con- gau-de - ant ca - tho- li - ci, le- ten- tur ci- ves

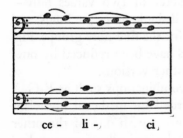

ce - li -, ci,

Ludwig's interpretation of this piece (in Adler *HdM*, I, 182) has been widely quoted; the only difference between it and the version

in Fig. 29a is that the values within each beat are rhythmically organized. See Fig. 29b, and note especially the five-note groups in
bars three and four.

FIG. 29B

Con - gau - de -   ant ca - tho - li -   ci, le - ten - tur

ci -   ves ce - li -   ci.

Dom Hughes has adopted a different method of transcription
(*NOHM*, II, 305–306) based on an attempt to have as many consonant vertical combinations on the first-beat coincidences of the
voices as possible. In so doing he adopts a modal rhythm; this is
seen in Fig. 29c.

Handschin has employed a still different method based on the
principle of having a measured character of two values only—
longs and breves—in the upper part. All single notes are longs, and
notes in ligatures are all breves, except for the five-note groups. Fig.
29d shows this method; the note values have been reduced by one-
half to facilitate comparison with the other versions.

Handschin points out that vertical combinations such as E-G-A
(over "le-" of "letentur") were regarded by medieval musicians
as consonances, as each voice is consonant with one of the other
two. The interval of the third, though theoretically dissonant, had
the force of a consonance because of its frequent use.

The upper part of Plate XXIII contains the two-part organum
Nostra phalanx, written in neumes that are easier to read than those

FIG. 29C

Con - gau - de - ant ca - tho - li - ci, le - ten - tur

ci - ves ce - li - ci

FIG. 29D

Con - gau - de - ant ca - tho - li - ci, le - ten - tur

ci - ves ce - li - ci

of *Congaudeant*. The text of the strophe underlying the music is as follows:

> Nostra phalanx plaudat leta
> Hac in die qua athleta
> Christi gaudet sine meta
> Jacobus in gloria,
> Angelorum in curia.

The Transcription of the Facsimiles

The lack of mensurality in the examples of early polyphony considered in this chapter makes the problem of their transcription superficially akin to that of Gregorian chant; but the coincidence of voices in polyphony is a factor which must necessarily be taken into account. While all efforts at transcribing these examples will necessarily be speculative, attempts at transcription will undoubtedly develop a feeling for the character of early polyphony which will be valuable for a consideration of the examples of modal notation in the next chapter. The following are suggested exercises in transcription:

Continue the transcription of the Verse *Dies sanctificatus* which follows the *Alleluia* of Plate XX in the manner of Fig. 26. The version of the plainchant given in the *LU* (409–410) should be used as a guide for the lower part. In reconstructing the upper part, the two principles to keep in mind are the observance of the pitch direction indicated by the neumes, and the selection of harmonic intervals most likely to have been used at this period. Re-read the discussion of Fig. 26.

Continue the transcription of *Jubilemus*, Plate XXI, in the manner begun in Fig. 27.

Transcribe the two conductus that follow *Lux descendit*, Plate XXII, in the manner of Fig. 28.

Transcribe the two-part organum, *Nostra phalanx*, Plate XXIII, in measured rhythm, organizing the individual note groups in the manner of Ludwig's version of *Congaudeant*, Fig. 29b.

4

MODAL NOTATION

▄▀

A
N IMPORTANT stage in the evolution of notation occurred in the late twelfth century, when a degree of mensurality came to be suggested by the pitch symbols. This
is the period of *modal notation*, in which the modal meters largely determined the rhythmical meaning of the notes. The
system of modal notation was ambiguous in some respects, however, and often indicated the rhythmic intent indirectly; for the
same notes and ligatures may have different meanings according
to context—a situation already encountered in medieval secular
monophony. The period to be dealt with in this chapter is somewhat earlier than that of the mensurally-written trouvère pieces,
and represents modal notation at a somewhat less advanced stage
than was described in Chapter 2. The principal monument of the
period is the set of four extant manuscripts which contain, in varying states of completeness, the collection called the *Magnus liber
organi*. The names of Leoninus and Perotinus, the compilers of this
"great book" of polyphonic music for the entire ecclesiastical year,
are the only ones known to us of what has come to be called the
Notre Dame School. Leoninus, the earlier of the two, may well
have been active before 1163, when the cornerstone of the great
cathedral of Paris was laid. The interpretation of the music of the
manuscripts which contain the Notre Dame repertory—known as
Wolfenbüttel 677, Wolfenbüttel 1206, Florence Pluteus 29.1, and
Madrid 20.486—like that of much of the music of the Middle Ages,
is not satisfactorily clarified by the writings of the medieval theorists, and there is considerable disagreement among modern re-

73

searchers over many essential details. However, we know enough to be able to transcribe a great deal of the Notre Dame repertory with a fair degree of certainty.

Most scholars transcribe this music in values in which the L is equal to the quarter note; in the transcriptions of trouvère and other thirteenth-century monophony, the L is usually represented by the half note. The reason is that in the modal period the beat (normally represented by the quarter note since the seventeenth century) was the *perfection*—that is, the perfect L, equal to three B's. Hence music of the modal period is usually transcribed in $\frac{6}{8}$ meter, each beat representing a perfection; this is a literal reduction of values from sixteen to one, as the L is equal to four whole notes. In the period of the trouvère manuscripts, however, a shift of values took place in which the B became the beat; this music is therefore usually transcribed in $\frac{3}{4}$ time with the B equalling the quarter note, a reduction of values from eight to one. This shift toward the smaller units to represent the beat continued down to the semibreve, minima, and semiminima (our present quarter note), the last becoming fixed as the beat from the seventeenth century to the present.[1]

The Basic Patterns of the Modal System

The compositions of the Notre Dame repertory are written in one of two general styles of notation: 1) the melismatic *organum* style, in which ligatures predominate almost exclusively, and in which the upper voice or voices execute continuous vocalises; 2) the syllabic *conductus* style, composed predominantly of single notes, in which ligatures are used only when a text syllable has more than one note, or in passages where a textless vocalise occurs. A melismatic line is written as much as possible in chains of ligatures broken only by rests which separate them into phrases called *ordines* (the plural of *ordo*). An ordo was a rhythmic pattern usually, though not always, followed by one or more repetitions of itself. The manner in which the notes of each ordo were arranged in ligature was the principal means of expressing the modal rhythm which

[1] See Apel, *NPM*, 343, and Sachs, "Some remarks about old notation," *MQ*, 1948, 365.

dominated twelfth-century polyphony. The basic principle of ligature notation expressing modal rhythm was the *binaria*, which is assumed to represent the rhythm B-L in practically all circumstances.

The six rhythmic modes, each illustrated with an instance of an actual ordo in that mode, are given in Fig. 30. With the exception of the fifth mode, they do not always appear in such regular formations as these; certain irregularities are frequently introduced into the ligature successions both for the sake of rhythmic variety and also because irregularities are sometimes unavoidable because of repeated notes. The characteristic feature of each mode may be summarized as follows.

Mode 1: ♪ ♪♪ ♪ , by far the most widely used, and presumably the oldest and the one from which all the others evolved. It is the *trochaic* meter of classical poetry—LB—and is expressed by the ligature arrangement 3-2-2, etc.; that is, a series of binarias beginning with a ternaria.

Mode 2: ♪♪ ♪♪ , the classical *iambic* meter—BL—whose accent falls on the B, which is not an upbeat. It is expressed by the ligature arrangement 2-2-3; that is, a series of binarias ending with a ternaria.

Mode 3: ♪· ♪♪ , originally the *dactylic* meter ⌐∪∪ ♪ ♪♪ , which was modified to allow for its use with the other modes. For this reason the last note of the pattern was considered to be an altered B, even though it had the same time value as the L of the first and second modes. It is expressed in ligature patterns by 1-3-3, etc.; that is, by a single note followed by one or more ternarias.

Mode 4: ♪♪ ♪· , the classical *anapest*, modified from ∪∪⌐♪♪♪ . This mode exists almost only in theory, it is so rarely used. Its ligature pattern is the opposite of the third mode, being 3-3-1, a series of ternarias ending with a single note.

Mode 5: ♪·♪· , the classical *spondee*, used mostly in the tenor. This mode was expressed in two ways, both of which are seen in Fig. 30. It may appear in uniformly moving, separately notated L's, or in a series of ligatures separated by incises. The use of ligatures to express L's was contrary to the fundamental principles of modal notation, but its use in this manner in the tenor was a convention that was recognized and allowed by the theorists.

Mode 6: 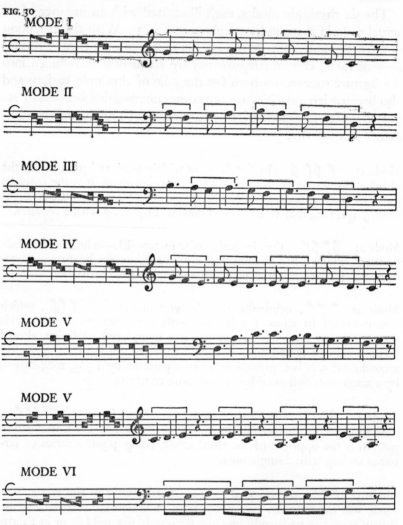, consisting of all B's, is used in organum almost exclusively in the upper parts, and usually for only short stretches. Its ligature pattern is 4-3-3; that is, a quaternaria followed by a series of ternarias. It is the classical *tribrach*.

FIG. 30

Although this system of six modes was recognized by medieval theorists, in actual practice only the first three appear to have been the standard patterns of the modal period. The second mode was less frequently used than the first and third. The fourth mode is al-

most never seen, and the fifth and sixth are hardly modes at all, in
view of their uniform rhythm, although there is a theoretical convenience in including them in the modal scheme.[2]

Rhythmical Modifications of the Basic Modal Patterns

Variations from the regular ligature patterns of the rhythmic
modes are brought about in one of two ways: 1) by deviations
within an ordo from the regular ligature successions; and 2) by the
addition of the plica. Both these methods are frequently used for
the purpose of replacing an imperfect L with two B's—a process
known as *fractio modi*, the "breaking up" of the mode.

In Fig. 31a, the normal L of the third ligature becomes a B, since
it is followed by an "irregular" ternaria, that is, one which appears
in a first-mode ordo elsewhere than at the beginning. When this
occurs, the L with which the binaria ends shares half its value with
the first note of the ternaria that follows it.

FIG. 31

The same rhythmical effect is produced by the plica, as may be
seen in Fig. 31b; the plica shares half the value of the L of the
binaria to which it is attached.[3]

[2] Medieval theorists distinguished between perfect and imperfect ordines. A
perfect ordo was one that ended on the first member of the modal pattern
(ſ ƀſ ƀ|ſ); an imperfect ordo ended on the last member of the pattern
(ſ ƀſ ƀ). This distinction has no practical significance, however. This may
also be said of the classification of the ordines according to the number of complete mode patterns they contained; thus in the first mode the first ordo would
be ſ ƀſ , the second ordo ſ ƀſ ƀ|ſ , the third ſ ƀſ ƀ|ſ ƀſ , etc.

[3] It is noteworthy that many such passages occur in compositions extant in more
than one manuscript in which the same rhythm is expressed by the plica in one
version and by a binaria in another. In the passage quoted in Fig. 31, however,
the plica could not have been used as it cannot by its nature represent a repeated
note.

Not every irregularity in ligature patterns means a change in rhythm, however; these are sometimes caused by repeated notes, which cannot be written in ligature but only in adjacent ligatures or by single notes. Fig. 32 shows three ways in which repeated notes are treated; all the irregularities in the ligature successions of the example are due to the presence of repeated notes falling at awkward places. (The climacus figure in Fig. 32a is considered the same as any other ternaria from a rhythmical standpoint.) Note the following points in the illustrations of Fig. 32:

a) There is no deviation from the modal meter.
b) It is impossible to begin with the usual ternaria.
c) The context from which this example is taken requires that the first perfection be in uniform eighth-note movement, which is ordinarily expressed by the quaternaria; since the repeated notes make the use of a quaternaria impossible, two binarias are used instead.

FIG. 32

A process is also employed in modal notation whereby the opposite effect of fractio modi is produced—that is, where a L that is normally imperfect in the modal pattern becomes perfect. This has been appropriately called by Willi Apel *extensio modi*, the "enlargement" or "lengthening" of the mode. The effect of extensio modi is to momentarily change the prevailing modal pattern into the fifth mode; fractio modi changes it into the sixth mode. Perfect L's, when not part of a modal pattern, are expressed by single notes. A primary rule of modal notation operates here—namely, that L before L is perfect; otherwise the prevailing ternary meter would be thrown off. The problem of repeated notes arises in *extensio modi* too, and many cases that appear to be L-before-L are due to repeated notes. The context will usually reveal what rhythm is called for.

Semibreves form another rhythmical modification of frequent occurence in the *Magnus liber*, where they are used in the literal sense of the word—"half-breves."[4] The semibreve (hereafter referred to as the S) is expressed in modal notation in two ways: 1) by the plica when it is attached to a B; 2) by the special form of ligature known as the *conjunctura* (or *currentes*) when the ligature consists of more than three notes.

The way in which the plica has the effect of making two S's out of the B to which it is attached is seen in Fig. 33a, in which the rhythm without the plica would have been [notation] . Since the plica shares the value of the note to which it is attached, and since analysis of the example shows this to have been a B, sixteenth notes necessarily result.

FIG. 33

The conjunctura, which is more frequently used than the plica for indicating semibreves, always appears in descending scalewise formation and in groups of from three to eight, or even more; in counting the notes of a conjunctura, the main note that the diamond-shaped notes follow is included in the ground. Three- or four-note conjuncturas are treated like any ligatures with the same number of notes. When a four-note conjunctura or ligature occurs within an ordo, S's result, as in Fig. 33b. The principles by which the rhythm of this illustration is ascertained may be analyzed as follows:

[4] Historically, these notes began as embellishing or "chromatic" notes (in the rhythmical meaning), but during the Franconian period they came to be subject to the same principles of perfection, imperfection, and alteration in relation to the B as the B had to the L, and thus to have the value of a third of a B.

1) In the normal course of a first-mode ordo, only binarias occur, after the initial ternaria; the last note of each binaria is a L.

2) When an irregular ligature, binaria or ternaria, is introduced, its first note (or notes) is (or are) shared by half the value of the L of the previous ligature.

3) If the irregular ligature is a ternaria, the L of the previous ligature becomes two B's, as in Fig. 31a; if it is a quaternaria, the L of the previous ligature still shares half its value, but the first two notes of the quaternaria become S's, as in Fig. 33b.

4) The last note of the irregular ligature thus remains a L, unless it is itself followed immediately by another irregular ligature, in which case the same process occurs. Thus the last note of the first quaternaria of Fig. 33b is a B, whereas the last note of the second quaternaria is a L.

The rhythmical organization of conjunctura groups of five or more notes is conjectural, as there are no rules stated by the theorists about them. The best musicological opinion of the present time is that they were performed in a fast but not precisely measured rhythm.[5] It occasionally happens that such conjunctura groups will have the value of more than one perfection, but this can be determined only by the context.

Rests are indicated by the incise marks which denote the divisions of the ordines, and have the value of either a L or a B, according to which seems more fitting; sometimes they are treated as a sort of phrase mark without time value, in which case they are indicated by a comma above the place where they occur. Distinction in the length of the line to indicate different rest values was a later development.

The Styles of Modal Notation

Modal notation is used in various melismatic and syllabic styles in the compositions of the *Magnus liber;* each style is illustrated in the facsimiles of Plates XXIV through XXXIV. The melismatic style of modal notation includes:

[5] See M. Bukofzer in *Notes of the MLA,* 1955, 234. The simplest solution in transcription is to join the notes of all such groups (except the last note) with a beam.

1) *Organum duplum*, the oldest, representing historically a continuation and development of the St. Martial melismatic style. Its notation consists of sustained tenor notes of indefinite duration set against a melismatic duplum with a highly irregular arrangement of ligatures which fall only occasionally into stretches of the usual modal patterns. This style presents the greatest problems of rhythmical interpretation to scholars today, a point that will be discussed below.

2) *Clausula*, that section of an organum which is based on a short chant melisma; it does not have a complete text, only an incipit. In a clausula the character of the notation is that of a measured succession of notes in the tenor against a duplum consisting of more or less regular ligature groupings. Nearly all organa dupla have one or more sections in clausula style.

3) *Organum triplum* (and *quadruplum*), in which the two (or three) upper parts are in ligature arrangements like those of clausulae; the tenor notes are either long and indefinite in value, or measured, like the clausulae tenors.

The syllabic style includes:

1) *Conductus*, in which single-note writing predominates in all voices. This style, like organum duplum, has been treated from conflicting viewpoints, chiefly because of the fact that in modal notation single notes are indifferently written with or without a tail. The rhythm of conductus must therefore be approached in some way other than through the note symbols themselves.

2) *Cauda*, the style of which is seen in the textless interludes and postludes of the embellished conductus which are written as much as possible in ligature. As in conductus generally, there is little distinction of musical character among the various voices. Thus caudae combine the note-against-note texture of conductus with the melismatic notation of organum.

Another style of notation which appears but rarely in the manuscripts of the Notre Dame school is that of the *motet*. Those motets that occur in the Notre Dame manuscripts are almost without exception incomplete, lacking the tenor, and have only a single text; hence they are indistinguishable in appearance from the conductus. The early transitional conductus-motet is illustrated in this chapter, Plate XXVIII, but the motet is the style *par excellence* of the Franconian period, and its notation is dealt with fully in the next chapter.

Transcriptions of the facsimiles cannot be made on the basis of a literal application of the principles discussed so far in this chapter, because many inconsistencies occur in the notational patterns, even beyond those caused by repeated notes. Often the method of trial and error is the only recourse in bringing about the proper vertical alignment of parts. Theoretically, proper alignment is a matter of perfect consonances falling on the beginning of each perfection; actually, however, the "dissonance" of the third was used much more often in this position than the fourth. Dissonances such as the second fall occasionally on the strong beat in the manner of an appoggiatura. In general, the scribes seem to have made an effort at a graphic vertical alignment of notes in the manuscripts, but there is often a lack of consistency in this matter, too. It should always be kept in mind that the context is the dominating factor in each situation; and it has been suggested that a paraphrase of a common saying would be a good motto for the transcriber—"Let your context be your guide."

PLATE XXIV. Six Clausulae: *Regnat, Filia, Filia, Et inclina, Concupivit rex,* and *Ex semine* (Florence, Bibl. Med.-Laur. Plut. 29.1, fol. 168; thirteenth century)

Modal notation in polyphonic music is usually at its clearest and simplest in the clausula. The study of the modal facsimiles in this book is therefore begun with the set of six short clausulae on Plate XXIV, which is a page from the sumptuous Florence copy of the *Liber magnus.* These characteristic examples include a variety of rhythmical expressions within the limits of modal writing. In the first three clausulae, ostinato patterns of the second and third modes occur in the tenors; simpler fifth-mode patterns are used in the last three.

Regnat, which begins after the third rest sign in the duplum of the top brace, consists of one long ordo in the third mode, followed by a "free" ending in which the rhythmical meaning is less clear. Endings which depart from the usual ligature patterns are fairly common in music of the modal period, and probably are a notational reflection of the natural liberty with which performers treated the end of a piece. All irregularities in the ligature arrangements of the long ordo with which the clausula begins are the result of repeated notes, and hence do not indicate a break in the modal pattern. The beginning and probable ending are given in Fig. 34.

FIG. 34

The first *Filia* is in the second mode in both tenor and duplum; it has several rhythmical modifications that are brought about both by plicas and by the introduction of irregular ternarias in the ligature patterns. The irregular ternarias are not always immediately recognizable because of the exigencies of repeated notes. The fifth ordo from the end of the second brace is an excellent illustration of how semibreves are introduced into the rhythm, both by ligature changes in the prevailing mode—in this case by beginning the ordo with a quaternaria instead of a binaria—and by the plica at the end of the quaternaria. Fig. 35 shows the passage transcribed.[6]

The second *Filia* is based on the following rhythmic pattern ♪♩ ♪♩|♩· ♩ ♪ , expressed by the ligature sequence 2-2-1-1, and also occasionally by 2-3-1. That these two figures are rhythmically synonymous is shown by the very first ordo, where the two forms

---

[6] This version of *Filia* occurs in *W 1*, fol. 51v, beginning at the third brace. The passage quoted above is notated slightly differently there, and would be performed differently. In *W 1* there is no plica, and the ligature arrangement of the ordo is 4-3-3; consequently the rhythm would be ♩♩♩♩ ♩♩♩♪|♪♩ ♩·

FIG. 35

are used together, one in the duplum, the other in the tenor. Modification of the pattern is effected in the duplum by the use of ternarias and quaternarias. Like *Regnat*, this clausula has a free ending, possibly intended as it is transcribed in Fig. 36.

FIG. 36

Et inclina has a free introduction, as well as a free ending. Its tenor is a good example of the use of the ternaria to express the rhythm   . There is one exceptional ordo in which   is substituted; note the use of the duplex L there. The duplum is in the first mode, modified by passages of extensio modi. The beginning and probable end of the clausula are shown in Fig. 37.

Concupivit rex has a rhythmic design similar to *Et inclina*; after an eight-bar introduction, the same fifth-mode pattern is set up in the tenor and maintained until the end. An inconsistency occurs in the second ordo of the tenor before the end of the brace; the plica does not fit into the design, and is probably a scribal error. The ending offers less of a problem than those of the other clausulae in this Plate, and should be transcribed literally.

Ex semine, the last clausula, is based on a repeated rhythmic figure in the tenor which covers four bars   . Only two exceptions occur, one at the beginning, and the other at

FIG. 37

the sixth ordo from the end, where the ligature is repeated instead
of proceeding to the two duplex L's as in the other phrases, thus
bringing about an odd two-bar phrase. The duplum is in the first
mode. The plicated note in the second ordo before the end of the
last brace is a duplex L, like the one at the beginning of the clausula.
The beginning of the clausula is transcribed in Fig. 38.

FIG. 38

The tenor of *Ex semine* appears in the three-voiced motets of the later codices of Bamberg (fol. 15v) and Montpellier (fol. 100v). The latter has the same ligature arrangement as the Florence manuscript, while the former is in ternarias throughout in a simple fifth-mode pattern.

PLATE XXV. Organum triplum: *Alleluia*, Perotinus (Wolfenbüttel, Herzogl. Bibl. 677, fol. 6 and 6v; early fourteenth century) for the Nativity of the Blessed Virgin

The organum triplum *Alleluia* (Nativitas) on Plate XXV occurs on the last brace of folio 6 and the first brace and beginning of the second brace of 6v, reproduced here for convenience on the same page. This organum was said by Anonymous IV to have been written by Perotin.[7]

FIG. 39

[7] The entire codex of *W1* is reproduced in Baxter, *An Early St. Andrews Music Manuscript*. *W1* is thought to have been written down in Scotland in the early fourteenth century, although the contents stem from the Notre Dame period, that is, *ca.* 1180–*ca.* 1235. Its last fascicle (XI) is of English origin, and is probably later by about a half-century than the rest of the manuscript. See J. Handschin, "A Monument of English Medieval Polyphony," *Musical Times*, 1932, 510, and 1933, 697.

The tenor, moving at first in long sustained notes, makes a characteristic change to clausula style in the first half of the second brace, and returns to the long note pedal character in the middle of that brace. In the duplum and triplum, which are much alike in character, the third mode prevails up to the point where the tenor section in measured rhythm ends; at that point the first mode appears and is maintained until the end of the organum. The modal rhythms are occasionally varied with binarias to break up the perfect L of the third mode, producing short stretches of second-mode rhythm. Fifth- and sixth-mode passages also occur, and at one point semibreves—duplum, second brace, second ordo. Fig. 39 shows the beginning of the organum.[8]

PLATE XXVIa. Organum quadruplum; *Mors* (Wolfenbüttel, Herzogl. Bibl. 677, fol. 4v; early fourteenth century)

Mors appears on the bottom brace of four staves on folio 4v of W1. Tenor rhythm follows a repeated pattern ♪· 𝄾· |♪··♪· |♪· 𝄾·, but in two ordines note repetition prevents the use of ligature. The tenor melody is repeated about halfway through the bottom line. In the duplum there are five duplex L's, which the scribe has purposely written larger than the usual L's. Four of these occur in succession in the middle of the line; the other in the third ordo from the end of the line. The repeated notes in the third ordo of the quadruplum are in the first mode, as might be expected; this mode is corroborated by the mensurally precise version of this same composition in the Montpellier manuscript (see *Polyphonies*, I, fol. 58v).

The Special Problem of Organum Duplum

The modal compositions considered so far have all had some stable rhythmic element which served as a reliable guide to their interpretation. This element often lay in the uniform motion or pattern repetition of the tenor; even in pieces in which the tenor

---

[8] This *Alleluia*, transcribed from the slightly different version in Montpellier (*Polyphonies*, I, fol. 9), is in Parrish-Ohl, *Masterpieces of Music*, 24; see also Ursprung's *Die katholische Kirchenmusik*, 123. The few differences in *Mo* appear to be "corrections" of the dissonances in *W1*, although the first of the two introductory chords in *Mo* has been changed to a sharp dissonance.

notes were of indefinite duration—as in the first part of the organum triplum *Alleluia*—the upper parts were in a fairly strict meter and rhythm, and their rhythmical character was clearly reflected in the arrangements of their ligatures.

A different situation exists in those sections of organa dupla where the tenor does not have the measured rhythm of the clausula, and the upper part does not have ligature successions which fall into recognizable patterns. It is generally considered that organum of this type is the oldest kind of polyphony represented in the Notre Dame repertory and is a direct outgrowth of the St. Martial style seen in *Jubilemus* (Plate XXI). The principal difference between the two lies in the kind of neumes employed in their writing— one of them being in Aquitanian neumes and the other in square notation—and a striking feature of the Notre Dame organa dupla, compared to the other styles of square notation used at Paris, is their highly irregular arrangements of ligatures and single notes in the organal passages. Medieval theorists, in writing about organum duplum, stress its "flexible" and "irregular" character; some refer to it as "*sine mesura.*"

A reconsideration of certain passages in the treatise of Anonymous IV has led Willi Apel to the formulation of the "consonance principle" in transcribing organa dupla.[9] The essential feature of this interpretation is that a note of the duplum is long if consonant with the tenor, the consonances being the unison, octave, fourth, fifth, and major and minor thirds; it is short if dissonant. Further details include making the first and last note of each ordo long; if the former happens to form a dissonance with the tenor, the latter remains silent until a consonance occurs. Also, each penultimate note of an ordo is a L, whether consonant or not. Conjuncturas are to descend quickly, but are preceded by a L. When two successive notes of the same pitch occur a *longa florata* is to be used, but the meaning of this is utterly obscure; it may refer to a special performance effect.

The result of applying these principles is a rhythm somewhat like the mensuralist rendition of Gregorian chant. It should be

[9] The treatise is *De musica mensurabilis,* and the particular passage is in Ch. VII, "De modis irregularibus" (CS, I, 361). See Apel's "From St. Martial to Notre Dame," *JAMS,* 1949, 145.

noted that this manner applies only to the purely organal sections;
clausulae within the organum are rendered as described above. Even
passages within the organal sections that are in a "normal" kind of
ligature succession are rendered in the usual manner rather than by
the consonance principle.

PLATE XXVIb. Organum duplum: *Viderunt omnes* (Wolfenbüttel,
    Herzogl. Bibl. 677, fol. 21; early fourteenth century)

The organum duplum *Viderunt omnes* occupies the upper three
braces of folio 21. It is transcribed in Fig. 40a according to the
consonance principle, by W. Apel, up to the end of the word
"Viderunt."[10]

FIG. 40A

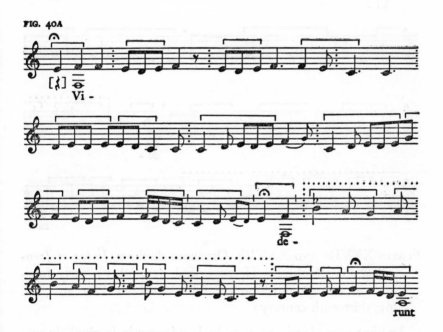

This interpretation has been disputed by those who hold that
only modal rhythm prevails in organum duplum, and that the "irregular rhythm" referred to by the theorists is merely a liberty allowed the performer to lengthen the L and shorten the B in first-

[10] *Ibid.*, 147.

mode rhythm: ♩♪♩♪ instead of ♩ ♪♩ ♪ .[11] The same section of *Viderunt* seen in Fig. 40a is shown in Fig. 40b transcribed by William Waite, who believes that modal rhythm is the *sine qua non* of all Notre Dame music. A comparison of the two transcriptions clearly reveals the difference between the two methods; almost the only point of correspondence between them is the passage written in regular ligature configurations, which is under the dotted brackets in the transcriptions.[12]

FIG. 40B

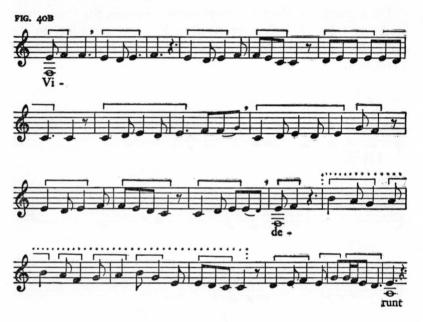

PLATES XXVIIa AND XXVIIb. Organum duplum: *Judea et Jerusalem* (Wolfenbüttel, Herzogl. Bibl. 677, fol. 13; early fourteenth century; and Florence, Bibl. Med-Laur. Plut. 29.1, fol. 65; thirteenth century)

Another example of organum duplum is seen in facsimile in two different versions—those of Wolfenbüttel (Plate XXVIIa) and Florence (Plate XXVIIb)—which are printed together to facilitate comparison. Also for comparison, the passage in this organum which occurs just before the Verse *Confitemini* is shown in three different

[11] See William Waite's "Discantus, Copula, Organum," *JAMS*, 1952, 77.
[12] From *The Rhythm of 12th Century Polyphony*, 67.

transcriptions in Fig. 41—by Apel in Fig. 41a (*JAMS*, 1949, 153); by Waite in Fig. 41b (*The Rhythm of 12th Century Polyphony*, Transcription 2); and by Wooldridge in Fig. 41c (*Oxford History of Music*, 1929, 122). The values are reduced four times in the last transcription.

Apel's transcription is made according to the consonance principle; Waite's is strictly metrical; and Wooldridge's is partly literal and partly arbitrary.[13] Franco of Cologne used this organum to illustrate one of the characteristics of organum duplum. He wrote about it: "Whatever is long requires concord with respect to the tenor; if a long occur as a discord, let the tenor be silent or feign concord." This statement confirms Apel's approach.[14]

FIG. 41

Conductus

The syllabic style of notation in conductus is essentially the opposite of the melismatic organum style, for conductus are written pri-

[13] Wooldridge used *Flo* in making his transcription, while the others used *W 1*, but there are practically no differences between the two manuscripts in this section of the piece.

[14] *Ars cantus mensurabilis*, SR, 158. See also M. Bukofzer's penetrating review of Waite's *The Rhythm of 12th Century Polyphony*, in *Notes of the MLA*, 1955, 232, in which some of the questions connected with the notation of Notre Dame music are considered at length, including the problem of whether the different notation of the same passage in different manuscripts indicates different rhythm or mere graphic variation.

marily in single notes, and ligatures are used only when more than one note is set to a syllable. The fact that it cannot be determined from their appearance whether single notes in modal notation are L or B has raised a problem in the transcription of conductus that is analogous to the one of free versus modal rhythm in secular monophonic music written in nonmensural notation. As a consequence of the ambiguity of the single notes, conductus have been transcribed in one or the other of two different manners—either one in which single notes are all rendered as equal L's in value and ligatures are treated in equipollentia to the L; or one in which the single notes are considered as falling into a modal pattern—usually the first mode—so that successive notes receive alternating L and B values. The first method has been called the "isochronous" or "isosyllabic" method, the second the "modal" method. Later mensural versions of the same conductus that appear in the early Notre Dame manuscripts have corroborated the modal interpretation, as these later versions are in definite modal rhythm; but it has also been claimed that this evidence is not conclusive, that conductus rhythm was probably not modal in the earlier period.

However, a circumstance has been noted in the Notre Dame sources which seems to make the case for modal interpretation there, too, almost irrefutable, at least in those conductus that have caudae. The notation of the caudae, being in ligature, conveys definite modal rhythm, and these sections have been transcribed modally even by those who treat the syllabic sections isochronously. Certain of these caudae have sections that repeat note-for-note parts of the syllabic sections; there hardly seems to be any reason for believing that different rhythms would be employed for the same music within the same composition. It is also noteworthy that the rhythm of the melismatic caudae in such conductus corresponds to the meter of the verse in the syllabic sections. This was pointed out by Manfred Bukofzer (*Bulletin of the AMS*, 198, 63), who also noted that there was a precedent for the use of different notational forms for the same music in sequences and their melismatic repetitions.

PLATE XXVIII. Conductus: *Sol sub nube* (Wolfenbüttel, Herzogl. Bibl. 677, fol. 110v and 111; early fourteenth century)

This two-voiced conductus for the Nativity occurs on the last two braces of folio 110v and the first two braces of folio 111, which are printed together on Plate XXVIII. An isochronous transcription of the beginning of the piece by L. Ellinwood is given in Fig. 42a.[15]

FIG. 42A

The method used by the transcriber is easily understood. In equipollentia, binarias are treated as B-L, ternarias as B-B-B. When the closing cauda toward the end of the fourth brace is reached, the ligatures are transcribed literally, as in Fig. 42b. The importance of this passage lies in the fact that the last six notes of the part bearing the text, which are single notes, are immediately repeated at the beginning of the cauda, but in ligatures of the first-mode pattern. The conclusion is all but unavoidable that the rhythm in these two passages must be identical, and that all the sections with text,

---

[15] From Ellinwood, "The Conductus," *MQ*, 1941, 192. In the example quoted, the note values of Ellinwood's transcription have been halved. Ellinwood has not included the plicas that occur in the quoted passage.

as well as the caudae, should be treated in modal rhythm. The transcription of the beginning of *Sol sub nube* according to the modal method is seen in Fig. 42c.

FIG. 42B

Non fu - it cor - rup -

ta.

FIG. 42C

Sol sub nu - be la - tu - it,   Sed e - clip - sis ne - sci- us,

Cum se car - ni mis -   cu - it,

The text of the rest of the conductus is as follows:

> Summi patris filius,
> Maritari voluit verbum patris altius,
> Nubere non potuit caro gloriosius.
> Gaude nova nupta, fides est et veritas,
> Quod a carne deitas non fuit corrupta.

PLATE XXIX. Conductus: *Veri floris* (Madrid, Bibl. Nac. 20.486, fol. 129v and 130; thirteenth century)

The conductus *Veri floris* occurs in polyphonic settings of either two or three voices in no less than seven different manuscripts of the late twelfth and early thirteenth centuries. It is characteristic of the short, simple type of conductus without caudae. The facsimile on Plate XXIX is of the last three braces on folio 129v and the first brace of folio 130 of the Madrid manuscript, in a two-voiced setting. The capital *V* of the first word of the poem is lacking; this is not at all an unusual occurrence in medieval manuscripts.

The notation of the piece in *Ma* contains several examples of an unusual note-shape that is not found in the other Notre Dame manuscripts—the note with a descending tail at either end and an angular twist in the body of the note, such as the two instances in the first brace, lower voice, over "figura" and "produxit." Anglès, who has transcribed this conductus modally, renders these notes like any other single note.[16] Their significance may lie in some special manner of performance. It is noticeable that they always fall on the L of the modal pattern, although single notes also fall in this position, including a few with tails, like the L of a slightly later period. There are several examples of the plica in the double-note form. The third and fourth notes of the duplum, second brace, over "pu-" of "pura," were probably intended to be in ligature, for there is one single note too many for the text syl-

---

[16] See *La Música a Catalunya fins al Segle XIII*, 262. Anglès has collated the *Ma* version of this piece with those of *W1*, *W2*, and *Tortosa*. Dom Hughes has transcribed it isochronously (*NOHM*, II, 330–332), collating it with these versions and also with others in the Br. Mus., Florence, and St. Gall. The existence of this piece in so many codices suggests its great popularity during the Notre Dame period.

lables at this place. The beginning of the conductus, interpreted modally, is given in Fig. 43.

FIG. 43

Ve - ri flo - ris sub fi- gu - ra, Quem pro-du - xit ra-dix pu - ra,

The remainder of the text reads:

> Cleri nostri pia cura
> Florem fecit misticum,
> Preter usum laicum,
> Sensum traens tropicum
> Floris a natura.

PLATES XXX AND XXXI. Conductus: *Presul nostri* (Wolfenbüttel, Herzogl. Bibl. 677, fol. 65 and 65v; early fourteenth century) [17]

The composition reproduced on these two plates is an elaborate example of the conductus style that is called the *embellished conductus* because of the several textless caudae which appear as interludes between certain lines of the poem and also at the beginning and end. It contains several problems of notation of a kind that has not arisen in previous examples; it is a challenging study in modal notation, although its difficulties are principally connected with the cauda sections. In the short excerpts that are transcribed in our discussion of this piece, the binaria is not always transcribed in its literal meaning of B-L; whenever these exceptional renderings are used, they are suggested by the rhythmical context in which they occur.

The text of the poem, with indications of the distribution and proportions of the caudae, is as follows:

[17] *Presul nostri* exists in a two-voiced version in the Madrid Codex B.N. 20.486, fol. 115, which contains the two lower voices of the *W1* version with but few and insignificant differences.

Cauda I, 18 bars

Presul nostri temporis
Patriem presidium

Cauda II, 5 bars

Emulandi decoris
Et virtutis pretium

Cauda III, 10 bars

Sanguinem patricium

Cauda IV, 3 bars

Actus augens Hectoris
Vires fragium hostium
Annis dignus Nestoris

Cauda V, 11 bars

Probis prestans premium

Cauda VI, 15 bars

The sections of the piece with text are relatively simple to transcribe. Each is marked off from the cauda preceding and following it by rests (which are also occasionally used within the sections with text to indicate the beginning of a new word), and the trochaic meter of the verse implies a first-mode rendition of these sections. The notes to which the first syllable of "Presul" is sung are about two-thirds of the way through the beginning brace; they come immediately after the last rest in that brace and are not in vertical alignment.

The opening cauda is remarkable for the use of a motive that appears quasi-imitatively in all voices, beginning in the duplum, and also for the use of hocket just before the first line of text. (Hocket is almost invariably indicated in modal notation by a series of alternating rests and single notes.) The first and last bars of cauda I are seen in Fig. 44a.

The end of folio 65, which falls in cauda IV, also suggests a short hocket passage. The most difficult passage of the entire conductus is in brace three of folio 65v, including not only cauda V but its junction with the previous section with text. Discrepancies appear to exist between the tenor and the upper two parts; but these disappear if the modal rhythm is continued in the tenor after the word "Nestoris" up to the rest. In the cauda that follows, there appears to be an overlapping of short phrases between the two upper parts. The passage is given in Fig. 44b from the word "Nestoris."

The final cauda is fairly clear and straightforward, the only ambiguous factor being the rests, which are sometimes of L and sometimes of B value. The choice, as usual, is determined largely on the

FIG. 44A

FIG. 44B

Ne - sto-ris

basis of consonance. The five-note currentes group at the end of the next-to-last ordo covers three perfections: ♪ ♭♪ ♭ ♪ ♪·. The beginning of the final cauda appears in Fig. 44c.

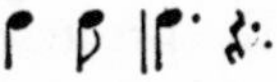

FIG. 44C

PLATES XXXII AND XXXIII. Motet: *Ave gloriosa mater* (London, Br. Mus. Harl. 978, fol. 9v and 10; thirteenth century)

The last two examples of modal notation to be considered in this chapter are not from the group of Notre Dame sources from which the previous pieces were selected. They are the last illustrations in this book of vocal music written in the score-like, horizontally superimposed arrangement in which nearly all music in modal notation is written. In the following, Franconian period, the method of writing the individual parts in a consecutive, juxtaposed manner, was adopted and became the rule in polyphonic music.

The motet *Ave gloriosa mater*, on Plates XXXII and XXXIII, is found in a number of manuscripts, of which the oldest is Harley 978, the source for our facsimile.[18] The Harley manuscript is of

---

[18] Actually, this motet does appear in one of the Notre Dame sources (*W2*, fol. 140), but only as a two-part conductus, lacking the tenor of the other versions. It is seen as a fully developed classical thirteenth-century motet in wholly mensural notation in the codices of Bamberg (fol. 1), Montpellier (fol. 89v), and Las Huelgas (fol. 100v). The versions in *Ba* and *Mo* are practically identical; *Las H* differs somewhat from them. The tenor and motetus of the Harleian manuscript are the same as in these three, except for details. The triplum of the Harleian manuscript is quite different, however; it is closely similar in rhythm and melodic character to the motetus, whereas in the other manuscripts the triplum has the flowing character of the sixth mode throughout. (See Handschin, *ZfM*,

British origin, as the composition may be itself. The motet is of the greatest interest from the point of view of both notation and style, as it has progressive characteristics in both areas, and represents a transitional stage in the formation of the motet—the great art form of the Ars Antiqua.

The upper parts are in syllabic notation, but of a kind that differs somewhat from Continental writing: the shape of the single notes is predominantly that of the L; and there are occasional tailless notes which illustrate a typical British mannerism of writing such notes diagonally, giving them a shape similar to the S. In neither case do these symbols have mensural significance in this manuscript.

Stylistically, *Ave gloriosa mater* has features of both conductus and motet; like a conductus, there is similar rhythm in all the parts; like a motet, it has a textless tenor part, written separately at the end of the piece, and the presence of two different texts. The additional tenor part at the end of folio 10 has always been an unaccountable puzzling feature of the manuscript. It is not quite identical with the tenor part in the score just above the text, and this fact caused earlier investigators to believe that the piece was in four voices, the tenor with the brace being a slightly embellished version of the other. A more likely explanation is that the two tenor parts provided alternate vocal or instrumental versions of the tenor, which meant that the piece could be performed either as a conductus—in which case all parts would be sung—or as a motet—in which case the tenor would be performed instrumentally and an instrumentally-notated part written in ligatures was therefore provided.

The tenors represent a somewhat varied version of the "Domino" section of the plainchant *Benedicamus domino*, a salutation for the First Vespers of solemn feasts (*LU*, 124); the Bamberg and Montpellier manuscripts have the word "Domino" as the incipit of the tenor of this piece. Halfway through the motet—from the last ordo on folio 9v, corresponding to the beginning of the second line in the separate tenor part—the tenor melody is repeated in

1928, 516.) The French paraphrase below the Latin text is peculiar to the Harleian among the manuscripts containing this motet. The piece also exists in four other manuscripts, in libraries at Paris (Mazarine and Arsenal), Munich (Bavarian Nat.-Bibl.), and Darmstadt (Hessian Nat.-Bibl.).

FIG. 45A

A - ve glo - ri - o - sa ma - ter sal - va - to - ris,

Du - ce cre - a - tu - re, vir - gi - ne Ma - ri - e,

A - ve spe - ci - o - sa vir - go

Chas - te, nette et pu - re et sanz

another variation of the original chant; also the tenor takes on a slightly different rhythm at this point, as the ligatures of the instrumental tenor show. The rhythm of the first section is that of the simple three-note, fifth-mode pattern which was discussed above in the clausula *Et inclina*. There is a strange discrepancy, however, between the two tenors—the one in the score begins with this fifth-mode rhythm, but then takes on the same first-mode rhythm of the upper parts. Dom Hughes, in his transcription of this composition (*EEH*, II, 29), used this conductus rhythm for the tenor throughout, even in those places where only fifth-mode rhythm is indicated. The beginning of the motet is given in Fig. 45a, in which the additional tenor part of folio 10 is on the bottom staff.

The second section also presents another rhythmical problem. In the separate tenor, the three-note pattern has changed to one of five notes; the ligatures and rests suggest the pattern ♩ ♩ ♩ ♩ |♩· ⁊·. This is the way it appears in all the later mensurally-notated versions in which the rhythm is expressed in the tenor. But a different rhythm seems to be implicit in the score after "virgo virginum"; it definitely suggests triple meter if read literally: ♩ ♩♩ ♩♩ ⁊. Dom Hughes has transcribed it thus, though inexplicably in notes of twice the value of the first section. Thus two versions of the second section seem possible, both of which are shown in Figs. 45b and c. In spite of the fact that the rhythm of Fig. 45c is used in the later mensural versions of this piece, Fig. 45b seems preferable for the Harley version, for the verse rhythm changes at this point to masculine ending; also, the Bamberg and Montpellier versions take on a different musical character with their new sixth-mode triplum, for which the rhythm of Fig. 45c is more suitable.

The two texts are as follows:

Triplum

Ave gloriosa mater salvatoris,
Ave speciosa virgo flos pudoris,
Ave lux iocosa thalamus splendoris,
Ave preciosa salus peccatoris.
Ave vitis via, casta, munda, pura,
Dulcis, mitis, pia, felix creatura.
Parens modo miro nova paritura
Virum sine viro, contra legis jura.

Virgo virginum, expers criminum,
Decus luminum celi domina,
Salus gencium, spes fidelium,

Lumen cordium, nos illumina.
Nosque filio tuo tam pio
Tam propicio reconcilia,
Et ad gaudia nos perhennia
Duc prece pia virgo Maria.

FIG. 45ᴮ

Vir - go vir - gi - num ex - pers cri - mi - num

Por - te de sa - lu vus estes res - ci - tu

c

Vir - go vir - gi - num ex - pers cri - mi - num

Por - te de sa - lu vus estes res - ci - tu

Motetus

Duce creature virgine Marie,
Chaste, nette et pure et sanz vilenie,
Par vus est la dure mort a ceus finie
Ki humeine figure ont la deite vie.
Vus estes la rose d'espine nurie
Par ki est desclose la porte de vie.
Ka testuz gant pose fu pour la folie
Eve e Adam close ke plein furent d'envie.

Porte de salu vus estes rescitu,
Garaunt et escu cuntre l'enemi,
Vus estes le port, solaz et confort
A ceus ki la mort urent deservi.
Par ceo enchantant e tut en plurant
Mere al rei pusant de quer fin vu pu.
K'en vers ure enfant me seez aidant,
K'il me seit garant e eit de moi merci.

PLATE XXXIV. Polyphonic chanson: *Entendes tout ensambles*,
   Gautier de Coinci (Paris, Bibl. nat. fr. 1536, fol. 247v and 248;
   early thirteenth century)

An example of modal notation quite outside the Notre Dame
tradition is seen in this chanson by the *moine-trouvère* ("monk-
trouvère") Gautier de Coinci, who died in 1236 as Abbot at Vic-
sur-Aisne. This piece is a contrafactum—that is, one in which a
new text has been substituted for the original one—and is part of
Gautier's *Les Miracles de la Sainte Vierge*. In *Les Miracles* Gautier used some of the most beautiful of the secular trouvère melodies, to which he set new sacred texts of great charm and literary
skill. His *Miracles* were exceedingly popular in the Middle Ages,
as is indicated by the large number of existing contemporary manuscripts which contain them.

The strophe which underlies the music, and which is followed
by eleven other verses in the manuscript, is as follows:

Entendes tout ensambles et li clerc et li lai,
Le salut nostre Dame nus ne set plus dous lai.
Plus dous lais ne puet estre k'est Ave Maria,
Chest lai canta li angles quant Dix se maria.
Eve a mort nos livra, Ave aporta vie.
Mais tous nous delivra et mist a port ave.

This composition was written before 1220, according to Genn-rich, and its notation conveys far less in the way of rhythmic sug-gestion than any of the previous examples discussed in this chapter.[19] In fact, it is almost only from the text itself that any kind of rhythmic shape can be given to the music, as in the modal rendering of monophonic trouvère song in nonmensural notation; its tran-scription into modern notation will necessarily be more arbitrary than that of any of the other examples of modal notation in this chapter. A striking feature of the composition is the number of sharp dissonances occurring on strong beats—the notation is clear enough to dispel any doubt that this is so. Note especially the bottom brace of folio 247v in this regard.

The factors of text rhythm, modality, equipollentia, consonance, and so on, indicate that the transcription of this piece may follow that of Fig. 46a, the beginning of the piece.

FIG. 46A

En - ten - des tout en - sem - ble et li   clerc et   li   lai

One of the most difficult places to transcribe in this chanson is the melisma on "Eve," folio 248, second brace. Being textless, the melisma is all in ligature, which ordinarily offers a fairly clear sug-

FIG. 46B

Eve

[19] *Troubadours, trouvères* . . . in the series, *Die Musikwerk*, Cologne, 1951. Gennrich's transcription of this piece (p. 28) differs in several details from the passages in Figs. 46a and 46b.

gestion of the rhythm. In this passage, however, the ligatures are ambiguous in character, and like the portions with text, offer several alternatives. Fig. 46b shows a likely possibility.

The Transcription of the Facsimiles

The transcription of modal notation is one of the most intriguing exercises in the whole range of notations, and is a source of both despair and satisfaction to the transcriber. The rhythm is in the note symbols; sometimes it is clearly defined, but is often latent and elusive, and must be dug out by the sheer effort of trying various possibilities. It should be evident after studying the facsimiles and following the analyses in this chapter that the meaning of the ligatures, and even of the single notes, is flexible and variable, and that rhythmical import is governed by particular situations. There is a considerable range of difficulty in the various examples discussed in this chapter; but all of them may be transcribed when an understanding of the underlying principles of modal notation has been achieved, with a fair degree of probability that the results in most cases will approach what the composers intended. The facsimiles in the plates fall into certain general categories, and it is suggested that their transcription be taken up in the following order.

Plates XXIV, XXV, and XXVIa contain the examples of clausula, and organum triplum and quadruplum; in these there is not much doubt about the general rhythmical character, nor are alternate interpretations likely except in minor details.

Plates XXVIb and XXVII illustrate the rhythmically ambiguous nature of organum duplum. The first of these facsimiles might be transcribed in two ways—either by following the consonance principle or by using modal rhythm. These two approaches are illustrated in Figs. 40a and 40b. Plate XXVII offers an opportunity to compare two versions in modal notation of the same piece; any differences in ligatures, notes, and so on, should be noted, and an attempt made to determine whether they suggest any differences in rhythm.

Plates XXVIII through XXXI illustrate three different conductus designs—one with a cauda only at the end, one with no cauda, and one embellished with a great many caudae. Our discussion of these facsimiles has indicated an almost certain modal rendition for Plates XXVIII and XXX–XXXI. Fig. 43, showing the beginning of Plate XXIX in transcription, is in modal rhythm; but for practice this facsimile should be transcribed isochronously, as well as modally.

Plates XXXII–XXXIII, *Ave gloriosa mater*, should be transcribed as begun in Fig. 45a up to the end of the first half of the piece; from this point on the rhythm of Fig. 45b should be used, for the reasons given in the discussion.

Plate XXXIV, although the simplest and most primitive of the polyphonic examples in modal notation, is also in some ways the most baffling. It is suggested that it be transcribed after the manners of Figs. 46a and 46b.

5

FRANCONIAN NOTATION

▄▄▄

The Franconian System

T HE LATTER half of the thirteenth century, usually referred to as the period of Franconian notation, gave rise
to the first true mensural notation, in which the various
note shapes employed conveyed in themselves specific
and definite meanings of duration. This system began to take shape
during an experimental period that began in the second quarter of
the century, and was codified in the celebrated treatise of Franco of
Cologne—the *Ars cantus mensurabilis* (*ca.* 1260)—a work which
long maintained a position of authority among musicians, even after
the system it describes was outgrown.[1]

Many striking changes distinguish the manuscripts of this period,
one of the most conspicuous being the adoption of a part arrangement of the voices in place of the score arrangement of modal notation. In the new scheme, the two upper voices individually occupy
each of two facing pages—or each of two columns on a single page
—while the tenor is on the bottom staff of the page, running underneath both the upper parts, as in most of the facsimiles with which
this chapter will deal (Plates XXXV–XLVI). This arrangement
was a direct result of the domination of the motet style, in which
each of the upper voices was provided with its own text. Motet style
is characterized by the continued use of a plainsong tenor, textless
except for the incipit indicating its source, usually written in modal
ligatures; a freer and more varied notation is used for the syllabic

[1] Franco's entire treatise is translated in *SR*, 139–159.

motetus and triplum. Sometimes, as in the example on Plate XLIV, a secular song is used as the cantus firmus tenor.

Modal rhythmic patterns continue to be used in the upper voices, but they are freely alternated in one and the same voice, and very often are departed from entirely. As Franco wrote: "Nor need one attempt to determine the mode to which such a discant belongs, although it may be said to belong to the one in which it chiefly or frequently remains." [2] This independence of the note symbols from the modes is the most important single feature of the Franconian system; it means that each note or ligature can unmistakably transmit a definite rhythmical significance by itself, rather than by its position in a note group. The notes and ligatures continued to be subject to the principles of perfection, imperfection, and alteration, however; and these devices by which modal rhythm was expressed remained effective in mensural music long after the modes themselves became obsolete.

Although this chapter is entitled "Franconian Notation," it should be noted that the extant compositions which conform wholly to the principles set forth by Franco are actually relatively few; and this chapter will be concerned not only with these, but also with two other groups of manuscripts that for convenience may be called "pre-Franconian" and "post-Franconian." The pre-Franconian period, roughly 1225–1260, used a notation in which true mensuration is in the process of formation, but is not yet standardized in details. Its notation is seen in the Bamberg and Las Huelgas manuscripts, and in the earlier part of the great Montpellier Codex.[3] The fully developed Franconian style of the late thirteenth century is represented principally by the later part of *Mo* (Fascicles VII and VIII); the post-Franconian style appears in the motets of the *Roman de Fauvel*, ca. 1310. The notation of the last manuscript, though founded solidly on the Franconian system, goes beyond it in some respects, and represents a transitional style that is very close to the practice of the Ars Nova. The facsimiles

[2] *Ibid.*, 151.
[3] The dates assigned to these manuscripts actually place them later than the Franconian period, but the style of notation employed in them is that of the period prior to the date generally ascribed to Franco's treatise. A similar situation exists with *W1*, which uses a notational style of about a century earlier than the writing of the manuscript itself.

illustrating this chapter are drawn from the above-mentioned sources, as well as from other important contemporary manuscripts.

Single Notes, Ligatures, and Rests

One of the most significant new features of pre-Franconian notation was the graphic distinction of single note shapes, which were made either L or B by the addition or omission of a descending tail to the right. To the principles of perfection, imperfection, and alteration governing these notes, which were discussed in Chapter 2, the following refinements of the Franconian system should be added:

1) A L followed by a B may be made perfect if a dot is placed between the two. Called the *"punctus perfectionis,"* or dot of perfection, this mark was also used to separate successive S-groups.
2) A L followed by another L or its equivalent (and therefore perfect) may be made imperfect by a *preceding* B, or by a group of more than three B's.

The logic behind these principles is that the underlying movement of the music is by a series of perfections, each of which is three B's long under the new standard of values discussed in Chapter 2; a succession of three B's making up a perfection would not affect a following L, but four B's would carry over into the next perfection by one B, thus reducing a following L to imperfection. Likewise a single B which began a perfection would have the same effect.

The S became widely used, but always in groups of two or three; it did not acquire independence as a single note with the individual status of the L and the B until early in the fourteenth century. Semibreves are expressed in Franconian notation in various ways: by the diamond shapes derived from the conjunctura of square notation; by the plica attached to the B; and also by a device new in the apparatus of notation—the sign of *opposite propriety*, an upward tail attached to the beginning of a ligature which automatically caused the first two notes of that ligature to become S's. In pre-Franconian note values, the S takes the place of the B of modal notation. The B now becomes the beat, so that the examples in this chapter will be transcribed in $\frac{3}{4}$ or $\frac{6}{4}$ meter. Willi Apel has pointed out that compositions of this period which are lacking in the S groups ought more properly to be transcribed in the values of the modal period, but has himself refrained from doing so to avoid "a rather undesirable discrepancy" (*NPM*, 283).

A feature of some late thirteenth-century compositions which is present in Plate XLVI is the use of groups of four S's to the B; a dot is used to mark off these groups. This is believed to have been an innovation of Petrus de Cruce (Pierre de la Croix, fl. late thirteenth century), and such groups are called after him *Petronian S-groups*. They are usually used in the triplum of a three-voiced motet, giving a more flowing character to that part than that of the other voices. The Petronian S-groups sometimes include more than four S's to a B value.

There is an element of uncertainty about the rhythmical organization of the groups of two and three S's which has already been referred to in the discussion of the contemporary trouvère chansons (see p. 44 and p. 45, footnote 3). In the modal period, division of the B into S's was binary (⌐⌐, ⌐⌐⌐), but Franco wrote that the S had the same relation to the B as the B to the L; *i.e.*, he considered it ternary (♭♩, ♩♩♩). It has been questioned whether this was a reflection of actual current practice of the mid-thirteenth century or an innovation by Franco himself. A rule of thumb we may follow in this book is to consider the S's in the pre-Franconian sources as binary, those in later sources as ternary. This is more or less arbitrary, for the matter is further complicated by the fact that most manuscripts of this era are copies written down some time after the actual composition of the music itself, so that an older musical style often appears in an advanced kind of notation. Scholars have not been consistent in the question of B division; consequently, transcriptions of mensural pre-Franconian music published in recent years reveal several different practices: binary throughout; ternary throughout; binary for two-S groups and ternary for three-S groups, resulting in occasional passages of two-against-three; and indiscriminate use of either binary or ternary division within the same piece.[4]

---

[4] For example, the motet from *Ba* in Einstein's *Beispielsammlung*, No. 4. W. Apel, while advocating binary division of the B for *Ba* (*NPM*, 304), uses ternary

The ligature writing that came into use during the Franconian period was of the greatest importance because of the precision and variety of rhythmical expression that it afforded. The meanings that were attached to them by Franco remained valid as long as ligatures continued to be used. The system of ligature writing in mensural music is based on the two forms of the binaria of square notation —the podatus and the clivis—in their original, normal shapes, the rhythmical meaning of which when so written is B-L. By graphic modifications of one or the other or both of the notes in these two ligatures, any of the other possible combinations of B-L—L-L, B-B, and L-B—may be brought about, as is shown in the table of Fig. 47.

FIG. 47
LIGATURE SHAPES

		MODIFICATIONS	RESULT
♪	♪	None	B-L (♪ ♪)
♪	♪	First note only modified—in ascending ligature by adding tail; in descending ligature by removing tail.	L-L (♪·♪·)
♪	♪	Last note only modified—in ascending ligature by turning it to right; in oblique form (rare in ascending ligature) first note is essentially unchanged.	B-B (♪ ♪ or ♪ ♪ depending on context)
 ♪	♪	Both notes modified — in ascending ligature by adding tail and turning upper note; in descending ligature by removing tail from first note — last note modified by oblique shape of ligature itself.	L-B (♪ ♪)

Ligatures of more than two notes are combinations of a binaria with a single note or with other ligatures; the inner note or notes of any ligature of more than two notes is B, except when the ligature has opposite propriety.

The various ligature meanings shown in the table of Fig. 47 are based on the medieval concepts of *propriety* and *perfection* which the basic figures were said to possess when unmodified. That is, they had propriety if the first note of each ligature were B and perfection if the second were L. Therefore, when changes were made

---

division in his own transcription of a motet from that manuscript (*HAM*, I, No. 28g). Many other instances could be quoted that reflect the uncertainty about the value of the S, which must have been an inconstant factor throughout the thirteenth century.

that affected the appearance of either the first or last note, or both, four different rhythmic figures, including the unchanged ligature, were available. In the terms of contemporary theorists, these figures were as follows (in the order given in Fig. 47):

1) With propriety and with perfection (B-L).
2) Without propriety and with perfection (L-L).
3) With propriety and without perfection (B-B).
4) Without propriety and without perfection (L-B).

The word "propriety" was also used in reference to the frequently-employed addition of an upward tail to the beginning of a ligature, which caused the first two notes to become S's; in this case, they were said to have "opposite propriety." When this sign is applied to a ligature of only two notes, both notes are S's.

The plica is far less frequently encountered in the Franconian period than in modal notation, although it is not absent from the facsimile examples of this section. It came to have four standard and different forms:

◢ ◣ : tail to the right, descending or ascending = L.
◣ ◢ : tail to the left, descending or ascending = B.

If the L is perfect, the plica takes one-third its value; if imperfect, it takes one-half. In the B with plica the resulting notes are S's, and the same problem of their rhythmic interpretation arises that is inherent in any kind of S in this period.

The discriminating use of rests by Franco is one of the most significant of the refinements introduced into thirteenth-century notation. He recognizes six varieties, one of which is the "*finis punctorum*"—the double-bar of modern usage—which he says is "immeasurable"; so that there are in practice five rests of definite duration. The rests are shown in Fig. 48.

FIG. 48

The rests shown represent, from left to right, the perfect L, the imperfect L (and altered B), the normal B, the major S, and the minor S. The major S is the triplet quarter note whose value is two-thirds of a B; the minor S is the triplet eighth note having one-third B value. An important feature of the rests is that they were not subject to perfection, imperfection, or alteration. The immutable character of the rests is a factor that is often very useful in solving ambiguous or difficult passages in transcription.

Motet Notation Through the Roman de Fauvel

PLATE XXXV. Motet: *Cruci domini–Crux forma–Portare* (Bamberg, Staatsbibl. Ed. IV6, fol. 112; late thirteenth century)

The Bamberg Codex is the most uniformly notated of the pre-Franconian manuscripts. It is thought to date from the end of the thirteenth century, and its notation differs from the Franconian principles outlined above only in the occasional use of some ligature forms not recognized by Franco, and in the manner of indicating rests.[5] In *Ba* the rest indicating the perfect L covers four spaces, the imperfect L and altered B three spaces, the normal B two, the S one. No discrimination is made between the major and the minor S, which strengthens the assumption that binary division of the B is appropriate in this manuscript.

The characteristic motet from *Ba* reproduced on Plate XXXV has a tenor in a simple rhythmical pattern in which the chant segment used as a cantus firmus is twice repeated; the second repetition varies the cantus rhythmically by the use of a duplex L in alternating measures.

The upper parts are in a predominantly third-mode rhythm, in which it frequently happens that the same rhythmic pattern ♩ ♩ is expressed by both B-L and B-B, the second B being altered, even in close juxtaposition, as in the second and third lines of the triplum. A sign of perfection—a vertical line drawn through the staff—is used in the second and third lines of the motetus to make a L perfect that would otherwise be made imperfect by a following B. This line appears to be a rest, but the context shows that it is not; if it were it would have the value of a B, which occupies two spaces, like those in line five of the motetus and line eight of both motetus and triplum.

[5] Facsimile edition, P. Aubry, *Cent motets*, I, Paris, 1908. Aubry employs ternary division of the B throughout in his transcription of *Ba;* his rendition of the motet on Plate XXXV is in Vol. II, 40.

The S's occur in this motet only sparingly, always in descending scalewise fashion, and always followed immediately by a B, the three notes (S-S-B) being written close together as a group. In each of these groups the B is altered, so that the rhythm is always ♪♪♩ . As each group forms a perfection, the L that precedes it is perfect also. Only one example of the use of opposite propriety occurs—in the motetus at the end of the fourth line. Fig. 49 shows the beginning of the motet.

Cru - ci   Do- mi -   ni   sit cunc-tis   ho - ris laus

Crux for -   ma   pe- ni-ten-ci - e   gra-ci -   e

Portare

pa - ra -   ta

cla - vis cla - va

The text is as follows:

Triplum

Cruci domini sit cunctis horis laus parata,
Per quam homini salus est data,

Que sustinuit illum, qui rapuit omnium peccata.
Carne sua mortificata que in cruce fuit sacrificata.
Quam est ergo venerandum ac laudandum hoc signum,
Quod solum dignum vite fuit vere precium sustinere.

Motetus

Crux forma penitencie, gracie clavis clava peccati venie,
Vena radix ligni iusticie, via vite, vexillum glorie,
Sponsi lectus in meridie, lux plenarie, nubem lues iusticie,
Serenum consciencie. Hanc homo portet, hac se confortet,
Crucem oportet si vis lucis vere gaudia sustinere.

Tenor

Portare . . .

PLATE XXXVI. Instrumental motet: *In seculum breve* (Bamberg, Staatsbibl. Ed. IV6, fol. 64; late thirteenth century)

The facsimile on Plate XXXVI is one of a set of five instrumental pieces in motet style that form a sort of appendix to the *Ba* Codex. They are all based on the same plainsong tenor—from the melodic segment of the Verse *Confitemini* of the Gradual *Haec dies* which occurs over the words "in seculum" (*LU*, 779).[6] They are also distinguished from the other compositions in *Ba* in being written in the older score arrangement, presumably because they have no text.

The piece is an interesting combination of old and new practices. The tenor, for example, is based on a simple second-mode pattern, but this is not accurately expressed by the ligature forms throughout most of the piece; the proper Franconian ligature arrangement of binaria + single note + imperfect L-rest to express this rhythm is used only where it was forced on the scribe by the occurrence of repeated notes, as in ordines one, six, and seven of the second brace. The ternarias in the remainder of the tenor probably represent a persistence of the accepted convention of the modal period.

The upper parts are thoroughly Franconian, with the few exceptions noted below, and they feature the use of hocket throughout. The individual S's occur only in hocket formation; and they indi-

---

[6] The well-known *In Seculum viellatoris* is one of this set; see *GMB*, No. 20.

FIG. 50

cate that this piece was notated later than the vocal motets in the collection, for the alternating S-rests of the hocketing passages definitely convey ternary division of the B. This is seen immediately after the beginning, where the first S in the triplum is followed by a rest covering a full space, while the corresponding part in the duplum consists of a rest covering only part of a space, followed by a S. (See measure three of Fig. 50.) These can only be interpreted as major and minor S's and S-rests. The second S of the hocketing pair is altered, but the S-rests—like all other rests—are not subject to alteration. The scribe has been meticulously consistent in this detail in every one of the numerous places where hocketing in S's occurs. From this it is reasonable to assume that all S's are ternary, whether in hocket formation or not. Those brought about by the B with plica have the rhythm of ♪ ♪ , while pairs of the diamond-shaped S's are ♪ ♪ ; S's notated by the sign of opposite propriety also have the latter rhythm.

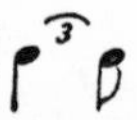

Certain of the ligatures in the upper parts are not in accord with the Franconian ligature system. These are:

1) Brace one: in the middle (C-D-C) and end (C-B-C), triplum. Brace two: second ligature (E-G-A), triplum. According to the context, these should all be B-L-B.

2) Brace three: last binaria before the end, triplum. This should be B-B, rather than B-L.

3) Brace two: just before second rest from end, motetus. The context requires L-B rather than B-B.

The beginning of the piece is seen in Fig. 50.

PLATE XXXVII. Motet: *Laus tibi salus–Laus tibi virgo–Tenor* (Burgos, Cod. de Las Huelgas, fol. 112; early fourteenth century)

The manuscript known as the Las Huelgas Codex, after the Cistercian convent of that name near Burgos, Spain, is a more heterogeneous collection than *Ba* and is in a less expert hand. However, in spite of certain local mannerisms, the ligature writing of *Las H* is much more in conformity with Franconian doctrine. The collection, which contains many pieces found in earlier manuscripts, was copied about 1325, according to Anglès, and includes nearly two hundred pieces—polyphonic organa, conductus, and motets, and a number of monophonic sequences.[7] It differs from *Ba* in its page arrangement, as it does not make use of parallel columns on the same page for the upper voices; in this motet, for example, the triplum occupies the upper three lines, the motetus is on the three lines under that, and the tenor is on the bottom line.

The tenor follows a simple first-mode pattern, and includes a few inconsistencies of notation. The ascending binaria in one case has an unnecessary descending tail (first ordo), but it is correctly written in the other instances in which it is used (fifth and ninth ordines). The descending binaria also appears in two forms—both

[7] Facsimile edition, H. Anglès, *El codex musical de Las Huelgas*, II.

with and without a descending tail on the second note of the ligature. The former suggests a binaria plicata, but plicas do not appear
ever to have been used in tenors; this same motet, with different
words, appears in both *Ba* (fol. 15) and *Mo* (fol. 44v), where there
are no plicas at these places. (The tenor of the *Mo* version may be
seen on Plate XXXIX, in the column to the right.)

The upper parts are more consistently notated, and present no
problems except the ubiquitous one of the rhythmical meaning of
the S groups. Anglès has transcribed this piece with binary division
of the B throughout (*Las H*, III, 220).

The rests are in accordance with Franco's rules, since the B-rest
covers one space.

Fig. 51 shows the beginning of the motet.

FIG. 51

Laus   ti - bi   sa - lus ho -mi - num, Splen-do - ris,   ful - go - ris,

Laus   ti - bi   vir - go vir - gi - num,   Pu- do - ris,   ho - no - ris,

The rest of the text is:

Triplum

Lux que contra morem
Redemptorem omnium filium
Portasti creatorem,
Cunctorum plasmatorem.

Motetus

Mater gerens florem
Que celorum hominum Dominum
Portasti salvatorem
Contra nature morem.

PLATES XXXVIII AND XXXIX. Motet: *Diex mout me fet–Diex ie fui ia–Diex ie ni puis–Et videbit* (Montpellier, Fac. des Med. H 196, fol. 378v and 379; late thirteenth century)

The great codex of Montpellier represents an even wider repertory and a greater time-span than that of *Las H*.[8] Its styles of notation range from modal notation in Fascicle I (fol. 1–22), through mensural notation with much of the uncertain ligature writing that characterizes *Ba* and *Las H* in Fascicles II–VI (fol. 23v–269v), to an advanced style of true Franconian notation in Fascicles VII and VIII (fol. 270–397v). Fascicle I has the Notre Dame score arrangement; the pieces in three voices of Fascicles II–VI have the triplum and motetus on facing pages with the tenor running along the bottom staff of both pages; those in four parts have the two upper voices on two columns on the left-hand page, facing the two lower voices which are similarly arranged on the opposite page. For Fascicles VII and VIII the arrangement used is the same as that in *Ba*.

The motet reproduced on Plates XXXVIII and XXXIX is one of the seventeen motets in four voices that comprise Fascicle II of *Mo*. It offers an opportunity to compare a piece in two different manuscripts, and also in two different versions; the three lower voices are essentially the same as those in the immediately preceding example from *Las H*, except for the text and a quadruplum that has been added in the column to the left of folio 44v.

The tenor expresses the same rhythm as that of the *Las H* motet of Plate XXXVII; but where the latter is written almost entirely in true Franconian style, the tenor in *Mo* is irregular in the manner of the tenor of *In seculum breve* (Plate XXXVI). As in that example the scribe has used correct ligature forms only when forced to do so by the exigencies of repeated notes.

In the upper parts there are several ambiguous ligature shapes, such as ascending binarias, unmodified in shape, that can only be read as B-B; likewise, the ascending ternarias are shown by context to mean B-B-B. In fact, there is only one Franconian ligature (in the third line of the triplum), whose final note, being turned to the right, is *without perfection*, and hence is a B. At the very end of

[8] Facsimile edition, Y. Rokseth, *Polyphonies du XIIIᵉ siècle*, I.

the motet all voices are in rhythmical agreement except the triplum. The quadruplum and motetus read B-B-B-L, tenor reads L-L. The triplum, which reads L-S-S-S-L-L, is brought into agreement with the other parts only by substituting a B for the L on each side of the S-group.

An interesting situation is seen in the two ligatures over the word "sospir" in the fifth line of the triplum. The context shows that the two must not exceed the total value of three B's, but their value as written is four B's. The movement of the lower voices at this point is uniformly ♪ |♪ ♪ . The choice must be made, therefore, of reducing one or the other ligature in value by one B; Fig. 52 shows the two possibilities.

FIG. 52

sos - pir   sos - pir

From the standpoint of text the second version is preferable, but musically the first is better unless the binaria is regarded as an appoggiatura. Yvonne Rokseth transcribed this passage in the second manner (*Polyphonies*, II, 64), but used ternary division for the three note group (♪♪♪), and binary for that of two notes (♪♪), a principle she followed throughout the pre-Franconian part of *Mo*.[9] It is possible that her method represents historically a sort of halfway stage toward Franco's ternary division in both groups. It brings about occasional three-against-two rhythm, but there is no basis for deciding whether this rhythm was accepted performance practice in the thirteenth century.

The only rest employed in this piece is that of the B. The stroke used for this covers two spaces, but the scribe has not always been careful about the length of the line. A rest has been omitted at the end of line six of the motetus.

The plica appears in both double- and single-note forms. The two occur successively at the very beginning of the quadruplum, and are *plicae longae*, the first being perfect, the second imperfect.

---

[9] Rokseth used a scale of values of L = quarter note in her transcription of this particular motet, *Polyphonies*, II, 64.

The text reads:

Quadruplum

Diex, mout me fet sovent fremir quant la voi en esmai,
M'a mis mout en veille, por m'amie mout sospir sovent,
Car ele est bele a merveille comme rose est vermeille.

Triplum

Diex, ie fui ia pres de ioir, or n'i voi qui de moi
Guerir s'apareille de ce que i'aim sans mentir, sans partir,
Mes quant plus me traveille, plus l'aim, c'est grant merveille.

Motetus

Diex, ie ni puis la nuit dormir, qu'ades oi ne sai quoi
Qu'amours me conseille, que si me fet tresaillir et fremir,
Si que quant ie someille li maus d'amer m'esveille.

Tenor

Et videbit . . .

PLATES XL AND XLI. Motet: *Amor potest–Ad amorem–Tenor* (Montpellier, Fac. des Med. H 196, fol. 378v and 379; late thirteenth century)

This motet from the last Fascicle (VIII) of *Mo* illustrates the fully developed Franconian style, and has several features of unusual interest. In the two facsimile pages on which it is reproduced, the tenor continues from the end of folio 378v to the bottom staff of folio 379, ending just before the word "Aptatur"; the triplum and motetus continue on to the textless postlude on the first three lines of folio 379, which is characterized by a continuous use of hocket. The rest of the music on this page represents the beginning of another motet (*Ave mundi–Ave salus–Aptatur*).

The composition is one of the rare thirteenth-century examples of music written specifically in duple meter. In these pieces the music does not proceed by the usual perfections of three B's, but rather in metrical groups of two B's, so that the division of the L into B's is understood to be imperfect throughout. Considerations of perfection and alteration do not arise in compositions in duple meter. Duple meter is recognized principally by the way in which rests are used. In the Franconian system of rests the imperfect L is represented by a line covering two spaces; in this motet a L is frequently followed by an imperfect L-rest. This can only be interpreted to mean that the piece is in imperfect meter or *modus imperfectus*, as it soon came to be called. ("Mode" in this connection refers to the number of B's in the L; if three, the mode is perfect, if two it is imperfect.) There are a few examples like this in *Ba* and *Las H*, although recognition of duple meter by the theorists did not appear until the early fourteenth century.[10]

FIG. 53

The tenor is an unusual one, consisting of an ostinato figure of three notes repeated a great many times, occasionally with a slight rhythmical variation. The ligatures are to be read literally; the two adjacent B's are the equivalent of an imperfect L, as the context of the two upper voices shows. The two short vertical strokes in the middle of the tenor staff on the second page represent a repeat sign; the tenor at this point returns to the beginning. When the upper parts are transcribed it will be found that the repetition will have to be shorter by two L's than the notated part to come out right.

Another feature of the motet that has not yet appeared in previous examples is the use of successive groups of S's. In these, each successive three-note unit is separated by a space (as in the bottom line, triplum, fol. 378v), but successive two-note units are separated

[10] See the section on "Duple time" by Dom Hughes in *NOHM*, II, 399; also Apel, *NPM*, 290, and Anglès, *La música a Catalunya*, 349.

by a dot (as in line five, triplum, and line six, motetus, fol. 378v). This was the "divisio modi" that Franco said should be used between successive S-groups whenever two S's stood for a B.[11] The rhythmical organization of the S-groups should no doubt be ternary throughout.

As in most of the compositions of the late fascicles of *Mo*, very few plicas occur in this motet; there are two instances of the B with plica—one in the motetus, line three, folio 378v, the other in the triplum, line three, folio 379, at the end of the first ligature.

Fig. 53 shows the beginning of the motet.

The rest of the text is as follows:

Triplum

Quia cepit minui
Fides et constancia
Que sibi restitui
Peritum iudicii
Petit cum instancia.

Motetus

Fides et constancia
Nam in hiis fundatur.
Hiis duobus igitur
Amor dum privatur,
Totus perit penitus
Et adnichilatur.

PLATE XLII. Instrumental dances: *Estampies reals* and *Dansse real* (Paris, Bibl. nat. fr. 844, fol. 104v; late thirteenth century)

Plate XLII is a facsimile of the last four of a set of eight Estampies, followed by a "Dansse," written on a couple of blank pages left in a thirteenth-century trouvère chansonnier. Although it is monophonic, the example has been included in this chapter because it is essentially Franconian in character, and because it illustrates notation of this period that is *sine litteris* and therefore written almost entirely in ligature. The single notes in these dances occur chiefly

---

[11] *SR*, 146. The term "divisio modi" does not refer here to "mode" in relation to L-B relationships, but rather to the rests or incise marks used to separate ordines.

PLATES

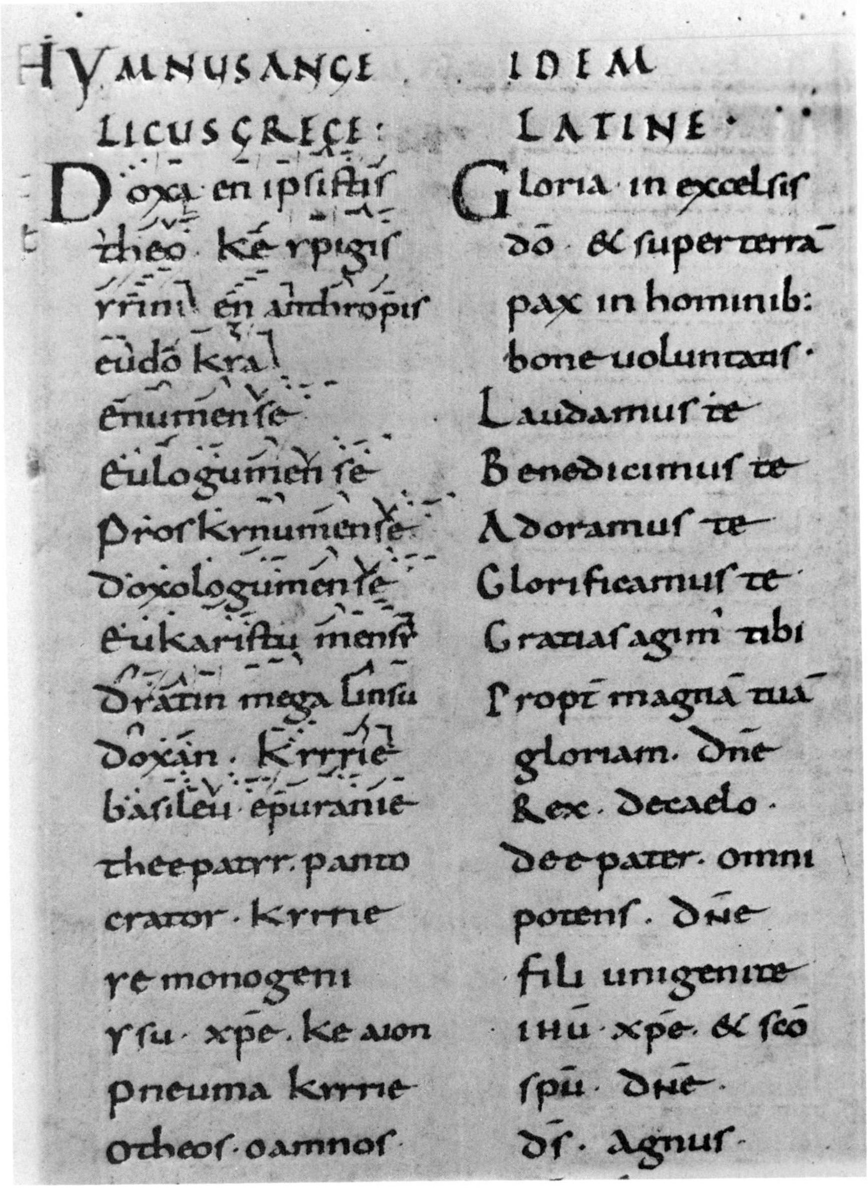

IDEM
LATINE

HYMNUS ANGELICUS GRECE	IDEM LATINE
Doxa en ipsistis	Gloria in excelsis
theo. ke rpigis	do. et super terra
rrini en andropis	pax in hominib:
eudo kral	bone uoluntatis.
enumen se	Laudamus te
eulogumen se	Benedicimus te
proskrnumen se	Adoramus te
doxologumen te	Glorificamus te
eukaristu mensi	Gratias agim tibi
oratin mega linsu	propt magna tua
doxan. Kyrie	gloriam. dne
basileu epuranie	Rex. de caelo.
thee patrr. panto	dee pater. omni
crator. kyrie	potens. dne
re monogeni	fili unigenite
ysu xpe. ke aion	ihu xpe. et sco
pneuma kyrie	spu. dne.
otheos oamnos	ds. agnus.

PLATE I. Paris, Bibliothèque Nationale, Lat. 2291, fol. 16. 9th Century

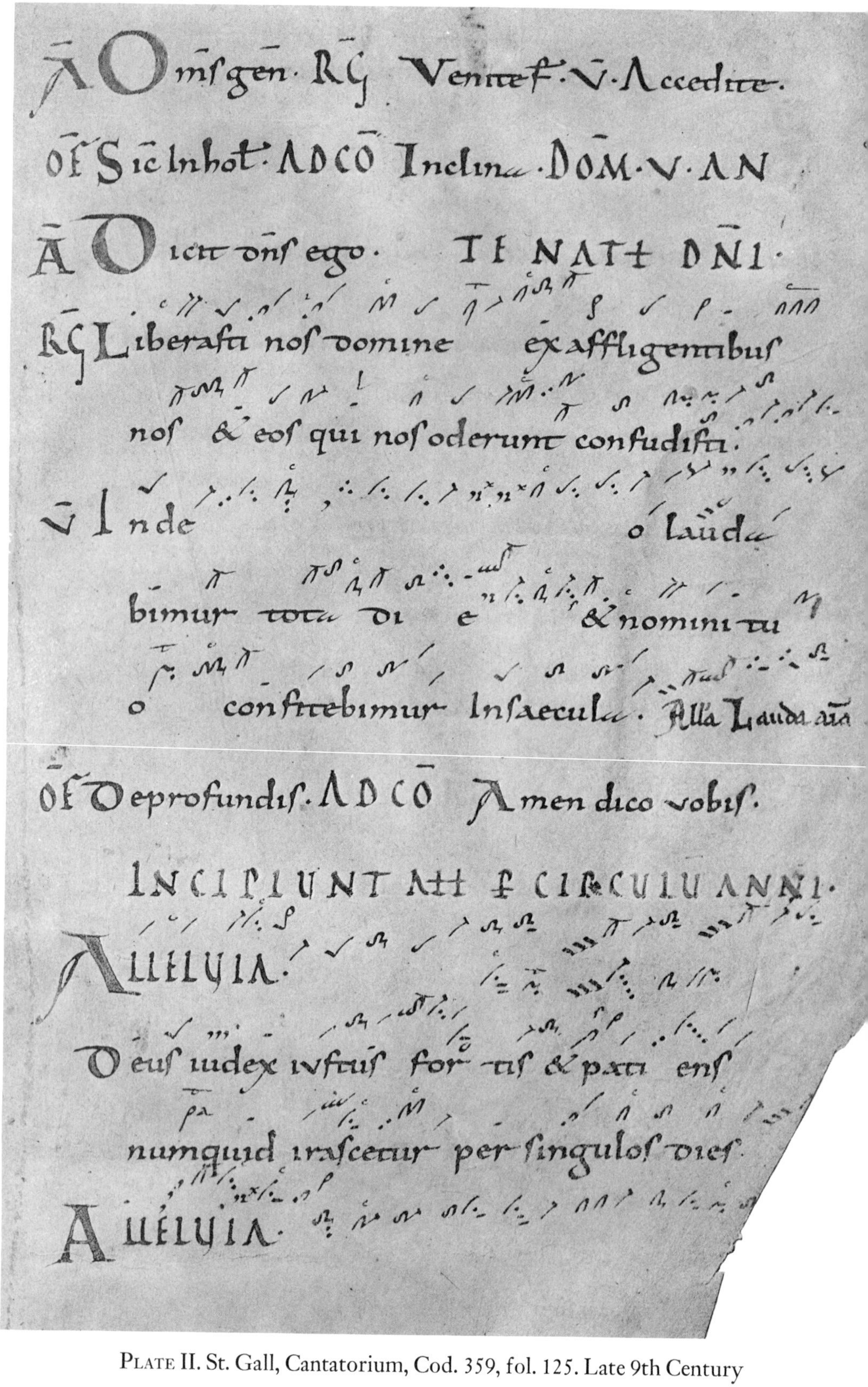

ĀO m̄ſ gēn RG̅ Venitteſ · v · Accedite .

OF Sic Inhot · ADCO̅ Inclina · DOM · v · AN

ĀO ict dn̄ſ ego · TE NATE DN̄I ·

RG̅ Liberaſti noſ domine ex affligentibuſ

noſ & eoſ qui noſ oderunt confudiſti ·

v Inde o laudā

bimur tota di e & nomini tu

o confitebimur Inſaecula · Alla Laudā aīa

OF De profundiſ · ADCO̅ Amen dico vobiſ .

INCIPIUNT Alt ꝯ CIRCULU ANNI ·

Alleluia ·

Deuſ iudex iuſtuſ for tiſ & pati enſ

numquid iraſcetur per ſinguloſ dieſ .

Alleluia ·

PLATE II. St. Gall, Cantatorium, Cod. 359, fol. 125. Late 9th Century

nominis tui · ut quicuq; eas sup se asperserint pro redeptione peccato
rum corporis sanitatem · animae tutelam pcipiant · pd AL OR
(S) qui non morte sed poenitentia desideras peccatoru · fragilitatem
humane condrationis benignissime respice · & hos cineres quos
causa preferende humilitatis atq; promerende uenie capiab; nris
tpori decernim benedicere tua pietate digneris · ut qui nos cine
rem esse & ob prauitatis nrae mentu in puluere reuersuros cognos
cim · peccatoru omiu uenia & pma penitentib; repmissa misericor

E xaudi nos domine qm benigna e misericordia tua scdm multitudinem I diu consequi meream · p
miseratronu tuarum respice nos domine · S S alu une fac u · XI iuxta ustibulu & altare plorabant sacdotes
& leui tae ministri domini & dicent parce dne parce populo tu o & ne dissipes ora clamantiu ad te do mine·
mutemur habitu in cinere & cilicio ieiunemus & ploremus ante dominum qui a multu misericors est
dmittere peccata nostra deus ñr ster · COLLECTA AD SCAM ANASTASIA
C oncede nobis dne qs presidia militie xpiane scis inchoare ieiu
nis · ut contra spiritales nequitias pugnatur · continentiae
muniamur auxiliis · p d AD MISSA AD scam sabinam ferens omniu domine & nihil odisti
eorum que fecisti dissimulans peccata hominum ppt poenitentiam & parcens il lis quia tu es dominus de us

P RESTA QS DNE FIDELIB; TUIS · VI noster · S miserere mei dñus·
ieiunioru ueneranda sollepnia & congrua pietate suscipiant ·
& secura deuotione pcurrant · pd · RM Miserere mei deus misere re
me quoniam in te con fidit a ni ma me a

U Mseruit decae lo ce libera ut me dedit in obpro brium conculcau
OF E xaltabo te domine quoniam suscepistme nec delectasti inimicos meos super re sme·
me domine clamau ad te & sana stione QD omine abstraxti stiab inferis animam
meam saluastime a descendentibus in la cum u E go autem dixi in me a bu
bundantia non mouebor in aeternum domine in uoluntate tu a p stitusti deo

F ac nos qs dne his muneribz offerendis SU P OBL ti meo uirtu tem·
conuenient aptari · quib; ipsius uenerabilis sacrameti celebram exor
Gaet dr · Q ui corporali ieiunio uitia coprimis PREF diuitu · p
mente eleuas · uirtute largiris & proemia · px CO Q ui me dutrabitur

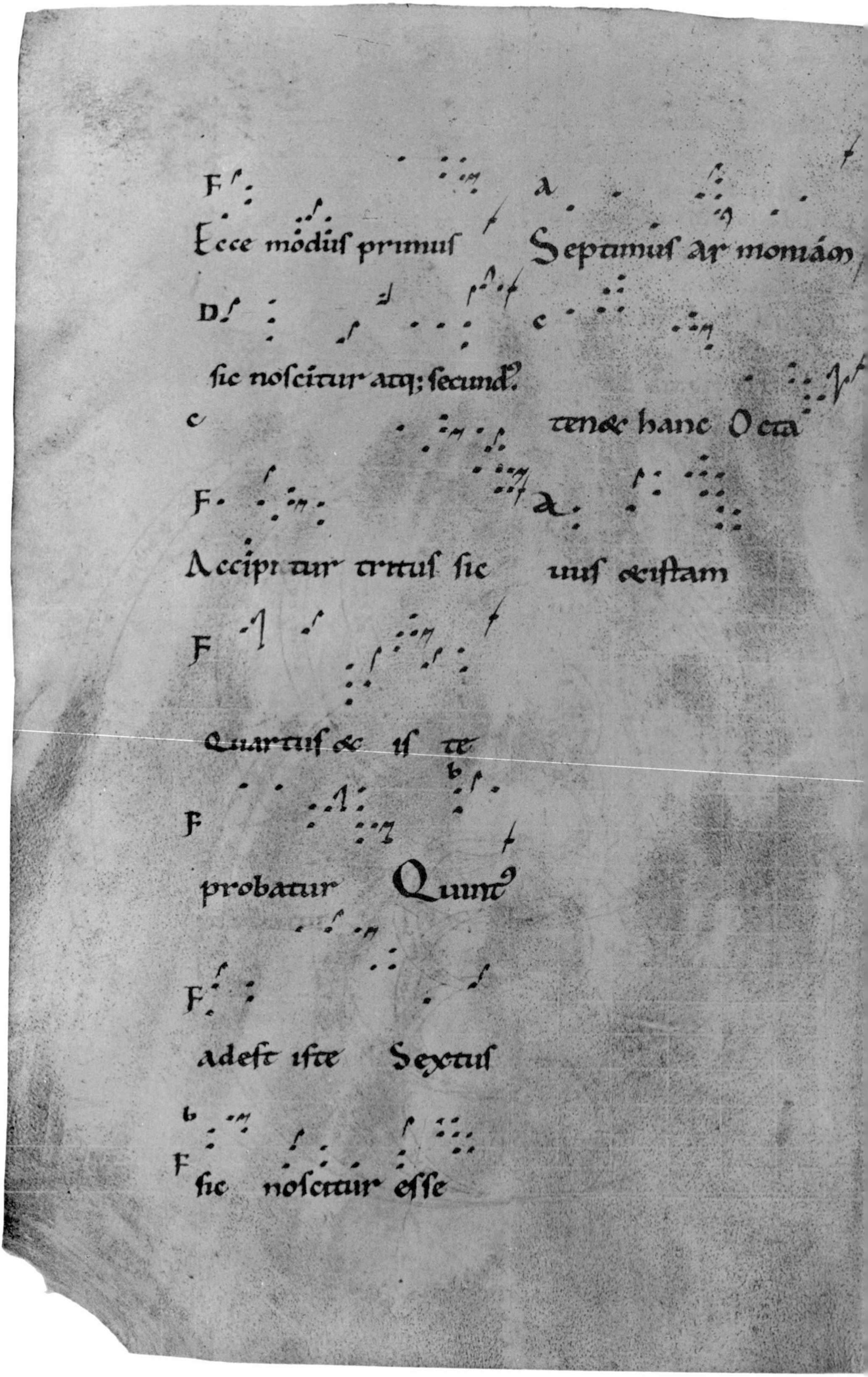

Ecce modus primus   Septimus ar monia

sic noscitur atq; secund?

tenæ hanc Octa

Accipitur tritus sic   uius cristam

Quartus & is te

probatur Quintus

adest iste Sextus

sic noscitur esse

PLATE IV. Paris, Bibliothèque Nationale, Lat. 7211, fol. 127v. Late 11th Century

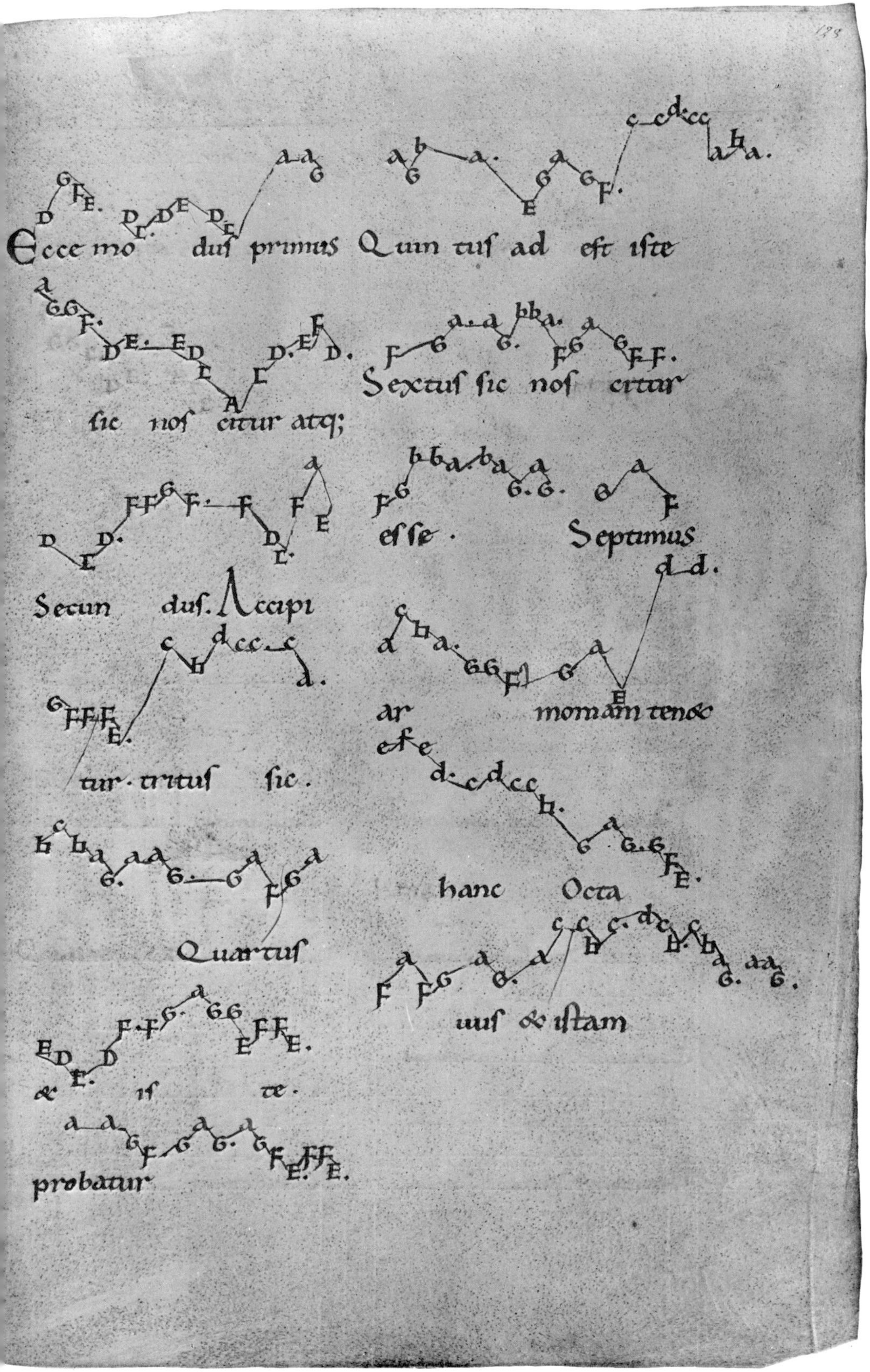

Ecce modus primus
Quintus ad est iste
sic noscitur atq;
Sextus sic noscitur
Secundus. Accipitur. tritus sic.
esse. Septimus
ar monia tenet
Quartus
hanc Octa
et iste.
uus et istam
probatur

PLATE V. Paris, Bibliothèque Nationale, Lat. 7211, fol. 128. Late 11th Century

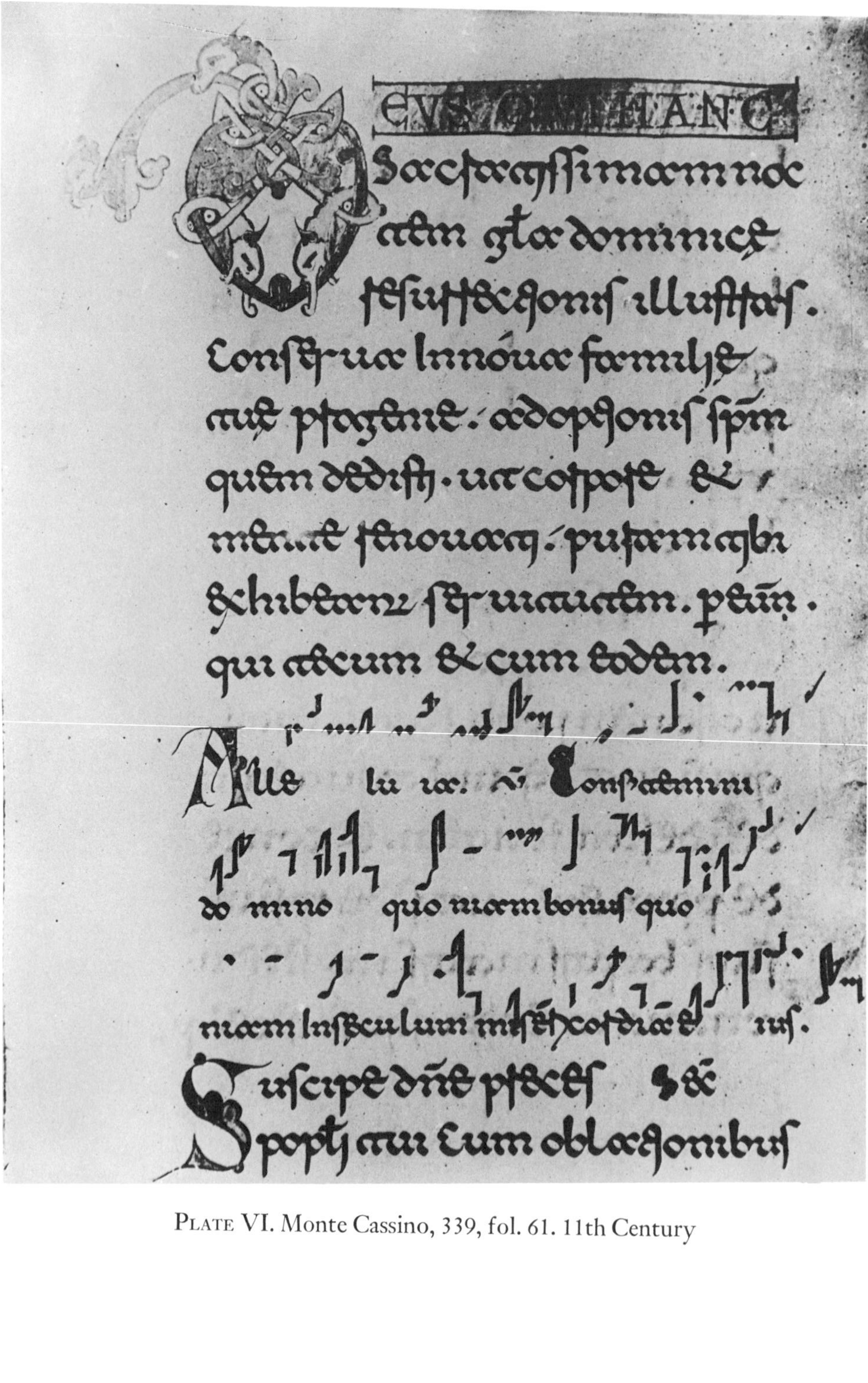

EVS OMN[I]ANC[?]

S[a]cratissimam noc
tem gl[ori]a dominic[a]e
resurrectionis illustras.
Construe Innoua familia[m]
tu[a]e pr[a]esent[a]e. adoptionis sp[iritu]m
qu[a]em dedisti. ut corpore &
ment[a]e renoua[n]t. puram eqbi
& hibere[n]t s[er]uiuate[m]. p[er] eu[m].
qui tecum & cum eodem.

Alle — lu — ia: C[on]firmini
do mino quia meam bonus quia
meam In s[a]eculum m[i]s[eri]c[or]d[i]a[e] e[ius]... ius.

Suscipe d[omi]ne pr[e]ces s[an]c[t]o
Spop[u]l[i] tui cum oblac[ti]onibus

PLATE VI. Monte Cassino, 339, fol. 61. 11th Century

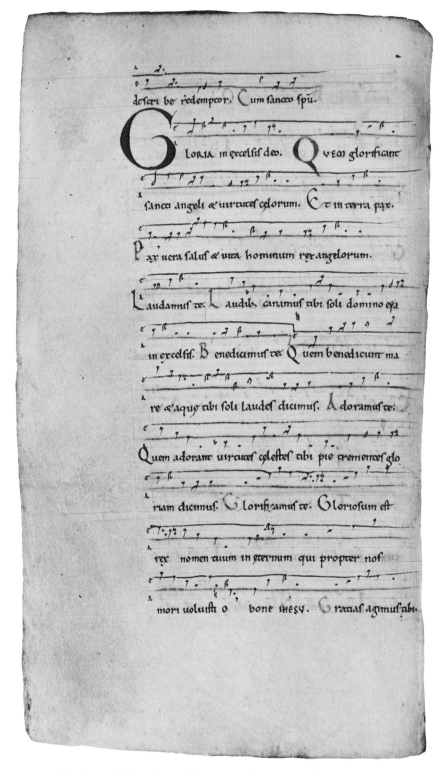

deseri be redempcor. Cum sancto spu.

Gloria in excelsis deo. Quem glorificant

sancti angeli & uirtutes celorum. Et in terra pax.

Pax uera salus & uita hominum rex angelorum.

Laudamus te. Laudib; canamus tibi soli domino eia

in excelsis. Benedicimus te Quem benedicunt ma

re & aque tibi soli laudes dicimus. Adoramus te.

Quem adorant uirtutes celestes tibi pie trementes glo

riam dicimus. Glorificamus te. Gloriosum est

rex nomen tuum in eternum qui propter nos

mori uoluisti o bone ihesu. Gratias agimus tibi.

PLATE VII. Paris, Bibliothèque Nationale, Lat. 10.508, fol. 32v. 12th Century

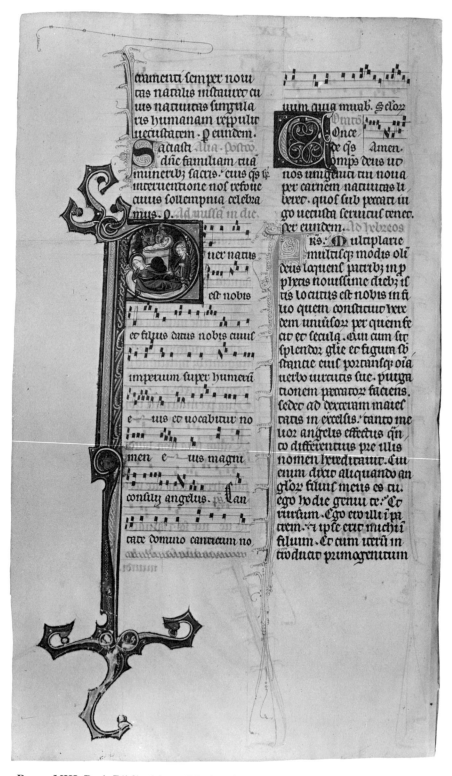

Plate IX. Brussels, Bibliothèque Royale, 4767, fol. 83. 16th Century

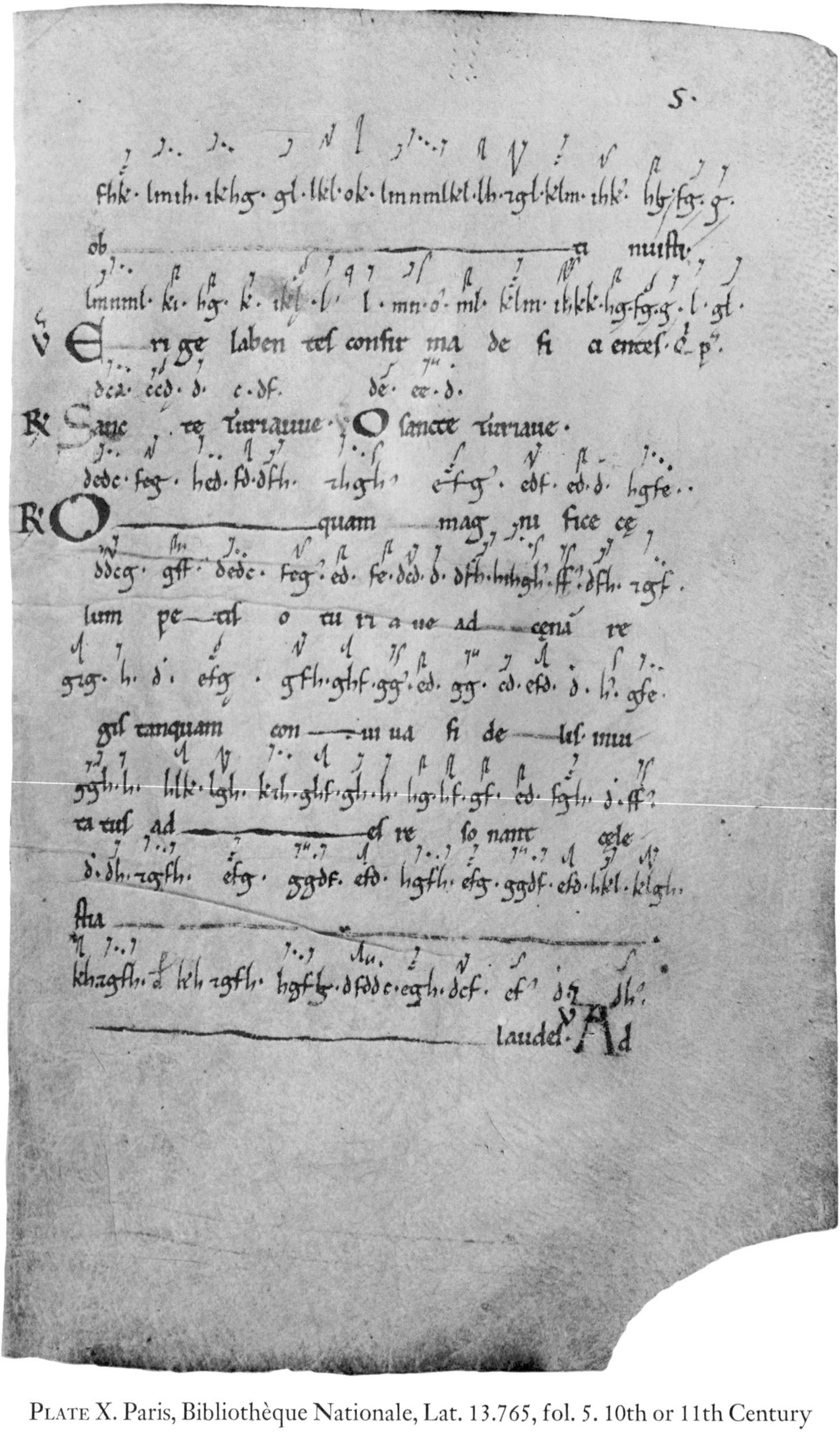

PLATE X. Paris, Bibliothèque Nationale, Lat. 13.765, fol. 5. 10th or 11th Century

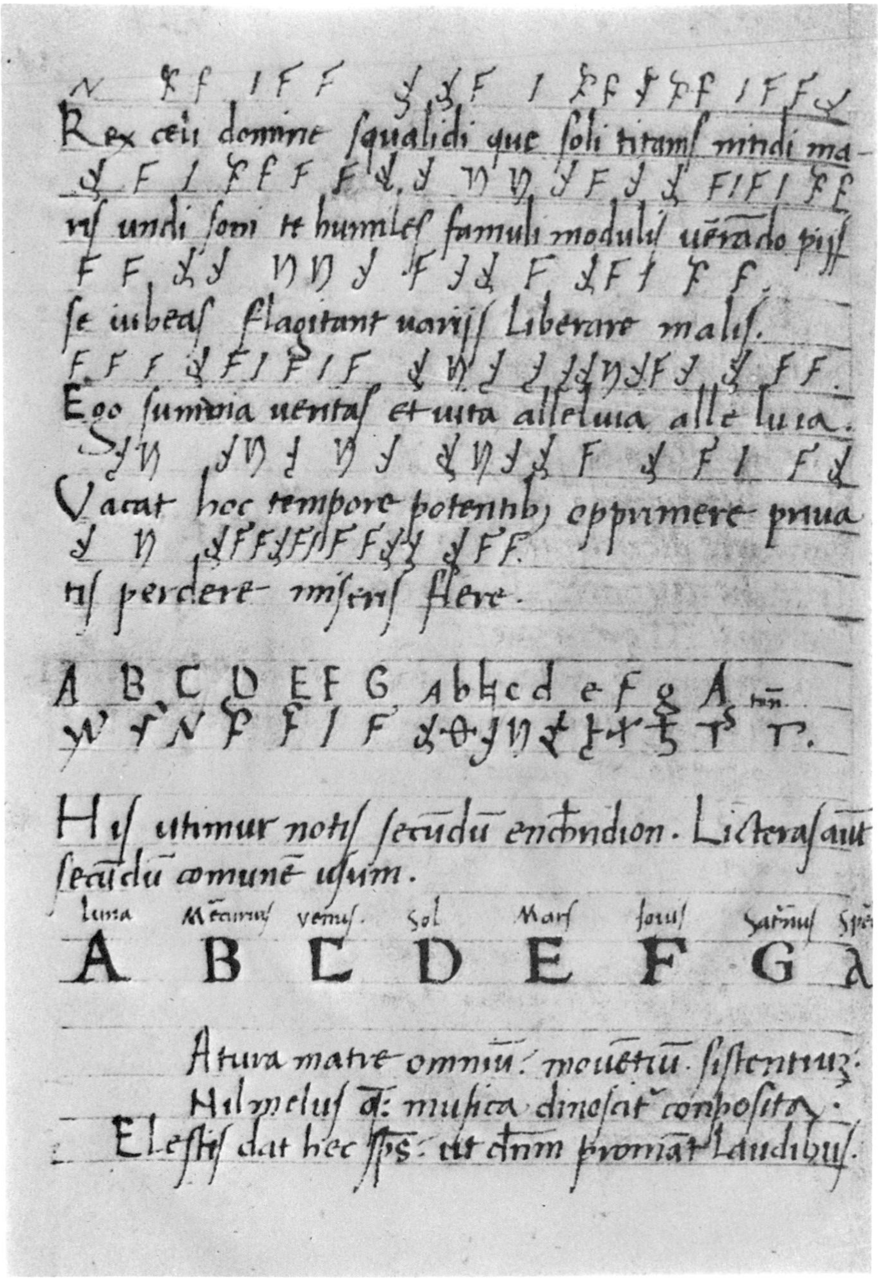

Rex ceu domine squalidi que soli titans mundi ma-

rus undi soni te humiles famuli modulis uerando pijs

se iubeas flagitant uariis Liberare malis.

Ego summa uentas et uita alleluia alleluia.

Vacat hec tempore potentibus opprimere priua

nis perdere miseris flere.

A B C D E F G a b ♮ c d e f g a

His utimur notis secundu enchiridion. Litteras aut
secundu comune usum.

luna   Mercurius   venus   Sol   Mars   Iouis   Saturnus   Spe

A B C D E F G a

Atura matre omnium mouentium sistentium
Hil melus d musica dinosat conposita
Electis dat hec sps ut dnm promat laudibus

PLATE XI. Paris, Bibliothèque Nationale, Lat. 7369. 15th Century (?)

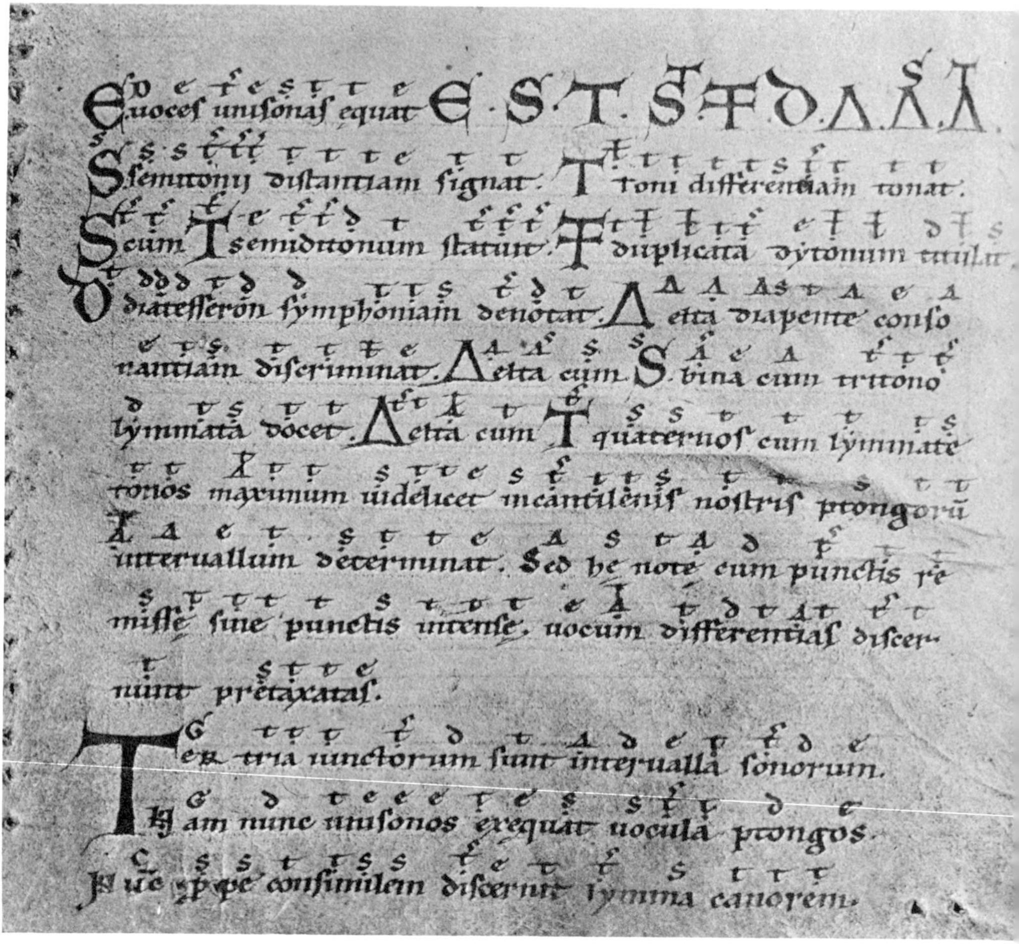
E uoces unisonas equat. E. S. T. S. T. D. Δ. Δ. Δ.
S semitonij distantiam signat. T toni differentiam tonat.
S cum T semiditonum statuit. T duplicata dytonum titulat.
D diatesseron symphoniam denotat. Δ etta diapente conso
nantiam discriminat. Δ etta cum S bina cum tritono
symmata docet. Δ etta cum T quaternos cum symmate
tonos maximum uidelicet in cantilenis nostris prongorum
interuallum determinat. Sed he note cum punctis re
misse sine punctis intense, uocum differentias discer-
nunt prefixatas.
Ter tria iunctorum sunt interualla sonorum.
Nam nunc unisonos exequat uocula prongos.
Nunc sepe consimilem discernit symma canorem.

Plate XII. Vienna, Nationalbibliothek, Hs. 2502, fol. 27v. 12th Century

me puet bie metir mel mauf z
ma gsetree. naime paf a droit
qui bee quil en portoit aueuir.
Dame qui a güt paor souent
lestuet esbahir. z panfera tel fo
lour dont ie ne me puis tenir.
sil est autre plesir. siert bie ma
poinne sauuee. qui soul de la
desitre me fait mon cuer esbau
dir. Nuf ne puet güt ioie a
uoir sil ne ta del maus apris.
qui touz iors fait son uoloir a
poinnes iert sinf amis. por ce
fait amors dolor. quil uuet le
guterredon rendre. ces q bien
seuent atendre z seruir a son
uoloir. Dame de tout mon
pooir mouttroi auos sanz con
tendre que sanz uos ne me pu
et rendre nuis bie ne ne puet
ualoir.   R. de Nauarre.

E touz mar nest mif

plaisanz fors soulement cil

pamer. mais cil est douz et

poignanz z delitous a pan

ser z tant set biau conforter

et de granz biens ta tant que

nuf ne sen doit oster. Ains
amis obedianz vuil a ma dame
en clmer. ie ne puis estre dolanz
quat ie oi de li pler tat me plait
a remenbrer que de touz mar mest
garanz sa beautez a recorder.
Amors qnt uos maue; mis
ire en uhe prison. mieuz ame
roie estre ocif que ieusse rean
con ter mar est bie saz raison
qui me plait qut me fait pris.
ne ta rien quier gariso Q ñq
il uos est amis dame me semble
raison. si ma utre amour so pris
z utre plaisant facon. z beautez
a tel foiso qui relprent a utre a
utre aiuf des lef piez en uisque
en son. Se de uos peuisse auoir
dame. i. pou plus beau seblat.
ie ne sauroie uoloir qrtre deu m
ci si güt. q de ioie auroie tant
q tuit autre home por uoir seroi
ent uf moi dolant Dame ou
toz mes biens atent. sachiez qnt
uos puis ueoir mis na si ioious
torment.   Roy de Nauarre

ame len dit que len

peut meur.

Dame seur toutes amee · de loi
au cuer sans trichier · bele et
bone ⁊ honoree · ie ne uos fai
losengier · loign sui de uie co
tree · ce me fait mlt esmaier ·
sen est lamor plus doublee ·
et ie ne uos os proier · tant uos
dout acorroucier · car ce ne ma
uroit mestier.

Nai pas la ioie oubliee · dou
douz termine premier · que
lamor me fu donee · dame
que touz iors requier · mes
tost me trefu uee · quant uos
plot a essaier · coment ire
est tost montee · la ou ioie
est en danger · sine men os
corroucier · car de seruir ai
mestier.

Amors a gi tant seignorie · seur
moi bien lema moustre · por
ce ne retrai ie mie · qua li
nace bon pence · et se madame
moublie · tant li prierai por
ce · quele reconoisse ⁊ die · q
iai loiaument amee · adonc
si soit pardone · se ie moroie
por le · Gaces brulles

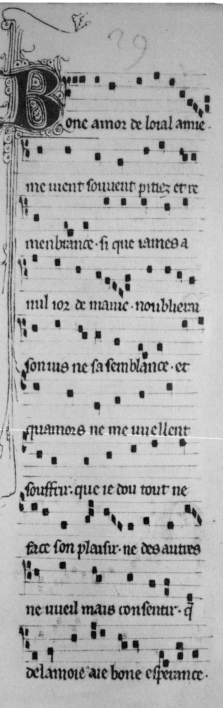

Bone amor de loial amie ·

me uient souuent pitiez et re

menbrance · si que ia mes a

nul ior de ma uie · noublierai

son uis ne sa semblance · et

quamors ne me uueillent

souffrir · que ie dou tout ne

face son plaisir · ne des autres

ne uueil mais consentir · q

de lamoie aie bone esperance ·

PLATE XIV. Paris, Bibliothèque Nationale, N. A. Fr. 1050, fol. 29. 13th Century

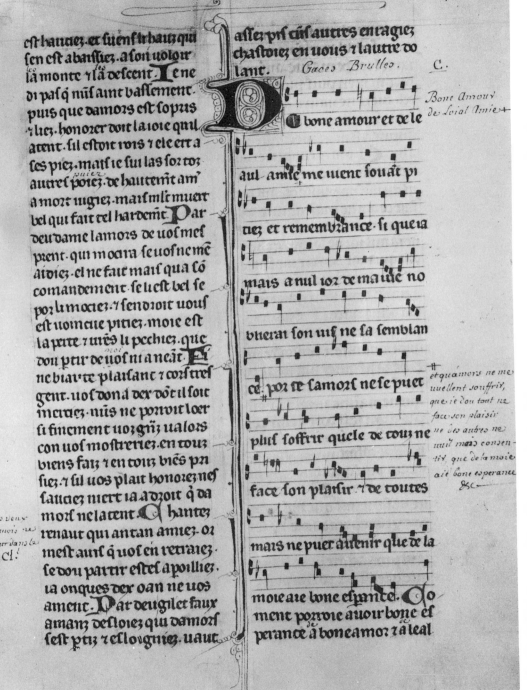

qʼl presente largent. si lo fait on enz entrer. mais ce
lui qui na neient na on cure de haster. ⁊ ie q̄ rien ne
present. por loz q̄ uint doutre mer fui bailliez tot ausi
ment. Certes or ai mot mesdit car rienſ ne li presentoie.
tp ai mis en mon escrit merueil moi ou ie pansoie. por
aler iusqa son lit mestoit mot corte la uoie.

Chastelains

Par quel forfait ne per quel mesprison mauez amors
si de uos esloignie. que de uos nai ne bien ne guerredon.
ne ie ne cruis qui de moi ait pitie. malement ai mon
seruise emploie cainz depar uos ne me uint se mals nō.
encor amors nel uos ai reproie mon seruise mais ore
men plaig gie. ⁊ di que mort mauez senz oquison.
Bien deussiez amors garder raison. de moi greuer qui
serui ⁊ proie. ai longuement en bone entencion. nō
quel nul ne me feistes lie. atort mauez si sanz ma
lassie. qant depar uos ne me uient se mals non. mici
ams tp mauez truaillie. ne me lassiez ensi deshseillie
q̄ ma dame ne me get de p̄son. Bele dame au droiz
mostre ⁊ raisons q̄ uos amez ure leal ami. alegiez moi
mon mal ⁊ ma dolor. q̄ ie sui cil q̄ mieuz uos a serui.

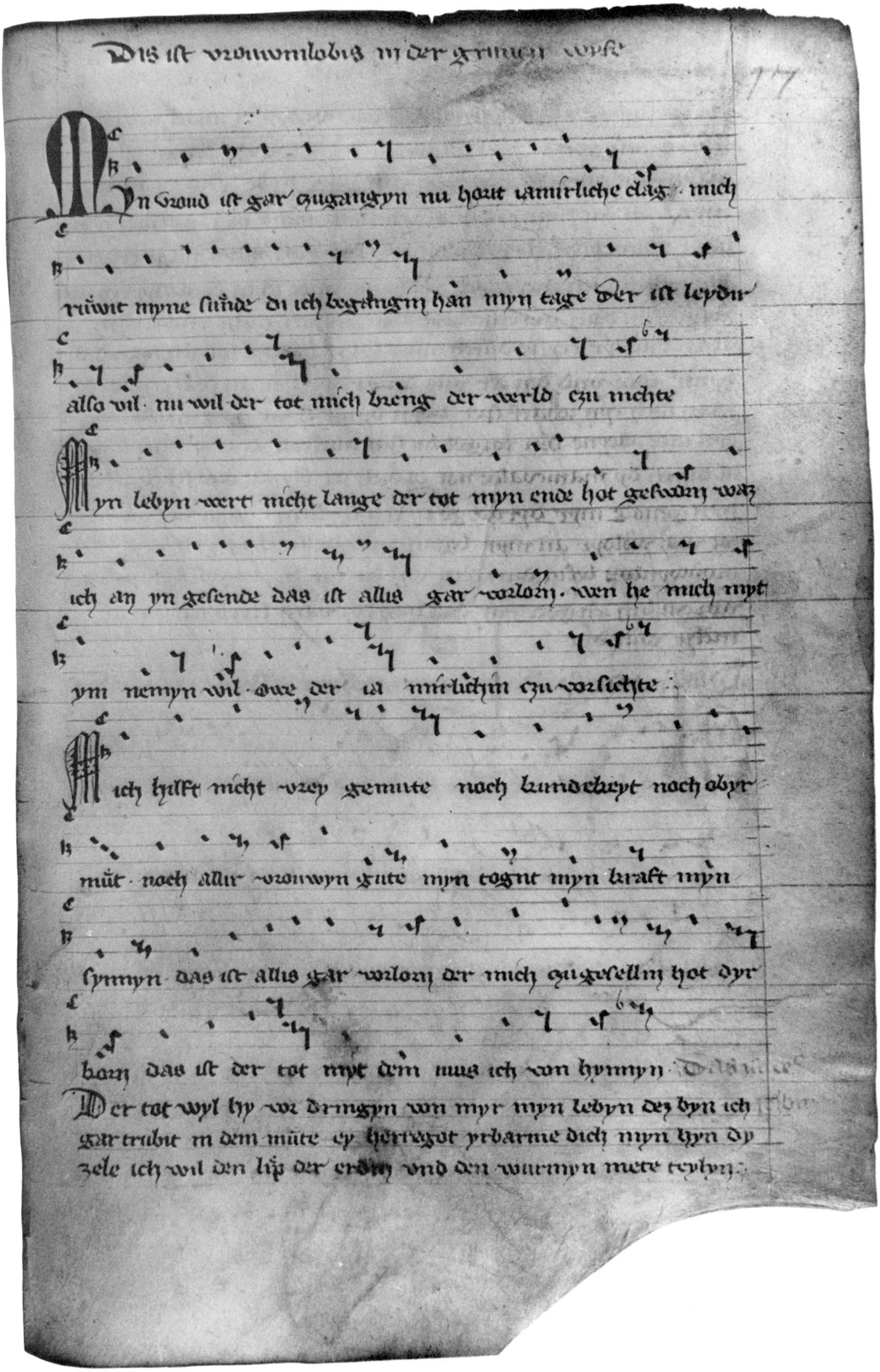

PLATE XVII. Vienna Nationalbibliothek, Hs. 2701, fol. 17. 14th Century

PLATE XVIII. Munich, Staatsbibliothek, Germ. 4997, fol. 19. 15th Century

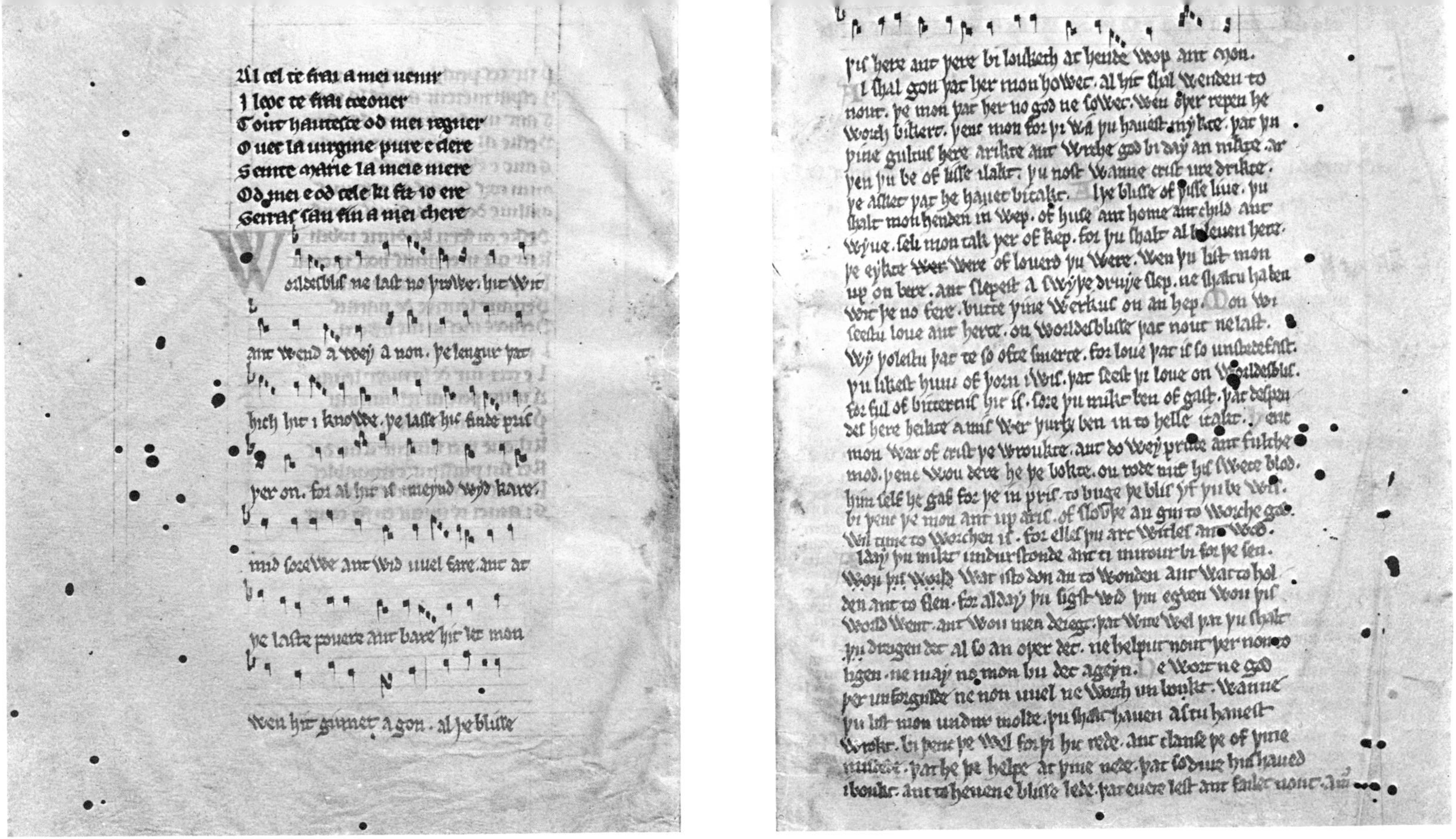

Plate XIX. Oxford, Bodleian Library, Rawlinson G 18 (14.751), fol. 105v and 106.
13th Century

PLATE XXa. Paris, Bibliothèque Nationale, Lat. 7211, fol. 9v. 11th Century

PLATE XXb. Paris, Bibliothèque Nationale, Lat. 10.509, fol. 89. 10th Century

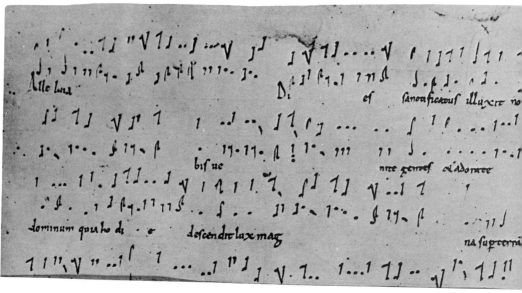

PLATE XXc. Chartres, Bibliothèque de la Ville, 130, fol. 50. 11th Century

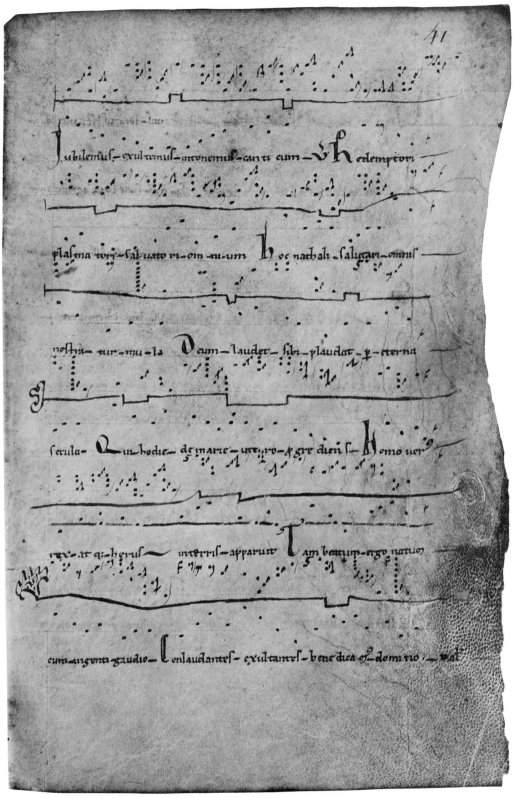

PLATE XXI. Paris, Bibliothèque Nationale, Lat. 1139, fol. 41. Early 12th Century

PLATE XXII. London, British Museum Add. 36.881, fol. 2 and 2v. 12th Century

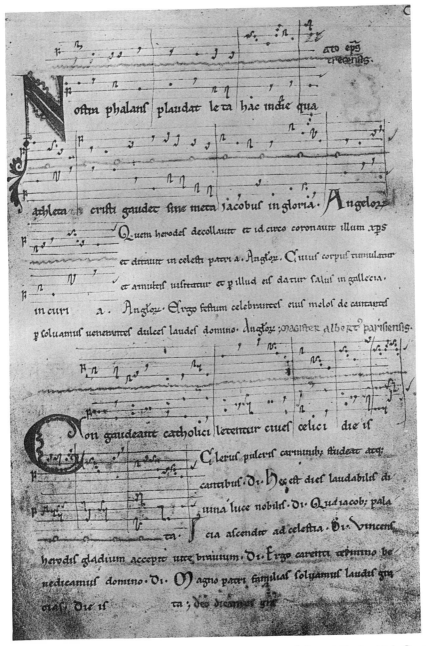

PLATE XXIII. Santiago de Compostela, Cod. Calixtinus, fol. 185. Early 12th Century

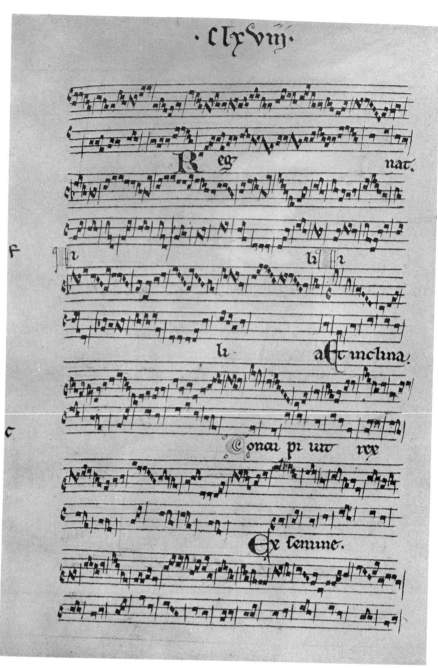

PLATE XXIV. Florence, Biblioteca Medicea-Laurenziana, Plut. 21.9, fol. 168. 13th Centu

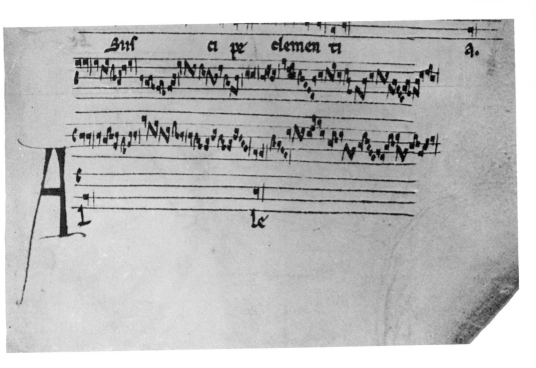

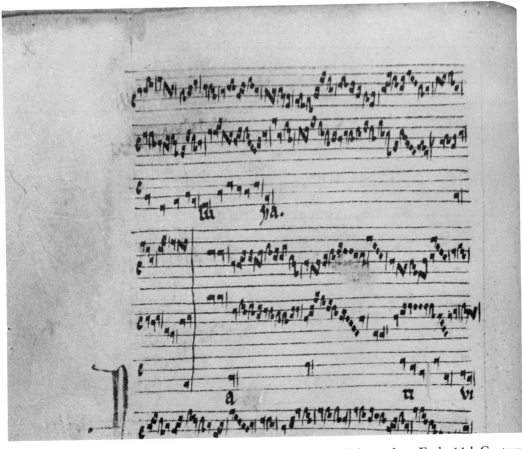

PLATE XXV. Wolfenbüttel, Herzog August Bibliothek, 667, fol. 6 and 6v. Early 14th Century

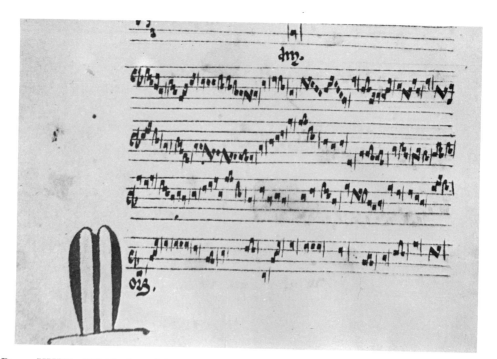

PLATE XXVIa. Wolfenbüttel, Herzog August Bibliothek, 677, fol. 4v. Early 14th Century

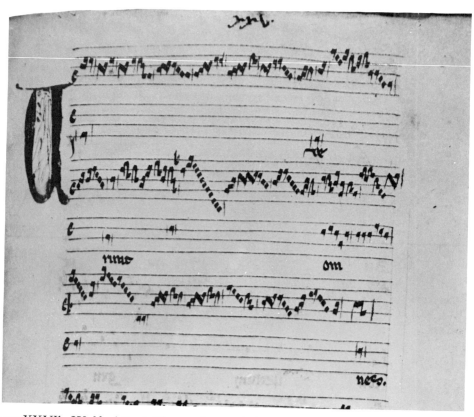

PLATE XXVIb. Wolfenbüttel, Herzog August Bibliothek, 677, fol. 21. Early 14th Century

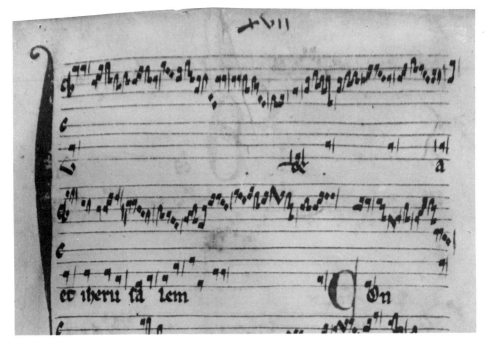

PLATE XXVIIa. Wolfenbüttel, Herzog August Bibliothek, 677, fol. 13. Early 14th Century

PLATE XXVIIb. Florence, Biblioteca Medicea-Laurenziana, Plut. 21.9, fol. 65. 13th Century

PLATE XXVIII. Wolfenbüttel, Herzog August Bibliothek, 677, fol. 110v and 111.
Early 14th Century

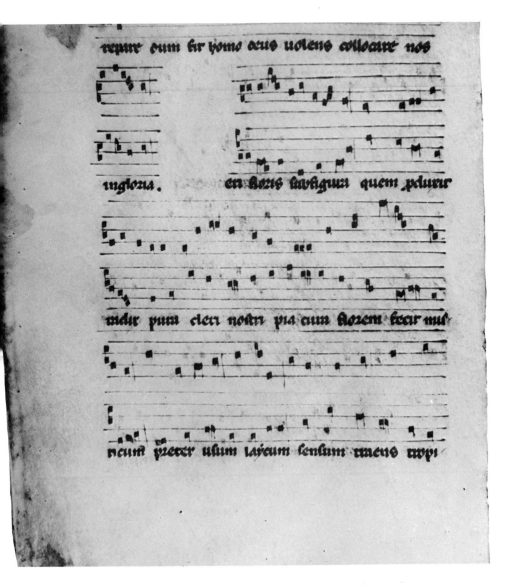

Plate XXIX. Madrid, Biblioteca Nacionale, 20.486, fol. 129v and 130. 13th Century

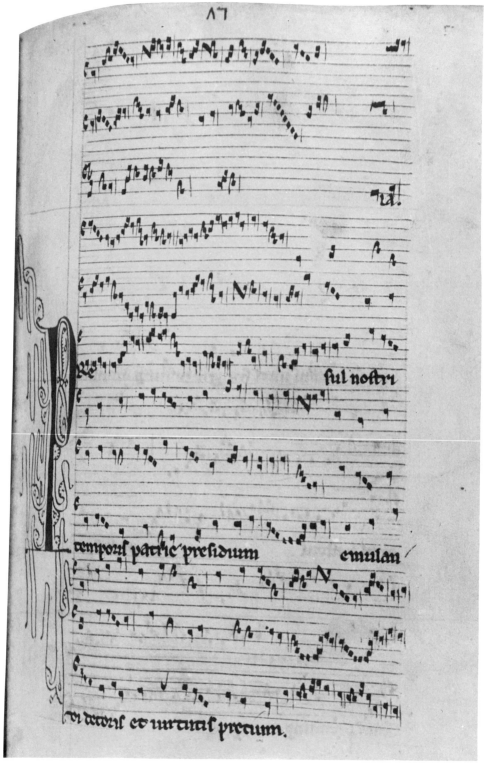

PLATE XXX. Wolfenbüttel, Herzog August Bibliothek, 677, fol. 65. Early 14th Century

PLATE XXXI. Wolfenbüttel, Herzog August Bibliothek, 677, fol. 65v. Early 14th Century

PLATE XXXII. London, British Museum, Harley 978, fol. 9v. 13th Century

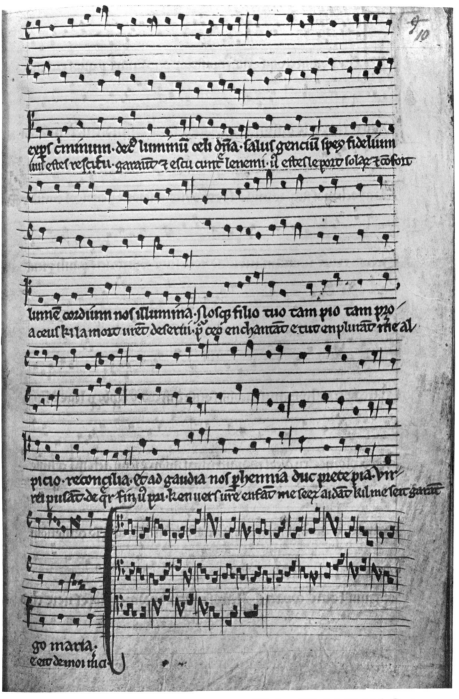

Corpus criminum. deus luminum celi domina. salus gencium spes fidelium

vus estes rescusu. garantu z escu cum lenemi. il estes le poro solaz z confort

lumine cordium nos illumina. sloscez filio tuo tam pio tam pio

a ceus ki la mort meo desertui. p cez enchantau e tuu enplunau me al

picio. reconcilia. et ad gaudia nos phennia duc prete pia. vn

rei pulau de gr finz il pri ken uers ure enfau me seez aidau kil me seit garau

go maria.
e ceo de mort ma

PLATE XXXIII. London, British Museum, Harley 978, fol. 10. 13th Century

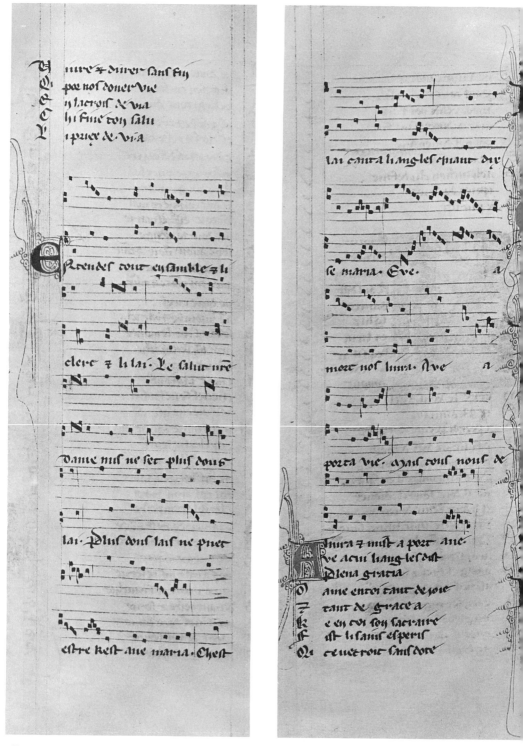

PLATE XXXIV. Paris, Bibliothèque Nationale, Fr. 1536, fol. 247v and 248. Early 13th Century

PLATE XXXV. Bamberg, Staatsbibliothek, Ed. IV 6, fol. 11. Late 13th Century

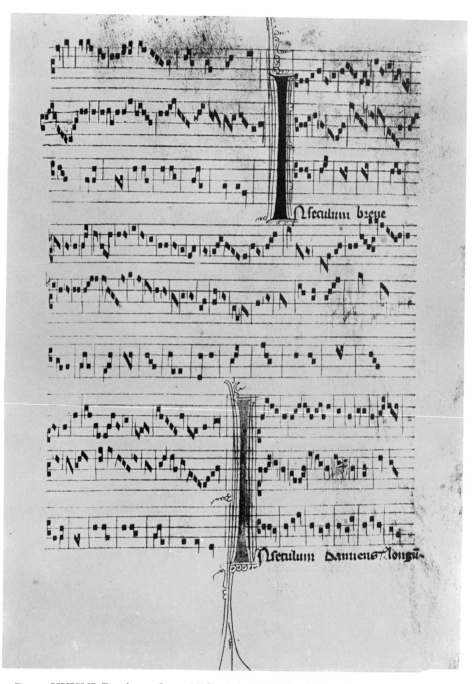

PLATE XXXVI. Bamberg, Staatsbibliothek, Ed. IV 6, fol. 64. Late 13th Century

PLATE XXXVII. Burgos, Codex de Las Huelgas, fol. 112. Early 14th Century

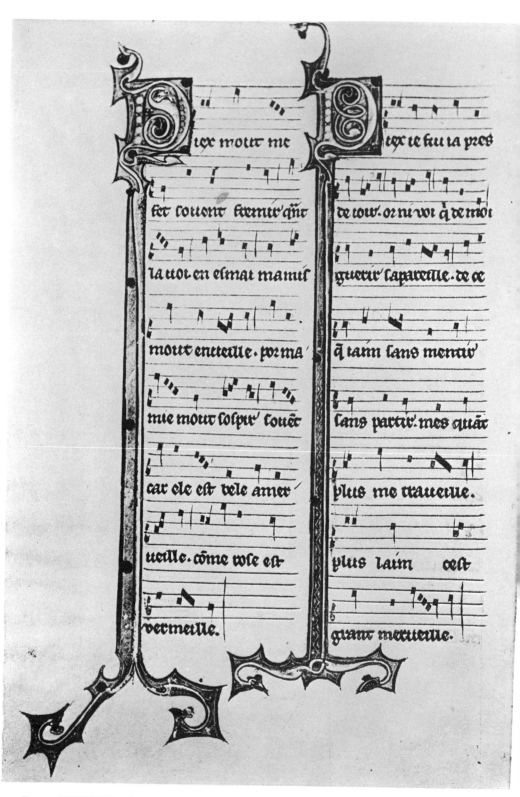

PLATE XXXVIII. Montpellier, Fac. des Medecins, H 196, fol. 44v. Late 13th Century

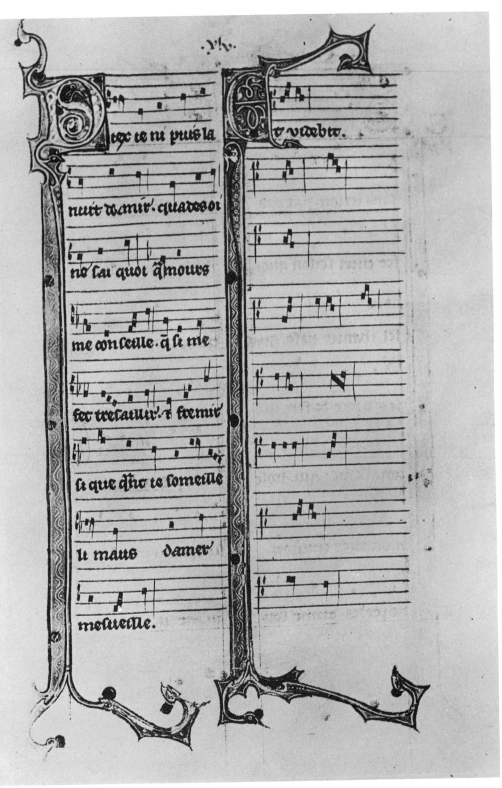

PLATE XL. Montpellier, Fac. des Medecins, H 196, fol. 378v. Late 13th Century

PLATE XLI. Montpellier, Fac. des Medecins, H 196, fol. 379. Late 13th Century

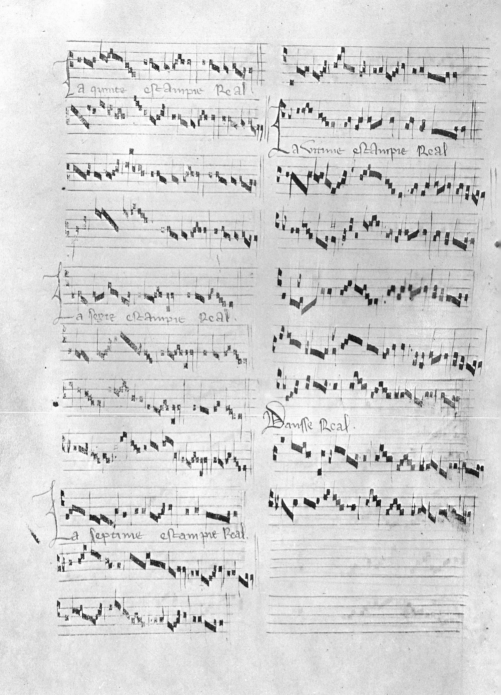

PLATE XLII. Paris, Bibliothèque Nationale, Fr. 844, fol. 104v. Late 13th Century

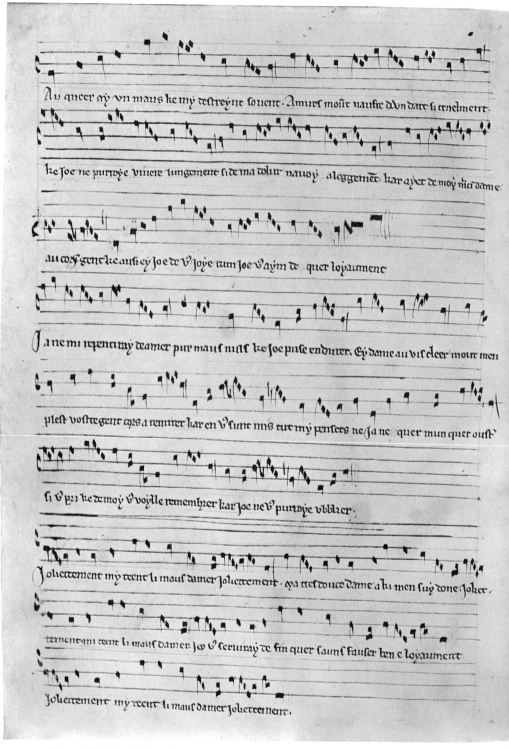

PLATE XLIV. Oxford, Bodleian Library, Douce 139, fol. 179v. 13th Century

PLATE XLV. Paris, Bibliothèque Nationale, Fr. 146, fol. 7. Early 14th Century

PLATE XLVII. Paris, Bibliothèque Nationale, Fr. 9221, fol. 161. 15th Century (?)

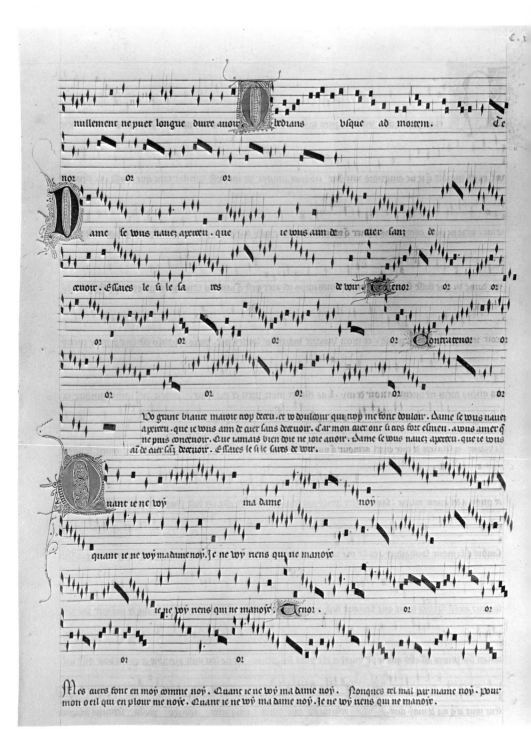

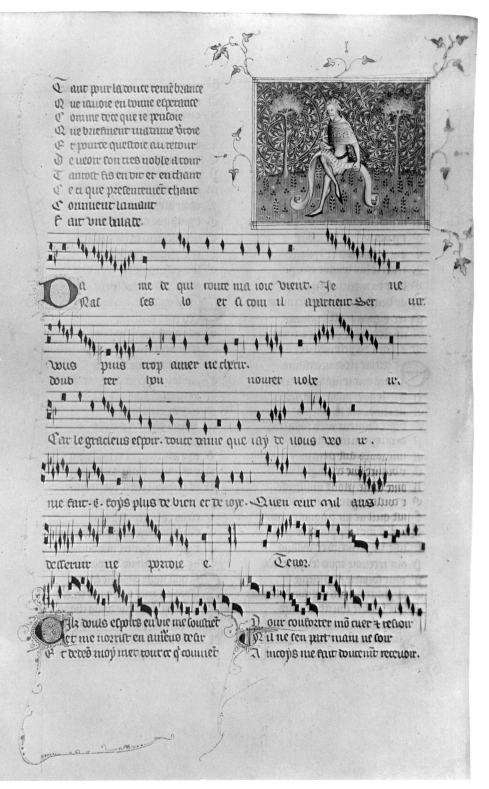

PLATE XLIX. Paris, Bibliothèque Nationale, Fr. 1586, fol. 47v. Early 15th Century

PLATE L. Paris, Bibliothèque Nationale, Fr. 22.546, fol. 131v. Late 14th Century

PLATE LI. Paris, Bibliothèque Nationale, Fr. 22.546, fol. 132. Late 14th Century

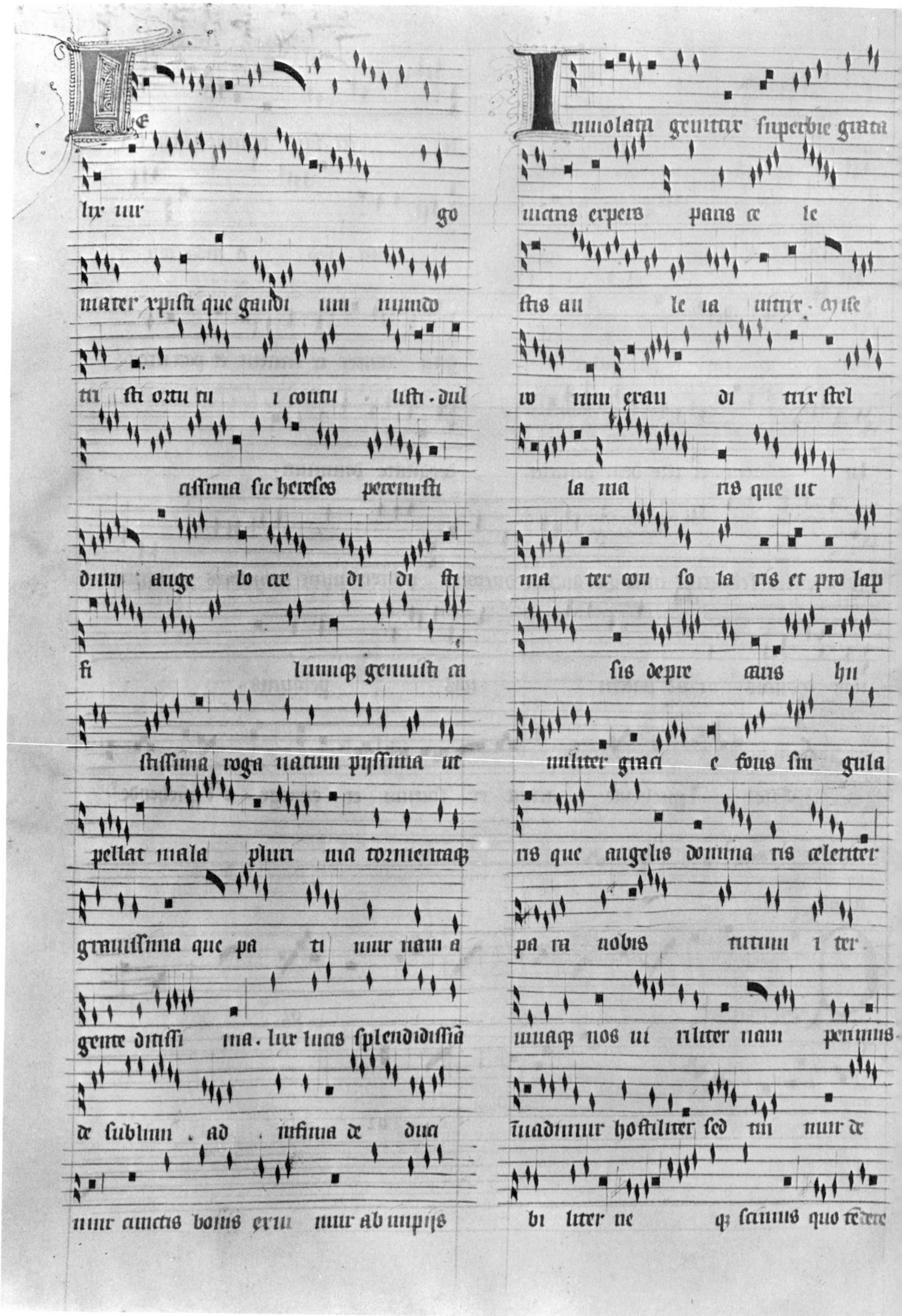

PLATE LII. Paris, Bibliothèque Nationale, Fr. 22.546, fol. 124v. Late 14th Century

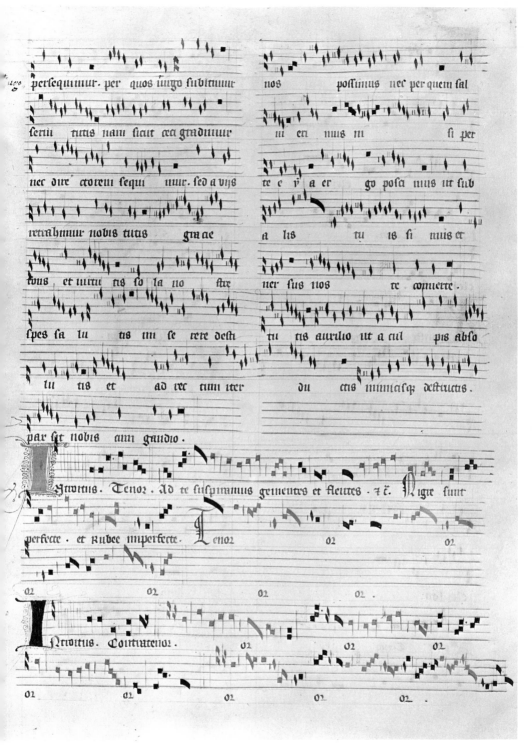

PLATE LIII. Paris, Bibliothèque Nationale, Fr. 22.546, fol. 125. Late 14th Century

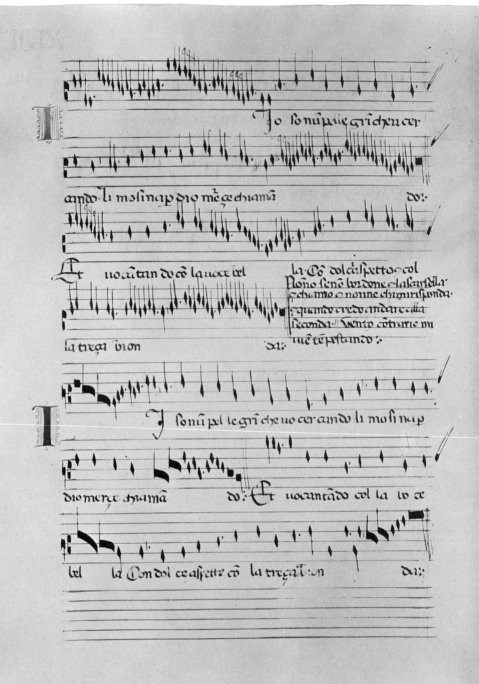

PLATE LIV. Paris, Bibliothèque Nationale, Ital. 568, fol. 42v. 14th Century

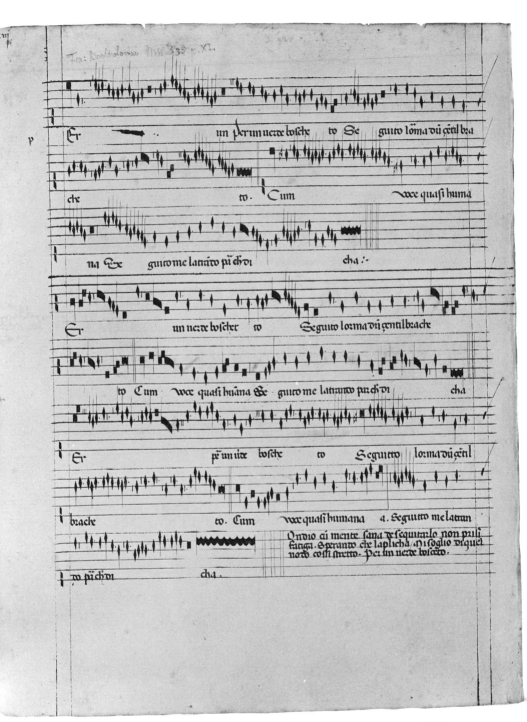

PLATE LV. Paris, Bibliothèque Nationale, N. A. Fr. 6771, fol. 23v. 15th Century

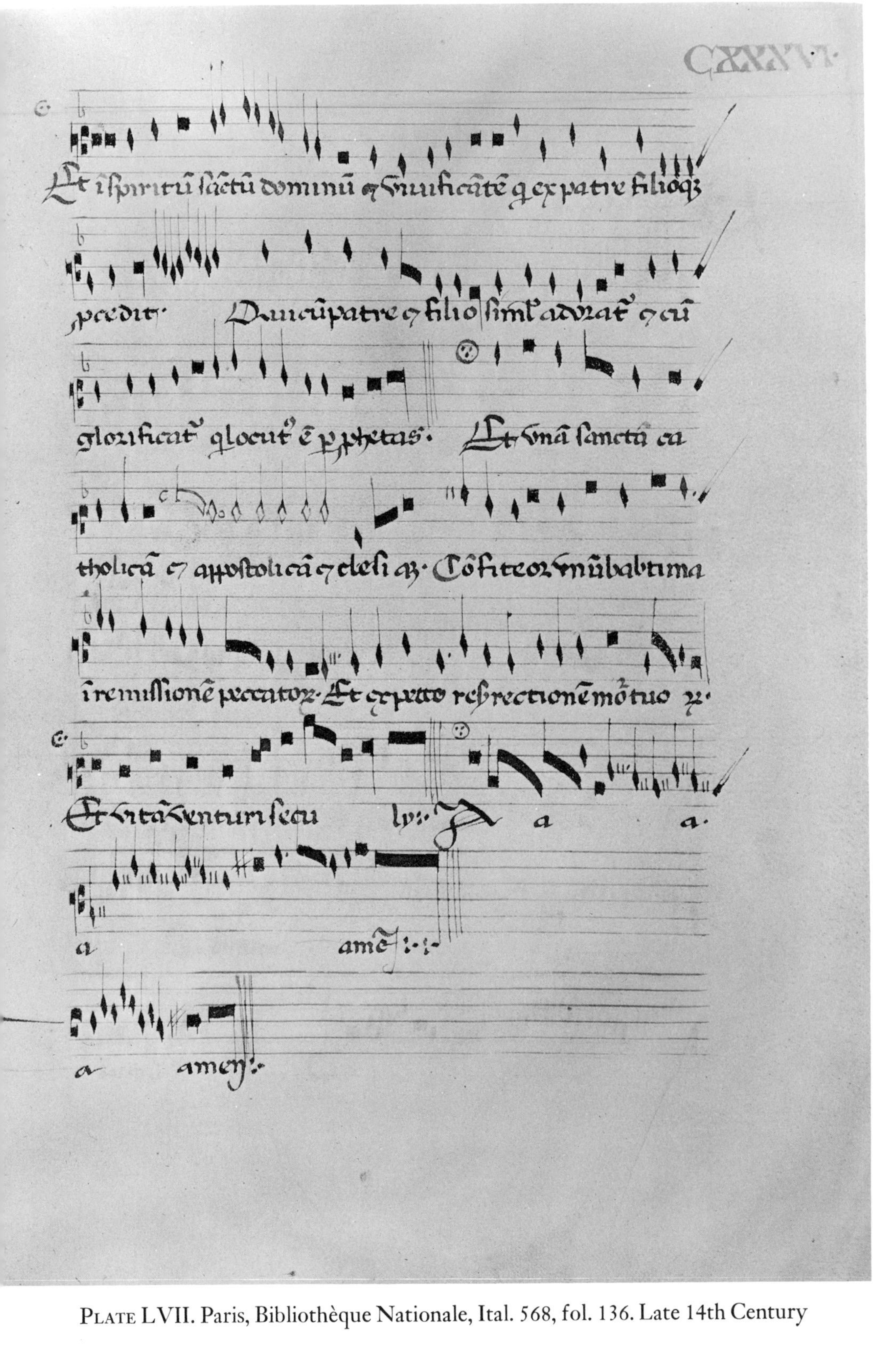

PLATE LVII. Paris, Bibliothèque Nationale, Ital. 568, fol. 136. Late 14th Century

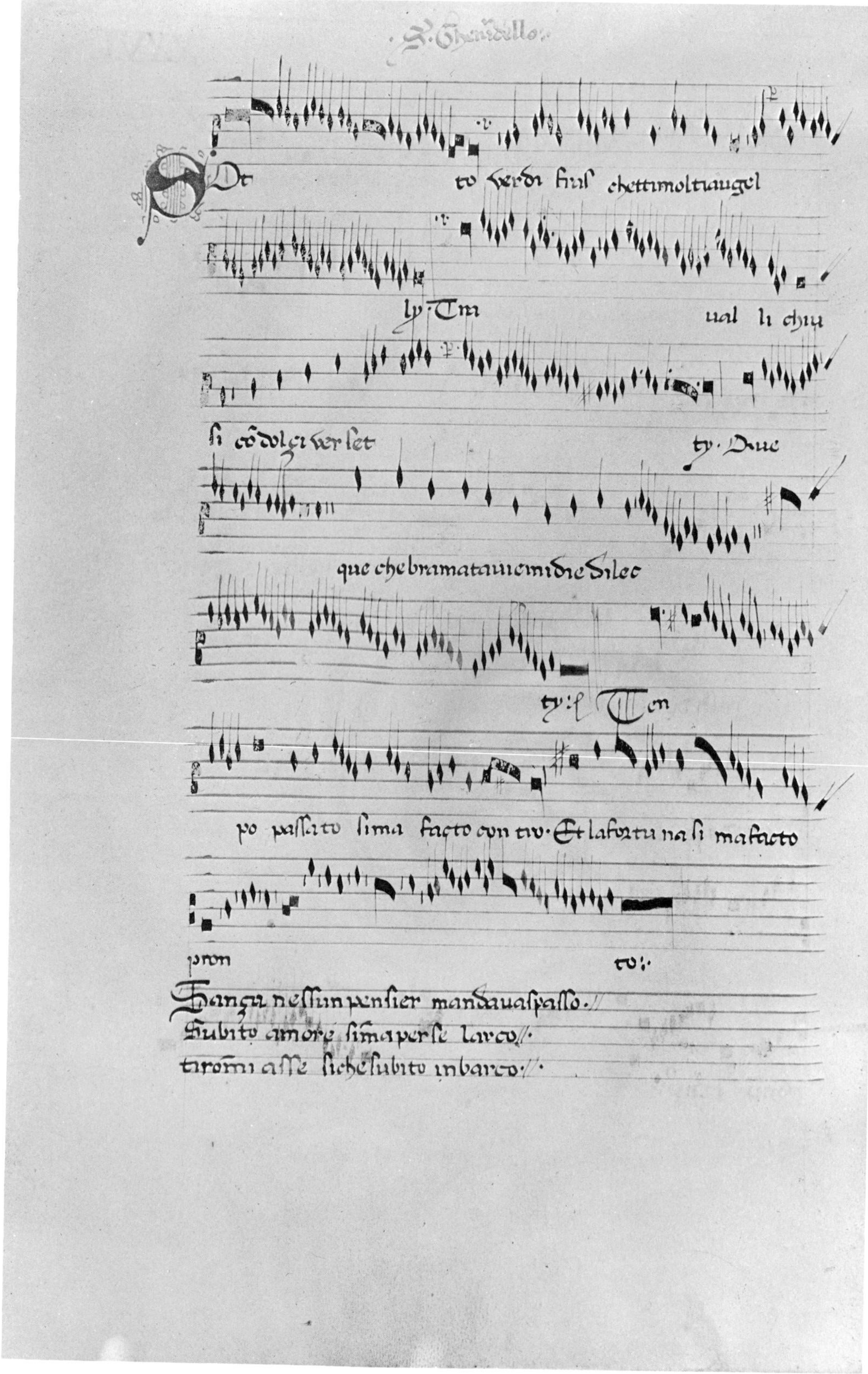

PLATE LVIII. Paris, Bibliothèque Nationale, Ital. 568, fol. 26v. Late 14th Century

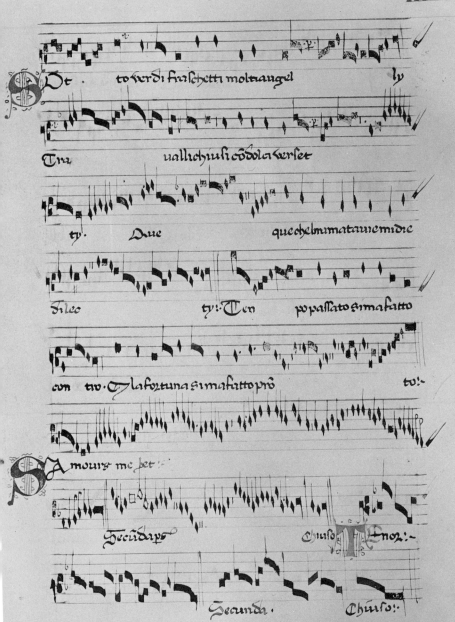

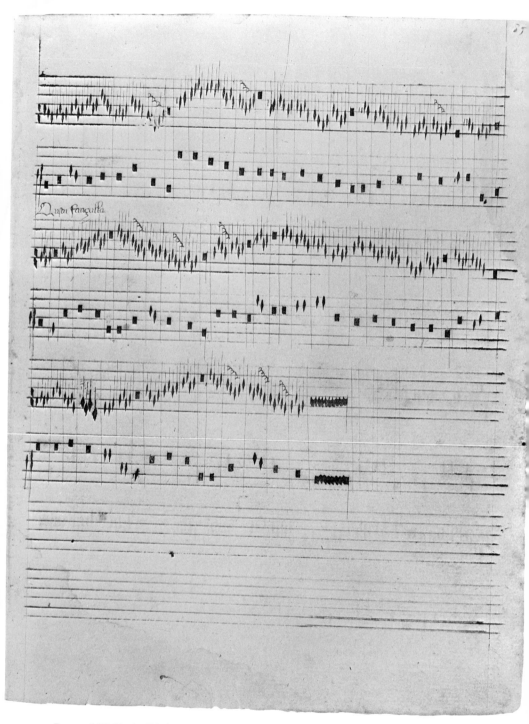

PLATE LX. Paris, Bibliothèque Nationale, N. A. Fr. 6771, fol. 85. 15th Century

PLATE LXI. London, British Museum, Arundel 28.550, fol. 43. Early 14th Century

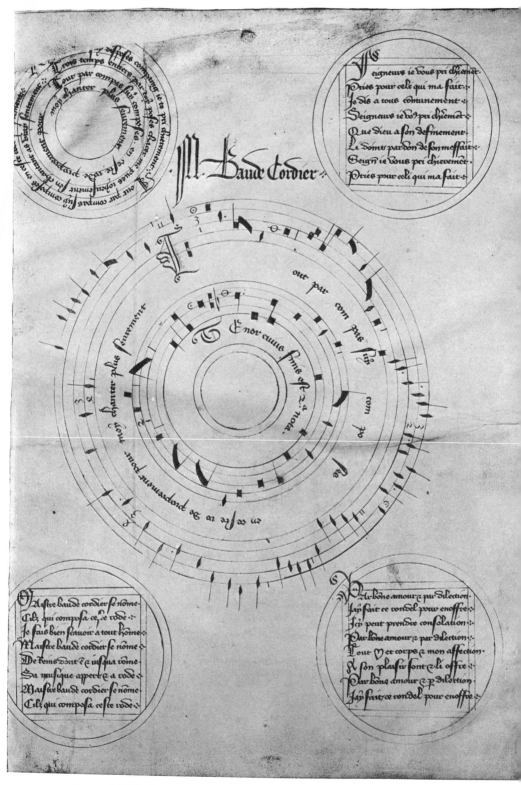

PLATE LXII. Chantilly, Musée Condé, 1047, fol. 12. Early 15th Century

by reason of being repeated notes, and also occasionally as a result of rhythmic exigencies.

The estampies are typical of the form of that dance, which consists of several sections called *puncta*, each punctum being repeated with *ouvert* and *clos* endings that correspond to the first and second endings of later music. The music of the endings of the first punctum of each dance is employed in all the subsequent puncta of that dance. The *quinte, sexte,* and *septieme* estampies each have four puncta, while the *uitieme* has five; each punctum occupies one line of music. Each punctum is performed in the following manner:

1) from the beginning up to the long vertical line through the staff, which is the equivalent of a repeat sign;
2) from the beginning to the short vertical dash that indicates the beginning of the phrase before the first ending;
3) from here—skipping the music between the two lines—to the final phrase, or second ending, between the long vertical line and the end.

The subsequent puncta of each estampie have the same music as the first punctum for their first and second endings.

The "Dansse" at the end follows a different design; it consists of three sections, each ending with the same phrase, but has no repeats, hence no first and second endings.

Certain of the dances begin on the up-beat. These are: 1) *sexte* estampie, first, second, and fourth puncta; 2) *septieme* estampie, third punctum; 3) *uitieme* estampie, first, second and fourth puncta. The other dances start on the first note of a perfection.

There is a certain ambiguity in the use of rests in this manuscript. The ends of phrases are marked off by short rest signs covering one space, and in most cases these can be transcribed as B-rests; but an exception occurs in the puncta of the fifth estampie, as the note preceding the dash is an imperfect L that fills out the perfection. The context shows that the note immediately after the dash must be the beginning of a perfection, leaving no room for a rest, so that the dash in this case only functions to mark off the phrase. On the other hand, a rest of two B's is clearly indicated in the first punctum of the seventh estampie by the dash covering two spaces.

The plica occurs frequently in the dances, attached both to single notes and to ligatures. When eighth notes are introduced—which is either by means of the plica attached to a B or by the sign of opposite propriety—the question of ternary or binary division again occurs.[12] It is quite possible that this was decided by the performer himself; a choice in the matter of rhythm is expressly stated by certain Ars Nova theorists, as will be discussed later on in this chapter. When the sign of opposite propriety and the plica are both found on the same binaria, as in line seven, column to the right, sixteenth notes are introduced into the rhythm (♪ ♪).

There are a few places in the manuscript that are incorrect or difficult to make out. These are:

1) Left column, line three, fifth ligature: there should not be a descending tail on the first note.
2) Right column, end of line two: a faultily-written ligature here is an ascending binaria reading F-G.
3) Right column, line four, third and fourth ligatures: these should be read as if joined together.
4) Left column, fourth line, first two ligatures: these are faded in the manuscript; they consist of a ternaria reading G-A-C, and a binaria reading D-E.

The first punctum of the *quinte* estampie is given in Fig. 54.

FIG. 54

The next two examples are from English manuscripts. They employ the distinctive English mensural notation of the thirteenth century, which differs in several respects from contemporary Continental notation. The most striking difference is the use of the diamond-shaped note for the B. The use of these notes in the modally-notated motet *Ave gloriosa mater* has already been mentioned above in connection with Plate XXXII as a British idiosyn-

[12] Aubry, in "Estampies et dances royales," *Le mercure musicale*, 1906, 169, used ternary division of the B throughout in his transcription of these pieces. The estampies that precede those reproduced in Plate XLII may be seen in facsimile in Beck, *Le Manuscript du Roi*, I, fol. 176v.

cracy. Another difference lies in the manner of writing S's in diamond-shaped groups in which the first of the group has a tail diagonally slanting to the left, indicating that not only this note but
those immediately following it are to be read as S's. This occurs
in the first line of the example on Plate XLIII, and in a great many
places in the following plate. Another difference from Continental
writing lies in the ambiguity that exists in the meaning of the ligatures. English notation lagged in adopting the progressive devices
that arose on the Continent, and eventually was superseded by Continental notation.

PLATE XLIII. Rota: *Sumer is icumen in* (London, Br. Mus. Harl.
978, fol. 11v; thirteenth century)

This celebrated composition has many details of extraordinary
interest from the point of view of notation. The date of the manuscript was the subject of a lively controversy between the late
Manfred Bukofzer and B. Schofield, Keeper of Western Manuscripts in the British Museum.[13] The really striking fact about the
canon, however, is that it once had a different form of notation
than it now has, which certain erasures and other alterations make
plainly evident. Because of the manner in which the alteration has
been made, it is possible to reconstruct the original notation, which
predominantly consisted of diamond-shaped notes with occasional
square shapes. The first part of the melody in its reconstructed form
may be seen in Fig. 55 (after Wooldridge, *OHM*, I, 1st ed., 329).
Comparison with the facsimile of Plate XLIII will show that some of
the diamond shapes were transformed into L's by being squared and
having tails added to them. Certain relatively insignificant melodic
changes were also made in the upper part.

Two different conclusions about the revised version have been
drawn. Wooldridge assumed that the alterations had been made to
change the piece from modal into mensural notation; while Bukofzer
(whose restored version in his '*Sumer is icumen in*', *A Revision*,

---

[13] See Bukofzer, '*Sumer is icumen in*', *A Revision*, 83, and Schofield, "The Provenance and Date of '*Sumer is icumen in*'," *The Music Review*, 1948, 81. On stylistic
grounds, Bukofzer believed it impossible that the Rota could have been written
earlier than 1280, and would rather have placed it "in the early period of duple
rhythm, that is c. 1310," while Schofield relied on paleographic evidence to show
that the date could be advanced to 1260, "but it is most unlikely to have been
written many years later."

FIG. 55

Su - mer is i - cu - men in   lhu - de sing cuc - cu. Grow - eth

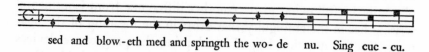

sed and blow - eth med and springth the wo - de   nu.   Sing cuc - cu.

p. 87, is almost identical with Wooldridge's) considered the first version to have also been mensural; he felt that the alterations were not made to "reform" the notation, but to change it from binary to ternary meter. He pointed out that the original version did not have the essential characteristic of syllabic modal notation, in which one note shape serves indiscriminately as both B and L; on the contrary, the L's of the original version were consistently treated as such. The other (diamond) shapes are meaningful only if considered as all B's, with two B's to each L. Had ternary rhythm been intended, the scribe would have alternated squares and diamonds. Fig. 56 shows the beginning of Bukofzer's transcription of the restored manuscript.

The *round*, or *rota* (a form of canon), is written on the upper

FIG. 56

Su - mer is   i - cum-en in,   Lhu - de sing cuc - cu.

Su - mer is   i - cum-en in

Sing   cuc - cu,   sing   cuc - cu   nu,

Sing   cuc - cu   nu,   sing   cuc - cu,

five staves; at the bottom of the page is the *pes* ("foot"), the name given to the repeated, two-voiced tenor motive written in the last two staves. The rubrics at the end of the canon and the pes give directions for performance; a clue to the notation lies in the reference therein to the length of the rest.

Canon rubric

Four companions can sing this rota, which should not be performed by fewer than three, or two, in addition to those who sing the pes. It should be sung thus: the others remaining silent, one begins with those who sing the pes, and when he reaches the note after the cross another starts, and so on with the rest. Each one pauses at the rests, but nowhere else, for the space of one long.

Pes rubric

One performer repeats this as often as needed, counting a rest at the end; the other sings this, with a rest in the middle, but not at the end, where he repeats the beginning at once.

The Reading Rota has elicited many speculations, among them the possibility suggested by Handschin that it may be "the earliest practical specimen of mensural notation we possess." Concerning duple rhythm, Handschin considered it unlikely that binary rhythm was used only at the time when it first appeared notated as such in Continental learned music of the late thirteenth century; he suggested that it suffered a "temporary banishment" in the late thirteenth century, to reappear in the period when actual examples occur in the manuscripts, such as the motet on Plates XL–XLI.[14]

PLATE XLIV. Motet: *Au queer ay un maus—Ja ne mi repentiray—Joliettement* (Oxford, Bodl. Lib. Douce 139, fol. 179v; thirteenth century)

The motet reproduced on Plate XLIV, which is thought to have Coventry as its possible place of origin,[15] occurs also in versions

[14] "The Summer Canon and its Background," *MD*, 1949, 74. Walter Odington, writing *ca.* 1300, seems to indicate that binary meter was an older practice that gave way to ternary; but he may be referring to the modifications of the third and fourth modes that were necessary to fit them into the modal scheme (*CS*, I, 235). Dom Hughes believes that if an early medieval piece is capable of being transcribed in either ternary or binary meter, the latter can be defended on the grounds that the notated form in which it appears was "the only way the notator could have written it with the materials at his disposal" (*NOHM*, II, 402).

[15] Dom A. Hughes, *Medieval Polyphony in the Bodleian Library*, 27.

that differ only in details in *Ba* (fol. 32), *Mo* (fol. 283v), and in a manuscript of Turin (Bibl. di S.M. il Re varii 42, fol. 24). The version in Douce 139, however, unlike the others, has a part arrangement similar to that of the example from *Las H* on Plate XXXVII.

The tenor is in the form of a rondeau; its text, exceptionally, is given in full. An unconventional form of the ascending binaria is employed to bring about the rhythm L-B in the tenor; instead of the usual modification made by turning the upper note to the right, the ordinary form is used, but with the lower note lengthened. Compare the ascending binaria in the tenor with those in the motetus.

A noticeable feature of the manuscript is the frequent incorrect use of a L for a B. In the upper parts examples of this occur in every staff. In one case the opposite occurs—a B is used in place of a L in the triplum, second line, first note. The general musical design of the piece, and the prevalence of first-mode rhythm suffice to indicate where most of these errors occur. Where they are not so obvious, comparison with the versions in *Mo* and *Ba* makes a reconstruction of the right rhythm possible. An outstanding instance of this occurs in the third line, where the six ascending notes that begin with A below middle C are in the following rhythm:

♪ ♪ ♪ ♪ |♪ ♪.

This is the first manuscript to be considered in which there are groups of more than three S's to a B-value. Actually, there are only two of these—the four-note ligature about two-thirds of the way through the fourth line, and another at the end of the fifth line. The organization of the notes in all the S-groups of the present example might well be rendered as Rokseth has done in her transcription of the *Mo* version of this motet; that is, by distributing the S's evenly over the B-value. Thus, two S's = ♫ , three S's = ♫♪ , and four S's = ♫♫ .[16]

The curious marks that occur near the beginning of staff three and in the middle of staves five and six are accidentals, consisting of a flat followed directly afterward by a natural sign. Plicas are used

---

[16] Rokseth used a scale of values of L = quarter note in her transcription of this piece (*Polyphonies*, III, 97). See also Aubry's transcription of the *Ba* version in *Cent motets*, II, 113.

sparingly; an ascending plica longa occurs in line four, and the plica brevis twice in succession at the beginning of line six and again toward the end of line eight. The phrasing is irregular; Rokseth attempts to make it clear through the use of an occasional half-measure.

The beginning of the motet is given in Fig. 57.

FIG. 57

Au   queer   ay   un   maus   ke   my   de -

Ja   ne   mi   re -   pen -   ti -   ray   d'a -

Jo -   li -   et -   te -   ment   my   teent   li

streint   so -   vent   A -

mer   pur   maus   nuls

maus   d'a -   mer   jo -

The text is as follows:

Triplum

Au queer ay un maus ke my destreynt sovent,
Amurs m'ont navsre d'un dart si cruelment

Ke joe ne purroye vivere lungement
Si de ma dolur n'avoy aleggement,
Kar ayet de moy merci dame au cors gent
Ke ausi ey joe de vous joye aim joe vous aym de quer loyaument.

Motetus

Ja ne mi repentiray de amer
Pur maus nuls ke joe puse endurer.
Ey dame au vis cleer
Mout men plest vostre gent cors a remirer
Kar en vous sunt mis tut my pensers
Ne ja ne quer mun quer ouster.
Si vous pri ke de moy vous voylle remembrer
Kar joe ne vous purroye ubblier.

Tenor

Joliettement my teent li maus d'amer, joliettement.
Ma tres douce dame a ki men suy donc.
Joliettement mi teent li maus d'amer.
Jey vous serviray de fin quer sauns fauser ben e loyaument.
Joliettement my teent li maus d'amer, joliettement.

The last two examples in this chapter are motets selected from among those interpolated in the *Roman de Fauvel*, and were written about or before 1310. According to Leo Schrade they are both the work of Philippe de Vitry.[17] While they are clearly Franconian in notational character, they also exhibit some features that are the result of influences that shaped the musical style of the Ars Nova. This influence is apparent in the use of modus imperfectus, which occurs in several of the *Fauvel* motets, including that of Plate XLVI, in the numerous S-groups—especially those four S's to the B—and also in the first appearance of tails added to S's which appear in many of these groups.

The use of imperfect mode has already occurred in a previous example, the motet *Amor potest* of Plates XL–XLI, where it was

---

[17] The attribution is indirect, and based on the fact that Philippe refers to the motet on Plate XLV in his *Ars Nova* (CS, III, 20), where he says that when rests of the value of three B's are found in one sign the mode is perfect, "as in 'Orbis orbatur.'" Schrade finds a kinship of text and musical style between this and the motet of Plate XLVI; the triplum of each begins with the same melody. See Schrade, Commentary to Vol. I, *Polyphonic Music of the 14th Century*, 33, and "Philippe de Vitry: Some New Discoveries," *MQ*, 1956, 330.

manifest from the context, especially from the use of imperfect B-rests, as it is also in *Orbis orbatus*, Plate XLV. But in the *Fauvel* manuscript the imperfect mode is sometimes specifically designated by certain expressions added to the tenor incipit, such as "ex imperfecte," or "canite imperfectis." One of the *Fauvel* pieces, *Adesto*, is cited by Philippe de Vitry in his *Ars Nova* (written between 1316 and 1325) as an example of both imperfect mode and imperfect time. Two motets have small vertical signs at the beginning which serve as a sort of meter sign to indicate duple time, although the use of such signs as a regular feature of notation did not occur until long after this period in France. Two other *Fauvel* motets use red notes to indicate a change within a piece from triple to duple meter, a device that came to be an important feature of the notation of the Ars Nova.

The interpretation of the Petronian S-groups in the *Fauvel* motets cannot be summarized easily because of the rapid changes which occurred in musical style during the early part of the fourteenth century. The normal rhythm of the groups of two or three S's was Franconian: two S's = ♪♩ ; three S's = ♪♪♪ . When groups of four S's or more began to be introduced, they were spread evenly over the B-value at first, so that a group of four S's would be ♪♪♪♪ , five S's ♪♪♪♪♪ , and so on. This interpretation is based on a statement by Jacob of Liége, writing in the second quarter of the fourteenth century as a defender of the "ancients" against the modern practices of his period (*SR*, 186).

A new factor entered into the performance practice of the period, however, when it was recognized that groups of two S's were sometimes performed by singers in such a manner that the first of the two S's was given the longer value. According to an anonymous treatise of 1279, the choice of rhythm for these notes (♪♩ or ♩♪) was "according to the will of the singers." [18] The rhythmic variety thus afforded was extended to the group of three S's, which were sometimes rendered as ♩ ♪♪ , and eventually these variants came to be represented graphically in the note symbols by means of a

---

[18] H. Sowa, *Ein anonymer glossierter Mensuraltraktat*, 51.

descending tail on the first of a group of S's. The tailed notes were called the *semibreves caudatae*, and many of these are seen in the motets of Plates XLV and XLVI, but it has been shown that the tails themselves are later additions to the manuscript of the *Roman de Fauvel*. Whether they were added for the purpose of bringing the motets into line with later practice or to make their original meaning more apparent is an open question. In the terminology of the period, the object of the tail was to modify *via artis* ("in an artificial manner") the rhythmical meaning that was inherent in the group *via naturae* ("in the natural manner"), that is, without the tail, by causing a lengthening of time value of the tailed note. The use of a tail may have been suggested by the analogous lengthening that caused a B-shape to become a L when a tail was added to it.

FIG. 58

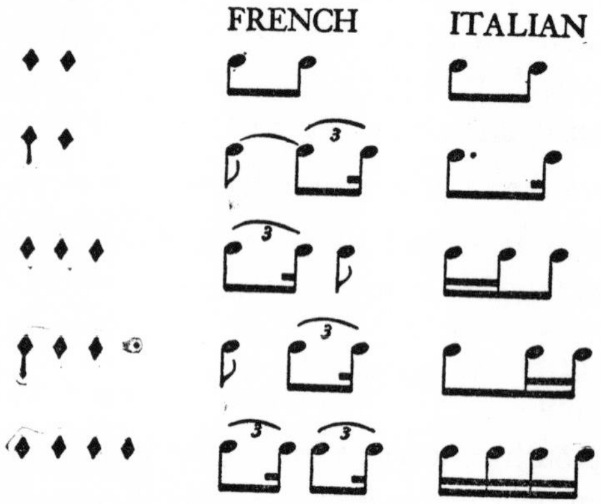

When a composition was in imperfect time, still more variety was given to the performance of the S-groups, for the singer had a choice of using either "French" or "Italian" rhythm. This was fully explained by Marchetto of Padua, writing about a decade later than the time when the Fauvel motets appeared, and his account of the differences between the two is summarized in the table of Fig. 58. The Italian manner is an expression of the southern preference for simpler and more straightforward rhythms than those favored by the French.

Marchetto wrote that in order to know which is intended by the composer, "at the beginning of any composition in the French manner . . . there should be placed a G" [for "Gallic"], while "at the beginning of a part in the Italian manner there should be placed a Greek I" [for "Ytalian"].[19]

In his recent edition of the *Fauvel* motets as part of the volume *Polyphonic Music of the 14th Century*, Leo Schrade has transcribed them so that in those in which the S-groups do not exceed three in number the division of the B is binary in the two-S groups, and ternary in the three-S groups. In all those motets that include four-S groups, however, he always divides the B as if it were imperfect, and always in the French manner. The interpretation of the former category of pieces is somewhat questionable since in the matter of the binary division of two-S groups it is "un-Franconian," but the use of imperfect time in those compositions having four-S groups is justified by certain statements of theorists of the early fourteenth century. Robert de Handlo, for example, in a treatise of 1324 (*Regulae*, CS, I, 388), says that pieces with up to five S's in a B were in *more mediocre*, that is, in moderate speed; in them the two-S groups were equal, and those of three-S's unequal, meaning that the B was imperfect.

The motets of the *Roman de Fauvel* mark the last appearance of the plica in polyphonic music. According to Marchetto (*Pomerium*, CS, III, 181), the plica in the fourteenth century had become a shorter note, occupying only one-quarter of a B in tempus imperfectum, and one-third in tempus perfectum.

PLATE XLV. Motet: *Orbis orbatus–Vos pastores–Fur non venit* (Paris, Bibl. nat. fr. 146, fol. 7; early fourteenth century)

The motet is in perfect mode; the time, following de Handlo's statement concerning S-groups, is imperfect.

The tenor, which starts on the bottom staff of the left column and occupies the two lines of the middle column, makes use of a fourth-mode pattern throughout, each ternaria having the rhythm of B –altered B –perfect L. The tenor melody has a quasi-ostinato character. It consists of a fifteen-bar melody which is twice repeated; the melody itself is made up of three five-bar segments, each of which is almost identical with the others. (Text, John x:9.)

[19] Marchetto's statement recalls the curious rubric "manera francesa" which occurs in *Las H* (for example, in the conductus, *Mater patris*, fol. 147); Anglès considers this rubric means duple time, but this is not borne out by the notation itself, and may refer to the French rhythm shown in Fig. 58.

The triplum has no special difficulties, but it contains one scribal error, the dot after the first note in the fourth staff; the context shows that this is part of a group of four S's making up a B-value, the first of which is the note at the end of the previous staff.

The motetus has two lacunae, one occurring at the end of the third staff, where notes to the value of four B's are missing; the other is in the last staff, where a perfection of three B's is missing just before the L with the *signum perfectionis*. Schrade has attempted to supply the missing notes of the first of these places by using the same notes that occur in the corresponding passage above the tenor later on in the piece (measure 40). The missing notes of the other passage he derives from the "harmonic situation" of this and the other places where the tenor is the same (measures 11 and 26). The two restored passages are given in Fig. 59.

FIG. 59

The beginning of the third staff of the motetus is L-B-L, with no sign of perfection; the question as to which L is perfect is determined by the context, which, from the standpoint of harmony and rhythm, calls for perfection of the first L. The rhythmical meaning of the conjunctura-like figure in staves four and five is not certain, although the context makes it clear that the group has the value of an imperfect L. Wolf treated such notes as ⌐ ⌐⌐ , Ludwig as ⌐⌐ ⌐ . This is a question of whether the newer or older practice should be followed; in the modal and pre-Franconian periods the latter would have been used, but in view of the progressive character of this motet, the former seems justified.

The beginning of the motet, with the S-groups transcribed according to the French manner, is seen in Fig. 60.

The text reads as follows:

Triplum

Orbis orbatus oculus
In die cecus respitat,
Dum componendis seculis
Mitratus quisque militat

FIG. 60

Or - bis or - ba - tus o- cu- lis in di- e ce- cus re - spi -

Vos

Fur non venit, nisi ut furetur, et mactet,

tat dum com - po - nen - dis se - cu - lis

pas - to - res

et perdat.

Pro dicandis nepotulis
Et pauper Christum clamitat
Ieiuniis verbo populis
Clamat iam raucis faucibus
Ad cor redite, filii,
Sed cum surdis sint auribus
Et contemptores impii,
Induratis cervicibus
Et ausi temerarii,
Hus mox compellat vocibus;
Cur, similes aspidibus,
Audire non dignamini?
Mutis iam paret canibus,
Cur in gregem crassamini

Eius de pastis carnibus
Nec ut lupos armamini
Horum armati dentibus?

Motetus

Vos pastores adulteri
Et veri mercenarii,
Successores Luciferi,
Christi pseudo vicarii,
Vicini dato muneri,
A vero semper devii,
Ventris vacatis operi.

Tenor

Fur non venit, nisi ut furetur, et mactet, et perdat.

PLATE XLVI. Motet: *Quoniam novi probatur–Heu fortuna sub-dola–Heu me* (Paris, Bibl. nat. fr. fol. 30; early fourteenth century)

This motet is distinguished in two ways from the previous example: it is in imperfect mode, and the S-groups are as profuse in the motetus as in the triplum.

The tenor is seen to be in imperfect meter by the presence of several imperfect L-rests, as well as by the context of the upper parts. The scribe has placed a sharp sign just before the last duplex L, but this is an error, as an imperfect L-rest is what is required here. The tenor melody is derived from motives in the chant *Tristis est*, the Responsorium in the First Nocturn of *Coena Domini*.

The upper parts have no problems different from those of the preceding motet, but there are two errors in the motetus: the plica longa in the middle of the first line should be a B; and the B immediately following the group of four S's in the second line should be a L. Like the previous motet, this one has a number of four-S groups, so the time is considered to be imperfect here also. Schrade has used the French manner in his transcription of this piece, as he regards it as "the rhythm customary in Fauvel," but he implies the possibility of the manner employed in Fig. 61 (Commentary to Vol. I, *Polyphonic Music of the 14th Century*, 88). Italian rhythm

has been used in Fig. 61, not only to illustrate the difference between it and the French manner used in Fig. 60, but also because
it seems to be suggested by the general musical character of the
composition. Historically, either would appear to be correct.

FIG. 61

Quo - ni - am no - vi pro - ba - tur ex - i - tu

Heu   for -

Heu me, tristis est anima mea

quan - tum pro - sit in -   fla - ri spi - ri -

tu -   na

The text reads as follows:

Triplum

Quoniam novi probatur exitu
Quantum prosit inflari spiritu
Superbie quid plus appetere
Quam deceat et quam suscipere
Non liceat tantum quia scandere
Quod tedeat ut alter Icarus

Qui tanquam ignatus in mari fluctu
Ac jam submersus
Sic nec est reversus Pheton usurpato
Solis regimine sed ipso cremato
Vito conamine est exterminatus
Sic nimis elatus Ycari volatus
Affectans transcendere nostri Aman vincere
Rapinam Phetontis in Falcionis montis
Loco collocatus evertus a pulvere
Ymbre sepe lavatur, aura flante siccatur
Suis delictis in ymis
Non eodem cursu respondent ultima primis.[20]

Motetus

Heu fortuna sub dola que semper diastola,
    Usque nunc fuisti,
Promittendo frivola tamquam vera fistola,
    Nunc apparuisti.
Heu graciens prospera longe ponens aspera,
    Ubi primsisti,
Meditans in immensa gaza usque ad ethera
    Nomen extulisti.
Nunc tua volubili rota lacu flebili
    Nudum demersisti.
Velud Aman morior de te sic experior
    Quod me decepisti,
Quanto gradus alcior tanto casus gravior
    Hoc me docuisti.

Tenor

Heu me, tristis est anima mea.

The Transcription of the Facsimiles

In the Franconian period certain fundamental principles of mensuration were established which are still valid today; but for the
late Middle Ages some features of the system which later became
obsolete were of much greater significance, particularly the fixing

[20] The first word of the text of the triplum is considered by Schrade, after
Becker (*Fauvel und Fauvelliana*, Leipzig, 1936), to be "Aman," following Becker's
interpretation of the text as a metaphorical reference to the Old Testament story
of Haman; "Quoniam" would therefore be a corrupt reading of this name. The
theory is supported by several factors (including the text of the motetus) but
does not account for the number of notes at the beginning of the triplum melody.

of the meaning of the ligatures and of a system of using them with considerable flexibility through graphic modifications. The facsimiles considered in this chapter show a wide range of techniques of notation within the general framework of the Franconian system; these techniques range from those in which ligature writing had not yet crystallized into standard patterns, to those in which the system was in process of expansion to meet the demands of the new rhythmical style which characterized the fourteenth century, such as the use of smaller note values and of imperfect mensuration. Each of the facsimiles discussed in this chapter will afford valuable exercise in transcription; the transcribing of the entire set will convey strikingly a sense of the rapid evolutionary development that occurred during the period in which they were written. It is suggested that each be completed in the manner in which it is begun in the illustrative Figures. Unlike modal notation, there is really only one ambiguous feature about the writing of the Franconian period in general, and that is the rhythmical organization of the S-groups; a summary of the various ways in which they may be treated follows.

Binary division is advised for the motets *Cruci domini* (Plate XXXV), *Laus tibi* (Plate XXXVII, *Diex mout me fet* (Plates XXXVIII and XXXIX), and the instrumental dances (Plate XLII).

Ternary division should be used in the instrumental motet (Plate XXXVI), and the motet *Amor potest* (Plates XL and XLI).

Binary division for two-S groups and ternary for those of three S's is recommended for the motet *Au queer ay un maus* (Plate XLIV); the four-S groups should also be evenly distributed over the B.

The first of the Fauvel motets—*Orbis orbatus* (Plate XLV)—should be continued in the French manner; the second—*Quoniam non probatur* (Plate XLVI)—in the Italian manner.

The Summer Canon (Plate XLIII) should be completed in the manner of Fig. 56.

6

FRENCH ARS NOVA NOTATION

D URING the early part of the fourteenth century, Franconian notation became elaborated and codified into a system that was to endure for a very considerable period with relatively little essential change. Even the change to white notation which took place about the middle of the fifteenth century was not a real change, as no new principles were involved; the hitherto solid black notes were merely outlined as a result of the increasing use of paper for manuscripts. The French system of the Ars Nova is seen in its developed, classical form in the works of Guillaume de Machaut, whose active period covers the second and third quarters of the fourteenth century; the illustrations in this chapter are drawn exclusively from the manuscripts containing his compositions.

In the Ars Nova another shift of the beat to a smaller note value took place, a fact noted by contemporary writers such as Jacob of Liége, who stated that the S had now the same speed as the (perfect) B had previously. In transcribing the compositions discussed in this chapter, therefore, the S instead of the B will serve as the beat, and will be rendered as a quarter note in modern notation. Studies of the writings of medieval theorists have established the fact that the general tempo for the beat (or "tactus") remained about M.M. 8o, but that three different speeds were recognized—quick, moderate, and slow. These speeds were referred to by various terms, as: *cita, media,* and *morosa; velociter, medie,* and *tractim;*

lascivo, mediocre, and *longo;* and *minimum, medium,* and *maius.*
Jacob stated that even though music was performed in these different ways, "the notation remains the same in each case" (*Speculum musicae, CS,* II, 400).[1]

The Apparatus of Ars Nova Notation

French notation of the Ars Nova had as its basis a system of note division in which the Franconian L-B relationships of perfection, imperfection, and alteration were applied to each of four different sets of time values, or "degrees," as they were called by the theorists: these were the *maximodus, modus, tempus,* and *prolatio.*

FIG. 62

1st degree: Maximodus	81 Triplex L	54 Duplex L	27 Simplex L
2nd degree: Modus	27 Perfect L	18 Imperfect L	9 B
3rd degree: Tempus	9 Perfect B	6 Imperfect B	3 Minor S
4th degree: Prolatio	3 Perfect S	2 Imperfect S	1 Minima

Thus Johannes de Muris (*Ars Novae Musicae,* 1319) showed in a diagram—reproduced in essence in Fig. 62—how each degree from the largest to the smallest contains perfect, imperfect, and "unitary" notes: the smallest of these in each degree becomes the largest of a similar set of relationships in the next degree. The degree called prolatio contains a new note, the *minim* (hereafter designated as M), which came into wide use as a consequence of the shift of values in which the S became the beat. The numbers after each note in Fig. 62 indicate the number of minims in that note.[2]

[1] For further discussions of the question of tempo, see Besseler, *AfM,* 1926, 212 (quoted in *MMA,* 333); *NPM,* 343; Machabey, *La notation musicale,* 79; and Sachs, *Rhythm and Tempo,* 186; see also Sachs, "Some Remarks about Old Notation," *MQ,* 1948, 365.

[2] After the table in *SR,* 177. Note that the relationship of perfect to imperfect notes is that of dotted to undotted notes in modern notation, not that of triplets

The triplex L is listed by Muris to satisfy the theoretical urge for completeness and symmetry, but it is not found in the actual sources of Ars Nova music except in the form of rests. For this reason, the maximodus differed from the other degrees, as it was a grouping of a duplex L and simplex L, or three simplex L's, into a perfect maximode, rather than a division of a maxima into L's analogously to the other degrees. An example of the use of the maximode is seen in the tenor and contratenor of Plate LIII.

The persistent ambiguity of the smaller note values that existed in thirteenth-century music is done away with in this system in which imperfect mensuration in each degree is accepted equally with perfect. The principles of perfection, imperfection, and alteration continue to be valid for any perfect mensuration, but do not arise, of course, in those that are imperfect. A note that is sometimes, though rarely, encountered in French notation of the Machaut period is a further division of the minim—the *semiminim* ("half of the smallest"—hereafter designated by Sm). At first each minim was divisible only into two equal semiminims; but later the minim came to share perfect values also, thus following the earlier history of the semibreve. The shape of the semiminim was formed by adding a flag on the right of the stem of the minim.

As a consequence of the fact that each of the degrees could be either perfect or imperfect, regardless of the nature of any other degree, time signatures began to make their appearance, although they did not become a regularly established part of notation in France until the fifteenth century. The most important of the time signatures were the signs denoting the four different possible combinations of time and prolation—the "*quatre prolacions*" of Vitry—in which a whole circle represented tempus perfectum, and a broken circle tempus imperfectum. The prolation was at first indicated by three dots within the circle for the major (perfect) prolation, and two dots for the minor (imperfect), as in table *a* of Fig. 63. Examples of the use of these meter signs may be seen in the facsimiles of Plates LVI and LVII. Later, the group of three dots in the circle was replaced by a single dot to represent perfection, while the

---

to duplets. Perfect and imperfect mensurations were considered by contemporary theorists to have replaced the six rhythmic modes, which were obsolete by this time, of course. (See Anon. I, *De musica antiqua et nova*, CS, III, 338.)

absence of a dot showed imperfection, as seen in Fig. 63b. The last of the signs in Fig. 63b still remains in present-day notation and retains the same metrical significance. Other meter signs given in Fig. 63c indicated the modus, but these were used only infrequently. In the fourteenth century, meter signs of various sorts were far more common in Italian than in French music.

The dot came to be used in other ways besides marking off the perfection of S-groups or larger units. The most important of these was the *punctus additionis*, used only in imperfect mensurations, which functioned exactly as the dot in modern notation. This usage was another result of the equal importance of imperfect and perfect

FIG. 63

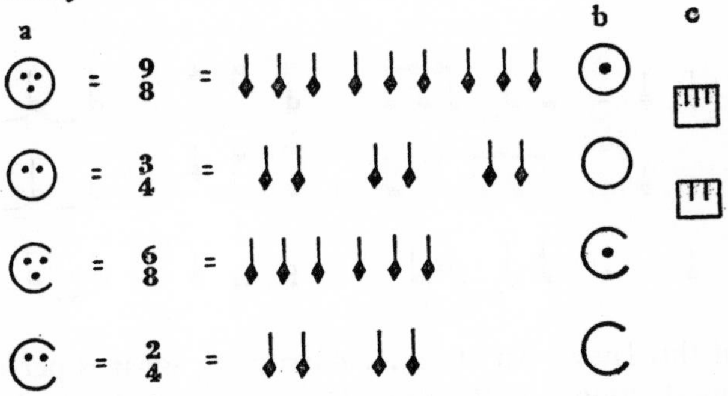

meter in the Ars Nova. Examples of the dot of addition may be seen in the first two lines of the Machaut piece *Dame, se vous n'avez aperceu*, on Plate XLVIII.

The dot was also considered to function as a *punctus demonstrationis* (a dot that "points out" or "singles out") in another Ars Nova innovation—syncopation. Syncopation was conceived of essentially as the "splitting" of a perfection of L, B, or S value into two parts, and then placing another perfection between the two parts. Thus a S could be placed within three M's, and the dot preserved the perfection of the inserted note, as in Figs. 64a and b. Actually this was a subtlety without much significance, for there are really only two kinds of dots—those of division and of addition —and the dot used in syncopation is essentially one of division. Later, syncopation came to be applied to imperfect as well as perfect mensurations, and the same principle applied to imperfect as well as perfect L, B, and S values. In perfect meters, if the latter part of a syncopation did not fill out a perfection, alteration was used to complete it; this is illustrated in Fig. 64c.

Another refinement indirectly related to syncopation was the extension of imperfection to notes that were two degrees apart in value—called *imperfectio ad partem remotam*. This meant that a L could be made imperfect by a S as well as by a B, and this principle could be extended even to notes three degrees apart (*imperfectio ad partem remotissimam*). Figs. 64d and e show a perfect L imperfected by a perfect S and M, respectively. While this came to be part of the common practice of the fourteenth century, it was held by Jacob of Liége to be one of the several ways in which "the practi-

FIG. 64

tioners of this [new] art are . . . corrupting what is perfect with many imperfections" (*SR*, 183). An example of distant imperfection occurs in Machaut's *Liement me deport*, on Plate XLVII, where the B toward the end of the first line (over the word "*pointure*") is followed by a M. See Fig. 64f.

The use of red notes is a very significant innovation of the Ars Nova, marking as it does the emergence in written music of the *hemiola* ("one and one-half"), that is, the use of time values in the relationship of three to two. Red notes were used at different times for different purposes; in the fourteenth century they were used to indicate a temporary change in the prevailing rhythm in which mensuration was transformed from perfect into imperfect as long as the red notes were continued. (This device came to be called *coloration*.) Since red notes are always understood to be notes of imperfect value, when they are introduced into a prevailing perfect mensuration, they cause a shift of accent. Red notes are used in the tenor

and contratenor of Plate LIII, for example, to effect frequent alternations in the maximode from perfect to imperfect. (The red notes
in the reproduction may be identified by their gray color.) Later,
when coloration came to be used freely in the upper parts, it was
often used to change tempus imperfectus with prolatio perfecta
to tempus perfectus with prolatio imperfecta; that is, to change
from $\frac{6}{8}$ to $\frac{3}{4}$ meter.

While red notes are almost never used in imperfect mensurations
in French Ars Nova sources, they were later as commonly employed in these as in perfect mensurations. In imperfect meters
the same underlying principle applies: the red notes bear the same
relationship to the black notes of the same species as they do in
perfect mensurations—they are *per se* reduced in value by one-
third—but the effect is to introduce a new time value into the
rhythm, since the black notes are already reduced to imperfect
values by being in an imperfect mensuration (♪ ♪ black $=$ ♪ ♪ ♪
red). Therefore, coloration in imperfect meters makes triplets of
duplets, while in perfect meters its effect is to cause a change of
accent. In the latter case the reduction of value in the red notes is
not so apparent because some of the black notes, normally perfect,
are usually made imperfect by context, and therefore have the same
value as the red notes; but in imperfect meters the reduction of
value introduces notes whose duration is different, and this can
be expressed only by coloration. Red notes, being imperfect, are
not subject to alteration; while black notes, if they are in a perfect
mensuration, are treated accordingly. In the mid-fifteenth century,
when the change from black to white notation took place, the use
of red notes was discontinued, and black notes were used to produce
precisely the same effects as the red notes had formerly been used
for.

The rests used in the Ars Nova are those of Franco: a line covering one space represents a B-rest, and those covering two and three
spaces are imperfect and perfect L-rests, respectively. Further rest
values are used for the larger and smaller values on either side of
these, however, and the signs for the major and minor S-rests are
abandoned. Fig. 65 shows the entire range of rests used; the values,

reading from left to right, are those of the perfect maxima; imperfect maxima; perfect long; imperfect long; breve; semibreve; minima; and semiminima.

FIG. 65

The Identification of Mode, Time, and Prolation

In most French manuscripts of the Ars Nova period there are no meter signs, but it is essential to know what the prevailing meters of a composition are before attempting to transcribe it. This is not always easy to determine, but there are certain features of the notation that are very useful in serving as general guides in this matter. These may be summarized as follows:

1) Rests are the most useful and reliable indications. The presence of rests of three B's, for example, always indicates perfect mode. Rests of two B's may indicate imperfect mode, although the mode is probably perfect if the rests are grouped together with a single B note. This manner of determining the mode is applicable to the other degrees as well, of course.

2) In a good many manuscripts the scribes have grouped notes in clusters of two or three or more. Frequently recurring successions of certain note combinations, such as B-SSS-B, or L-B L-B would almost certainly indicate perfect mensuration. Likewise, pairs of notes of the same species would suggest imperfect mensuration. This method of determining meter is useful, but it should be kept in mind that a two-note group can occur in perfect as well as imperfect mensurations through alteration of the second note.

3) The manner in which the dot is used is an aid in determining perfection or imperfection. If a dot appears to be one of addition the meter will be imperfect; if it is a dot of division the meter will be perfect.

4) The presence of red notes, which were used only in perfect mensuration in the French Ars Nova, is a certain indication of the prevailing meter.[3]

[3] For exhaustive details concerning the recognition of mensurations in an Ars Nova composition, see Wolf *GdM*, I, 150; Ludwig, *SIMG*, VI, 607; and Apel, *NPM*, 346.

The "Classical" Notation of Machaut

The compositions of Machaut that have been chosen to illustrate the practices of the French Ars Nova, which are analyzed on the following pages, have been selected for their variety of styles of notation, texture, and mensuration, and are arranged progressively from the simplest to the most complex.

PLATE XLVII. Three monophonic virelais: *Tuit mi penser, Mors sui se ie ne vous voi,* and *Liement me deport,* Guillaume de Machaut (Paris, Bibl. nat. fr. 9221, fol. 161; early fifteenth century?)

This plate and the one following are from the largest and most sumptuously written of five manuscripts in the Bibliothèque Nationale of Paris, each of which contains the complete works of Guillaume de Machaut. The other four (fr. 22545–22546, fr. 1584, fr. 1585, and fr. 1586) are from the fourteenth century, but this one (fr. 9221) may be from the early fifteenth century; it appears to have been copied for Jean, Duc de Berry. The first of the two pages reproduced here contains three monophonic virelais, only the last of which (*Liement me deport*) will be considered in some detail.

In transcribing these pieces it is essential to be aware of the virelai structure and its expression in both the text and music of the manuscript. The pattern is that of a recurrent refrain, between each statement of which is a strophe consisting of three verses. The first two of the verses are set to the same melody, which has first and second endings—sometimes marked as *ouvert* and *clos;* the third verse is sung to the music of the refrain. In *Liement me deport* the pattern is as follows:

1) Refrain: occupies the first line of music, and itself has *clos* and *ouvert* endings, like the strophe that follows;
2) Strophe: the second line of music, with two verses and two endings;
3) Third verse of strophe: sung to the music of the refrain. In this virelai, exceptionally, the scribe has not written out the music for this verse. The text of the verse is set down in the five short lines at the end of the second staff, and is continued at the beginning of the next line

up to the word "Liement," which marks the return of the refrain; 4) Refrain: with the words it had at the beginning.

The repeats—or *ouvert* and *clos* endings—are a feature of a good many of Machaut's secular pieces, and sometimes present problems, as the point where the first ending begins and ends is not often clearly indicated, nor is it always obvious. The *clos* ending sometimes repeats one or more notes of the *ouvert* ending, which is the case at the end of the refrain in *Liement me deport*, where the second verse on leaving "sa" on *g* does not proceed directly to the first note after the long vertical line, but repeats the note *a*, the last note of the first verse. The end of the refrain is given in Fig. 66; the note in brackets is not in the manuscript, but is necessary for its completion.

FIG. 66

The situation at the end of the second line is much simpler, as the vertical line covering the staff clearly marks off the last note of the first ending from the first note of the second ending. A comparison of the notes coming both after and before the line shows an identity of rhythm, and indicates what note should be quitted on the repeat when taking the second ending.

The meter of the piece can be determined without difficulty from the first few notes. The beginning of the piece with its succession of SMSM-rest followed by a group of six M's, points definitely to imperfect time and perfect prolation. The dots used are those of division. Alteration of the second note of a group of two M's occurs fairly often, and the one case of distant imperfection near the end of this Plate has already been mentioned earlier in this chapter. There appears to be an error in the manuscript: the S-rest immediately following the sole ligature in the piece was no doubt intended to be a M-rest; otherwise there would be an uncharacteristic half-bar too many in this section.

The text of the refrain and the first strophe of the virelai follow:

Refrain

Liement me deport par semblant, mais je port
Sans joie et sans deport, une si grief pointure
Dont je sui au droit port de mort, sans nul deport,
Se d'amours ne tel port qu'il me preingne en sa cure.

Strophe

Quar quant de vo figure la doulce pourtraiture
Dedans mon cuer recort,
Espris sui d'une arsure ardant, crueuse et sure,
Plaine de tout descort.

Car desir son effort fait de moy grever fort,
Mais j'ay cuer asses fort contre la blesseure.

Si ne me desconfort, car d'espoir me confort
Qui me donne confort en vostre doucour pure.

Liement, etc. . . .

Tuit mi penser, the virelai at the top of Plate XLVII, is in imperfect time and imperfect prolation, and begins on the second half of the third beat of the measure. In the notation of this piece in the other manuscripts of Machaut's compositions there is a M-rest at the beginning. As with most of the monophonic compositions, the scribe has not attempted to group the notes in a manner that makes clear what the meter is. There is an error in the second staff—the sixteenth note should be a S rather than a M. Unlike *Liement me deport*, the refrain of this virelai is written out, beginning after the line through the staff in the middle of the second line of music, and the two notes following the double bar at the end act as a guide to the beginning of the refrain melody.

The text follows:

Refrain

Tuit mi penser sont sans cesser
En vous amer et honnorer tres doulce creature.

Strophe

Nonques mes yeux saouler
De regarder et remirer vo gente pourtraiture,

Ne pos ne mon cuer oster
D'ades penser a vo vis cler et a vo bonte pure.

Ce fait doubler et embraser
Et aviver par desirer mon amoureuse arduie.

Tuit my, etc.

Mors sui se, the second piece on this page, is actually a two-part virelai; but through an oversight on the part of the scribe only the first seven bars of the tenor are given in the manuscript. The time is imperfect, the prolation perfect, and the dots are those of division. An interesting use of the dot to show imperfection of a B by a M both before and after the B occurs in the second measure. An error has been made in the second line at the second measure after the double bar; the context shows that there is a value of one M too many between the dot that indicates the end of the first measure and the first note of the third measure, which is the note g just before the S-rest. According to the other manuscripts, the first note of the second measure—the M on B-flat—is superfluous and should be disregarded.[4]

The text follows:

Refrain

Mors sui se ie ne vous voi, dame d'onnour
Car l'ardour qui ma doulour
Acroist en moy m'occira
Si com ie croy pour vostre amour.

Strophe

Si ne say que faire doy
Car riens de nulle part n'ay qui ma tristour

Esteigne ne mon annoy
Et bien say qu'onques mais n'oy tel ne greignour.

[4] Transcriptions and texts of both these virelais are in Ludwig, *Machaut, Werke*, I, 84–85.

Car tant seuffre et tant recoy
Plains de paour qu'ades plour
Dont tel m'atour, seul en recoy,
Que je ne mengu ne boy riens par savour.

Mors sui, etc. . . .

PLATE XLVIII. Two rondeaux: *Dame se vous n'avez aperceu*, and
Quant ie ne voy ma dame, Guillaume de Machaut (Paris, Bibl.
nat. fr. 9221, fol. 141; early fifteenth century?)

The first of the two rondeaux on Plate XLVIII is for a solo voice
and two accompanying instruments, the parts for the instruments
being marked "Tenor" and "Contratenor." All three degrees—
mode, time, and prolation—are imperfect in this piece. This is
manifested through the grouping of notes by the scribe, particularly
at the beginning of the cantus, where the seven notes following
the initial L could not be fitted into any other metrical pattern than
imperfect time and prolation. Also, the context of the opening bars
shows that the two B's in ligature of both lower voices equal the
L of the cantus, thus making the imperfect character of the mode
clearly apparent.

The imperfection of the mensurations being established, it follows that the dots are those of addition; the dot near the beginning
produces syncopation for a couple of notes. The dot after the two
B's in ligature near the end of the second staff is an error, and should
be disregarded. On the other hand, a dot is required above the first
of the two notes of the ligature that comes a few notes before this.
In the manuscript it looks as if a dot had been there originally, but
had been erased. The notes of the contratenor begin a short distance
before the word "Contratenor" appears.

In actual performance the rondeau has the following pattern:

1) The whole melody, which consists of two sections, with the refrain
verse:

> Dame, se vous n'avez aperceu
> Que je vous aim de cuer, sanz decevoir,
> Essaies le, si le sares de voir.

2) The first section of the melody, which goes to the long vertical line
near the beginning of the second line, with the following words (the
text is between this and the following rondeau):

Vo grant biaute m'aroit trop deceu,
Et vo doulcour que trop me font douloir.

3) The first section of the melody again, with the first part of the refrain verse.

4) The whole melody with the rest of the text that lies below the music:

Car mon cuer ont si tres fort esmeu
A vous amer que ne puis concevoir
Que jamais bien doie ne joie avoir.

The beginning of the rondeau is transcribed in Fig. 67.

FIG. 67

The second piece on Plate XLVIII is the two-part rondeau *Quant
ie ne voy*, which has a third part, a Contratenor, in the manuscript
of the Paris Bibliothèque Nationale fr. 22.546. Both time and prolation are imperfect, consequently all the dots are those of addition.
The dot immediately after the three-note ligature that appears about
two-thirds through the first line is an error, and should be disregarded.[5]

PLATE XLIX. Ballade: *Dame de qui toute ma ioie vient*, Guillaume
    de Machaut (Paris, Bibl. nat. fr. 1586, fol. 47v; early fifteenth
    century)

The ballade reproduced on Plate XLIX is from the series of seven
songs by Machaut that are part of the poetic cycle, *Remède de
Fortune*, in which each song illustrates one of seven different musical forms. In three of the codices in which the piece is found, in-

[5] *Ibid.*, 69.

cluding that from which the facsimile was made, it is in two voices; but in three other manuscripts it occurs in a four-voiced version, which includes a contratenor and a triplum in addition to the cantus and tenor of the two-voiced version.

The mensurations are imperfect mode, perfect time, and imperfect prolation. The time obviously consists of notes to the value of six M's, as seen in the very clear grouping by the scribe at the beginning and end of the first line. The question is whether the grouping is in two groups of three M's, or three groups of two M's. The latter is seen to be what is intended through the presence of a number of groups made up of three S's, or B + S, or their equivalents, and by the ending of the tenor part from the last B in line six up to the final L: this group is only divisible into measures by three. The imperfect mode is shown by the two L's in the first half of the bottom line; the context reveals that each of these has the value of two B's. Imperfect mode is further confirmed by the two-B rest following the second of the L's.

Three errors occur in the manuscript:

1) the fourth note after the L on the first staff, a M, should have been written as a S; it continues the syncopation begun in the previous S;
2) in the third staff a dot of addition is lacking after the second of the two S's over the word "douce";
3) the B-rest after the three-note ligature in the middle of the bottom line should be disregarded.

The structure of the ballade is a simple *aab* plan; this is indicated in the manuscript by the double line of text under section A of the music. The text underneath the bottom line of music is that of the second and third stanzas; the final line of each stanza is identical. The two A sections have *ouvert* and *clos* endings, but they offer no problems, as they are melodically identical. The first ending is over the words "trop amer ne cherir"; in the second there is a possibility of confusion because of the placing of the word "honourer." The first syllable of this word has been put under the first ending, and the rest of the word has been continued over into the second. In transcribing, the first syllable should be placed with the rest of the word under the first note of the second ending. The vertical lines in the middle and end of the second staff are not rests, but signs that mark the terminations of the first and second endings.

The equivalent signs in the tenor are seen after the first and second single L's in the bottom staff.

The text of the stanza under the music is as follows:

> Dame de qui toute ma ioie vient,
> Je ne vous puis trop amer ne cherir.
> N'asses loer si com il apartient,
> Servir, doubter, honourer, n'obeir
> Car le gracieus espoir, douce dame,
> Qui j'ay de vous veoir,
> Me fait c(ent) foys plus de bien et de ioye
> Qu'en cent mil ans desservir ne porroie.[6]

The beginning of the ballade is given in Fig. 68.

FIG. 68

PLATES L AND LI. *Sanctus, Osanna,* and *Benedictus* from *La messe de Nostre Dame,* Guillaume de Machaut (Paris, Bibl. nat. fr. 22.546, fol. 131v and 132; late fourteenth century)

The section of Machaut's famous Mass reproduced on Plates L and LI is in four voices, the triplum and motetus appearing on

---

[6] Any differences in spelling between the texts of the stanza above (or elsewhere in this chapter) and that of Ludwig's Machaut Edition are explained by the fact that Ludwig used a different manuscript as the basis of his edition.

Plate L, and the tenor and contratenor on the facing plate. The tenor is a cantus firmus, being the Sanctus from Mass XVII, and it follows the chant closely (*LU*, 61).

The mensurations are perfect mode, with imperfect time and imperfect prolation. The latter two meters are indicated by the frequent groups of four M's, by syncopated groups of MSM, and also by the hocketing passages in the triplum of lines three and four. Perfect mode is suggested by the groups of three ascending B's in ligature (triplum, end of second line), by the rest of three B's preceded by a L (motetus, line five, and tenor, line five), and also by the several places where a grouping is made of a B followed by a rest of two B's (as in the triplum, line five).

Unlike the previous examples in this chapter, the *Sanctus* and the motet that follow (Plates LII and LIII) are *isorhythmic* compositions; that is, their rhythmical organization is governed by isorhythm ("equal" or "same" rhythm), the use of a repeated rhythmical pattern which is most often applied to the cantus firmus tenor. The isorhythmic principle is also used—though more freely—in the upper parts. The principle is basically the same, except for the greater length of the isorhythmic pattern, as the repeated patterns (ordines) of the earlier modal rhythm. The recognition of the isorhythmic design of pieces so constructed is essential for transcribing them, and is often helpful in determining doubtful notes in a manuscript.

Isorhythm does not begin in the *Sanctus* until after the twice-repeated word "Sanctus," after which it is confined to the tenor and contratenor. The isorhythmic pattern (the *talea*) begins on the third staff in each of these parts, and is eight bars in length. The pattern followed by each of the two lower voices is seen in its rhythmic outline in Fig. 69a. This pattern occurs ten times throughout the course of the three sections in the facsimile. Alteration occurs frequently, as Fig. 69a shows.[7]

In the upper parts isorhythm is not strictly followed throughout the composition. There is, however, a general pattern of rhythmic activity in which the two upper voices parallel the eight-bar pattern

[7] See Gombosi's article, "Machaut's Messe Notre Dame," *MQ*, 1950, 204, which has elaborate analyses of the isorhythmic sections of the Mass, and also of some of the motets.

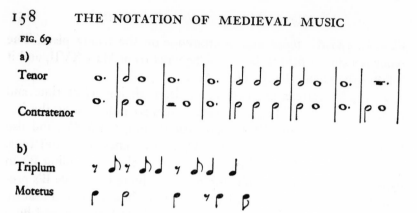

FIG. 69

a)

Tenor

Contratenor

b)

Triplum

Motetus

of the lower voices to a certain extent. That is, if each eight-bar segment is compared to the notes in the upper parts, it will be found
that the fifth and sixth bars of these consist of a hocket-like rhythmic figure, identical in each of these bars, which is the same in each
talea. The rhythm of this figure is given in Fig. 69b. The remarkable
symmetry of the composition is occasionally interrupted by an odd
bar between the statements of the talea.

FIG. 70

San   ctus.

San   ctus.

San   ctus.

San   ctus.

The allocation of the syllables of the text is not entirely clear in
this manuscript. There are many variants in the disposition of the
words in the manuscripts containing the Mass, and the contratenor

has a partial text which may indicate instrumental performance of this part.[8]

The text is as follows:

> Sanctus, Sanctus, Sanctus dominus deus sabaoth. Pleni sunt
> celi et terra gloria tua. Osanna in excelsis. Benedictus
> qui venit in nomine dominum. Osanna in excelsis.

The opening exclamation is transcribed in Fig. 70.

PLATES LII AND LIII. Motet: *Felix virgo–Inviolata genetrix–Ad te suspiramus–Contratenor*, Guillaume de Machaut (Paris, Bibl. nat. fr. 22.546, fol. 124v and 125; late fourteenth century)

This four-voiced motet is one of the most structurally complex of all Machaut's compositions, and has several features of notation that are of extraordinary interest. The piece is laid out quite differently on the page from the Mass: the tenor and contratenor are placed at the end of the second of the two pages on which it is written, and each of their staves runs across the page rather than in parallel columns like the motetus and triplum.

The over-all design of the motet is as follows:

1) A nonisorhythmic introduction, the end of which is marked by a double bar in each of the parts;
2) a section which is isorhythmic in the tenor and contratenor, but not in the upper parts (which continue in the same manner as before), and which consists of a talea, twice repeated, which ends at the following places on folio 125:

> Triplum: line four, the B-rest near middle of line;
> Motetus: line one, first note;
> Tenor: second line, after four-note ligature near beginning of line;
> Contratenor: bottom line, double bar;

3) another isorhythmic section, from the places indicated above to the end, in which the two lower parts repeat the music of the second section in diminution in which the time values are half those of section 1; the upper parts continue in the same manner as before.

A striking feature of the lower voices in the last two sections of the piece is a considerable use of red notes. (These notes appear gray in the facsimile.) As the rubric under the tenor states: *"Nigre*

---

[8] Guillaume de Van shows the variants in the placement of the text of the Sanctus in the various manuscripts in his edition of the Mass, ii and xvi–xx. His transcription of the Sanctus (p. 20–25) is so printed as to make its isorhythmic structure very clear.

sunt pefecte et rubee imperfecte"; that is, "The black [notes] are perfect and the red [notes] imperfect." [9]

The mensurations of the motet are rather involved. In the introduction, or *Introitus,* as it is marked, the upper parts are in perfect prolation and imperfect time. The mode is imperfect, but the upper parts each have one exceptional, simultaneously-sounding note— the dotted L near the beginning of line four of the triplum and the beginning of line three of the motetus (fol. 124v)—which form an odd measure of $\frac{2}{3}$, as may be seen in Fig. 71. The statement that the mode of the upper parts is imperfect seems to be contradicted by the five perfect-L rests at the beginning of the motetus, as rests covering three spaces are invariably an indication of perfect mode; but these rests are incorrect. They should have been written as five imperfect-L rests, and they are so written in two other manuscripts containing this motet.[10]

Since the time is imperfect and the prolation perfect, the upper parts will be transcribed in bars of four quarter notes, and each quarter note will be divisible into three eighth notes.

The lower parts are entirely in L's and B's, except for the last section, and are therefore at the rhythmical level of the maximode. For this reason, and to make the design of the piece clear, the lower parts are written in bars that are three L's in length, against bars of one L in the upper parts. Since the L's of tenor and contratenor are perfect, the perfect L-rests at the beginning of these parts are correct, even though they were incorrect for the upper parts. The place in the *Introitus* where the lower parts enter is given in Fig. 71.

In the section after the introduction, the two lower voices are so written that the tenor is in perfect mensuration (black notes) at the same time that the contratenor is in imperfect (red notes), and vice versa; or, in other terms, while one is in perfect maximode and imperfect mode, the other is in imperfect maximode and perfect

---

[9] According to Machabey there are only three pieces among the manuscripts of Machaut in which red notation is used (*Guillaume de Machault,* I, 90).

[10] Paris, Bibl. Nat. fr. 1584, and a manuscript once in the possession of the de Vogue family of Paris. The latter was the principal source used by Ludwig in preparing his Machaut edition, but it has since disappeared. Ludwig states incorrectly that the tempus of this piece is perfect (*Machaut, Werke,* III, 86), but transcribes it correctly as imperfect.

FIG. 71

que gau- di-um   mun -   do   tri -

ex - pers   pa -   ris,   ce -   le -

sti   or -   tu

stis   au -

mode. Each voice part makes one hemiolic shift of rhythm in each
talea, and the combined effect of tenor and contratenor is that of a
continual large-scale three-against-two movement. The rhythmical
design of the first talea is presented in Fig. 72. The lower parts
continue in perfections of three L's per bar, each bar equalling

three four-beat measures of the upper parts, as in the introduction.
The upper parts continue to be in imperfect mode and time, with
perfect prolation.

FIG. 72

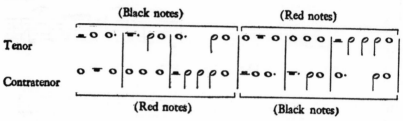

In the second section after the introduction, where the two lower
parts are in diminution, there is no longer any maximode, and the
alternation is between perfect mode with imperfect time and imperfect mode and perfect time. Each bar of the lower parts is equal
to a bar-and-a-half of the upper parts, which continue as before.
Fig. 73 shows the beginning of this section.

FIG. 73

The longa plicata in the motetus in the bottom line of the first
page should be a B, according to the context. The plica had become
quite rare by this time, and it has been suggested that it might very

well be rendered as a grace note just before the note that follows it.

The texts of the upper parts are as follows:

Triplum

Felix virgo, mater Christi,
Que gaudium mundo tristi
Ortu tui contulisti,
          Dulcissima;
Sic hereses peremisti,
Dum angelo credidisti
Filiumque genuisti,
          Castissima.
Roga natum, piissima,
Ut pellat mala plurima
Tormentaque gravissima,
          Que patimur;
Nam a gente ditissima,
Lux lucis splendidissima,
De sublimi ad infima
          Deducimur;
Cunctis bonis exuimur,
Ab impiis persequimur,
Per quos virgo subicimur
          Servitutis,
Nam sicut ceci gradimur
Nec directorem sequimur,
Sed a viis retrahimur
          Nobis tutis.
Gracie fons et virtutis,
Sola nostre spes salutis,
Miserere destitutis
          Auxilio,
Ut a culpis absolutis
Et ad rectum iter ductis
Inimicisque destructis
          Pax sit nobis cum gaudio.

Motetus

Inviolata genitrix
Superbie grata victris
          Expers paris,
Celestis aule janitrix,

Miserorum exauditrix,
Stella maris,
Que ut mater consolaris
Et pro lapsis deprecaris
Humiliter,
Gracie fons singularis,
Que angelis dominaris.
Celeriter
Para nobis tutum iter
Juvaque nos viriliter;
Nam perimus,
Invadimur hostiliter,
Sed tuimur debiliter
Necque scimus,
Quo tendere nos possimus
Nec per quem salvi erimus
Nisi per te.
Eya! Ergo poscimus,
Ut sub alis tuis simus
Et versus nos te converte.

Tenor

Ad te suspiramus, gementes et flentes
(a phrase from the anthem to
the B.V.M., *Salve regina, LU,* 279)

The Transcription of the Facsimiles

The notation described in this chapter will have been seen to be essentially an extension of Franconian notation, on which that of the French Ars Nova is solidly based. The innovations of the Ars Nova, apart from the shift of values representing the beat, consist primarily of the complete acceptance and incorporation of duple meter into the rhythmical system; the larger variety of note values; the use of variable meters at the different degrees from maximode to prolation; the dot of addition; and hemiolic rhythm, all of which are illustrated in the facsimiles discussed in this chapter.

Because of the greater variety and systematization of the Ars Nova notation, and also possibly because of Italian influence, it might be assumed that the French rhythm applied by performers to pieces in imperfect time, which was described in the last chapter in connection with the Fauvel motets, did not continue into the period of the Ars Nova. However, it should be recalled that as late as the eighteenth century, passages written out as successive eighth notes were said by Couperin to be performed as alternate dotted eighths and sixteenths (*L'art de toucher le clavecin*, 1716); and it would be interesting to speculate whether this represents the persistence of a long tradition. For the purposes of the study of notation, it certainly seems best to transcribe those Machaut examples that are in imperfect time with a literal translation of their note values.

7

ITALIAN ARS NOVA
NOTATION

▀▀▀▄▄▄

I N THE fourteenth century Italy emerged as a serious musical
rival of France, whose domination in theory and practice had
hitherto been unquestioned. Italian composers of the Trecento
adapted the new rhythmical techniques of late thirteenth and
early fourteenth century French art, and evolved for their own
purposes and tastes a form of notation that differed considerably
in some ways from French notation. Italian notation, whose origins
are not very well documented, remained in actual usage for about
a century. It was first expounded by Marchetto of Padua in 1318,
and its final statement appeared in a treatise by Prosdocimus de
Beldemandis in 1412.[1] The notation had certain inherent limitations
which caused the notation to become obsolescent by 1412, a circumstance deplored by Prosdocimus. In certain manuscripts, elements
of both Italian and French notation were combined, probably as a
result of the mingling of Italian and French composers at the Papal
court when it was at Avignon (the "Babylonian captivity," 1309–
1377). In some works by composers of both nationalities which
were written in the latter part of the fourteenth century, every possibility of rhythmical division and combination was explored, re-

---

[1] The essential passages by Marchetto that describe Italian notation are in *SR*,
160*ff*, in which the text used is from the *Pomerium* (*CS*, III, 170–78), and the
musical examples are from the *Brevis compilatio* (*CS*, III, 5–8). The treatise of
Prosdocimus is available in C. Sartori's *La notazione italiana del Trecento*.

sulting in intricacies of rhythm and of notation that have not since been surpassed.[2]

The System of Divisiones

Italian notation is based on a system of *divisiones* that represent meters of various kinds; this system is a continuation and further development of the system of S-groups set off by dots which was introduced by Petrus de Cruce, and which was abandoned as a regular feature of French notation. The fundamental unit on which the Italian system rests is the B, which was considered to be unchangeable in time value; the B acts as a measure, since any group of notes of smaller value is set off by dots into a cluster whose total value is that of a B. The dot thus functions as a barline, and within any given "bar" of each of the different divisions a great variety of rhythmical organization was possible.

Each B is subject to division and subdivision by two or by three, and by compounds of two and three; these divisions are equivalent to the meters of French notation. The system of divisions, with their Italian names, and their metrical equivalents in modern notation are given in Fig. 74.

The name of each division indicates the maximum number of minimal units contained in it; these names are indicated in compositions in which changes of meter occur by the initial letter of the name of the division. *Senaria imperfecta* and *senaria perfecta* are exceptions to this, however; they are marked *i* and *p*, respectively. Examples of the use of these letters are to be seen on Plates LVIII and LIX. Sometimes the meter is shown by the use of dots and circles, as in Plates LVI and LVII. When one division prevails throughout a piece, as in Plate LIV, no meter is indicated; the division usually becomes obvious after a brief examination, being identified by the number of notes in any measure in which all the notes are M's, as in Fig. 74.[3]

[2] In this chapter, only the more representative manuscripts of Italian notation (and of mixed Italian and French notation) are taken up, since the elaborately rhythmical examples are relatively few and occur during only a brief period. They form a special study beyond the scope of a general survey such as this, and have been treated in detail in the admirable work of Willi Apel, *French Secular Music of the late 14th Century*.

[3] In Marchetto's own illustrations these groups are all represented by S's, as

FIG. 74

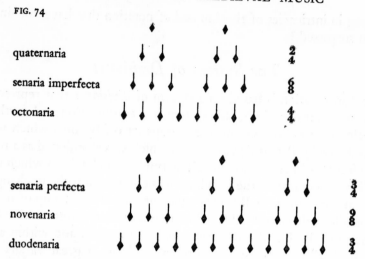

Most of the time a measure will have fewer than the maximum number of such notes in the division, and it is here that certain singular traits of Italian notation are manifested. The manner in which the notes of such measures are rhythmically organized hinges upon the concepts of *via naturae* and *via artis*, which have already been discussed in Chapter 5 in connection with the motets of the *Roman de Fauvel*. In Italian notation *via naturae* refers to the way of interpreting a group of S's set off by dots, which are fewer in number than all the minimal units in the measure, and in which the values are distributed in such a way that the longest value comes at the end. Thus, in a measure of quaternaria, such a group of three S's would be interpreted as two eighth notes followed by a quarter note.

The distribution of values in groups of less than the full number of M's in the division, *via naturae*, in the divisions of senaria imperfecta, senaria perfecta, and octonaria is seen in Fig. 75. These are after Marchetto, who does not explain the rhythm of four S's in senaria imperfecta; the interpretation of this group is recon-

---

in the Petronian S-groups; but in the actual sources the full measures of minimal units are given as shown in Fig. 74. The division of duodenaria, like senaria, may be either perfect or imperfect, depending upon the arrangement of notes within the measure. It is usually perfect, in which case it is transcribed as $\frac{3}{4}$ meter; if imperfect, the meter sign will be $\frac{12}{8}$.

structed on the assumption that the principle of having the long
values come at the end is applied to each of the two halves of the
measure. (See Wolf, *GdM*, I, 30.) Marchetto does not give similar
tables for novenaria and duodenaria, probably because measures in

FIG. 75

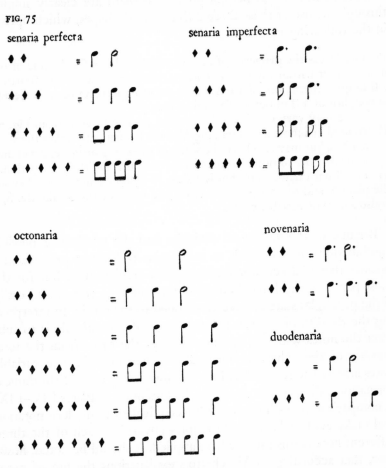

these divisions never occur without one or more tailed notes, that
is, they always appear *via artis*. He does give the formula for groups
of two and three S's for these divisions, however, which are shown
in Fig. 75.

When rhythms different from those of Fig. 75 are desired in any
given division, *via artis* (the "artificial" way) is used to produce

them through various combinations within a measure of the S with the M, or with a form consisting of the S with a descending tail (called by contemporary theorists the "semibrevis major"), or with both. The number of combinations possible through this means is enormous, but the principles governing them are clearly implied through the use of these three different note-shapes, which operate in the following manner:

1) The M has the property of always representing a fixed value of one minimal unit within any given division; that is, it is always one-fourth of a B in quaternaria, one-sixth of a B in senaria (perfecta or imperfecta), one-eighth of a B in octonaria, and so on.

2) The S may vary considerably in value, as may be seen from Fig. 75. When used in a measure containing M's, the S frequently takes the value of two M's, but may also have the value of three M's or more, depending upon the number of notes making up the measure and their formation.

3) The S with descending tail is a sign of further lengthening beyond the plain S, and often represents twice the value of the S; like the S, it is also a note of variable value.

Because of the variety of divisions and the number of possible combinations, it is difficult to summarize the Italian practice in a manner that will account for any given combination; but for the most part, the rhythmical configurations may be recognized easily if the principles stated above are applied to the music. In interpreting the rhythm of a given measure, a good general rule is to subtract the notes with fixed values—that is, the M's—from the total number of the values in the measure; then organize the variable notes among the remainder. Fig. 76 shows some typical rhythmical formations, all of which appear in the facsimiles of Plates LIV–LIX. A comparison of each group with its equivalent in modern notation will make evident how the principles governing each of the three different note forms involved are applied. It should be noted, however, that according to Marchetto's explanations the use of notes other than S's is unnecessary in some cases; the rhythm called for would have come about just the same *via naturae*. These cases probably represent a precaution taken by the scribe to make doubly sure that the correct interpretation will be made.

While the S, M, and S major form the basis of the Italian system, other note forms are also used for further rhythmical modifications.

FIG. 76

senaria imperfecta

senaria perfecta

octonaria

novenaria

The most frequently occurring of these is the M with a flag attached to the right of its stem. Two of these *semiminims* are the equal of one M. (See examples on Plate LVI.) These notes are also used in another kind of rhythmical embellishment in which they occur in groups of threes with their stems turned in the other direction, as illustrated in Fig. 77a. In this case the resulting triplets are the equal in value of two M's, so that the effect is that of coloration applied to duple meter. The direction in which the stems are turned is not always consistent; sometimes triplet flags go to the right, as in the facsimile of Plate LX, but the number of notes used makes clear which rhythm is intended.

Another note form that occurs in some of the Italian manuscripts is the white (that is, outlined) M, which produces the same effect as the triplet M's just mentioned. Instances of these occur in Plates LVI–LVII and LIX. These notes are used in the same manner as the red notes in the Machaut motet (Plate LVII); in fact, they are actually substitutes for red notes, and the use of these notes is also referred to as "coloration." In Italian notation, coloration reduces the value of the notes so treated, so that three white M's are the equal of two black M's. This principle is extended to make four white M's equal to three black ones, as seen in Fig. 77b.

In addition to the note forms that have already been described, Italian notation introduced a great many other special forms, most of which appear to have originated as a result of the restless search for rhythmical novelty that characterized some of the music of the late fourteenth century. These are forms that are never encountered

FIG. 77

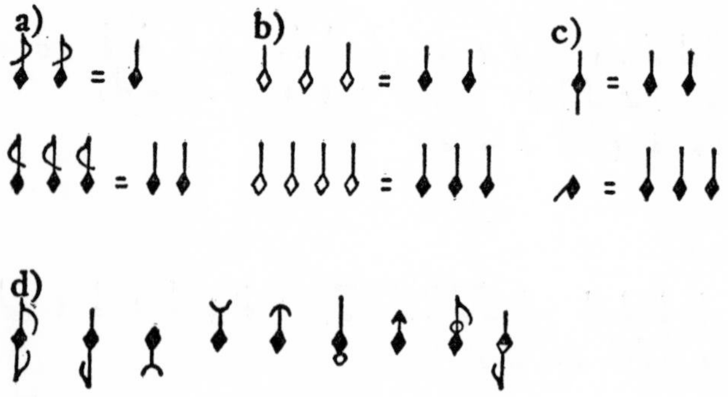

in French notation, and they disappeared with the return to a simpler style in the early fifteenth century. Only one of these is seen in the facsimiles of Italian notation: the S with both ascending and descending tails attached to the same note—called by some contemporary theorists the *dragma*—which had a fixed value of two M's, and which was usually employed to introduce brief hemiola into the division of senaria imperfecta. An example of the dragma is seen in the facsimile of Plate LVIII, in the middle of the second line. (See also Fig. 77c.)

The note under the dragma in Fig. 77c is an occasionally-used form which, as it happens, does not appear in any of the facsimiles of Italian notation. Like the dragma, it had a fixed value, in this case of three M's. Other notes which also do not appear in any of the facsimiles are shown in Fig. 77d to indicate the inventiveness of Italian composers in what Willi Apel has called the "mannered period" of the late fourteenth century. These do not exhaust the list, as various combinations of red, black, and white were used in a single note in the effort to capture every possible nuance of rhythmic variety.[4]

In certain pieces of the Italian manuscripts of the fourteenth century, the consistent and exclusive use of the dot of division to mark off measures of B-value is abandoned, and only the dot of addition is employed. This style of writing, which combines both Italian and French usages, is called *mixed notation*, and is represented in the facsimiles of Plates LVI–LVII and LVIII–LIX. In mixed notation, a special use of the dot was to set off a single note. The note was written with a dot both before and after it, and thus enclosed was often a syncopation. This usage recalls the French *punctum demonstrationis*. At other times, dots placed both before and after a single note function to prohibit alteration. Thus used, the pair of dots are essentially two dots of division applied to a value smaller than the B. An example of this use of the dot occurs in Plate LVIII in the middle of the second line, shortly after the dragma.

The rests used by the Italians were the same as those of French notation. It will be seen from the facsimiles that Italian scribes favored the use of a six-lined staff.

Secular and Sacred Trecento Writing

The facsimiles illustrating Italian notation are from two of the most important manuscript sources of the Trecento repertory. One of these—Paris, Bibl. nat. ital. 568—is thought to be the oldest of the manuscripts containing Italian music of the Ars Nova, and the one from which some of the other manuscripts were copied, notably the Codex Squarcialupi, named after its owner, a Florentine organist, Antonio Squarcialupi, 1417–80. The other—Paris, Bibl. nat. n. a. fr. 6771—is known as the Reina Codex, also after the name of a former owner, and is the only manuscript represented in this book which is written on paper rather than parchment. The Codex Squarcialupi contains only Italian compositions, and was probably

[4] For further examples of these special notes see Apel, *French Secular Music of the Late 14th Century*, 8, and NPM, 405; also Wolf, GdM, I, 302.

written in the late fourteenth century; the Reina Codex has works by both Italian and French composers, and was copied in the fifteenth century.[5]

PLATE LIV. Ballata: *Io son un pellegrino*, Giovanni da Firenze (Paris, Bibl. nat. ital. 568, fol. 42v; fourteenth century)

This two-voiced *ballata*, the famous Pilgrim Song of Giovanni da Firenze, is a clear and simple example of Italian notation. Several note groups show a full complement of M's, revealing that the division is octonaria. The rhythms of the various measures are readily determined. For example, the first measure of the upper voice has a total of three S's, the two M's standing for a single S-value; the S normally has the value of two M's in octonaria, but when only three are present, as in this case, the last is lengthened *via naturae*. The same process is applied to the next-to-last measure of the lower voice.

Fig. 78 shows the opening melisma of the ballata.[6]

FIG. 78

[5] For description and contents of these manuscripts see J. Wolf, *GdM*, I, 250 and 260; also L. Ellinwood, *Francesco Landini*, xvii.
[6] A different rhythm is given the opening bar in the transcription of *Io son* in *HAM*, I, No. 51, but it is one for which there seems to be no justification in the manuscript. The same transcription also omits the final eighth note of measure six.

In the performance of the ballata (a form derived from the French virelai), the voices first sing straight through both the *prima* and the *secunda pars*. The music of the second part is then repeated to the second strophe, which is written in at the end of the fourth staff. (The first line of this second strophe is just above the top line of the staff, and should not be confused with the line of text just above it, which is part of the first strophe.) The first part is then repeated to the text of the third strophe, and then again to the refrain text. The complete text follows:

Refrain

Io son un pellegrino che vo cercando limosina
Per dio merce chiamando.

Strophes

E vo cantando colla voce bella,
Con dolce aspetto e colla treccia bionda.

Non ho se no'l bordon e la scarsella,
E chiamo, chiamo e nonne chi mi risponda.

E quando credo andare alla seconda
Vento contrario mi vien tempestando.

PLATE LV. Ballata: *Per un verde boschetto*, Bartolinus de Padua (Paris, Bibl. nat. n. a. fr. 6771, fol. 23v; early fifteenth century)

The three-voiced ballata of Plate LV illustrates an inherent ambiguity of Italian notation, especially in senaria imperfecta, that has caused some scholars to treat this division differently from the manner described previously in this chapter.

The meter itself is relatively easy to determine; the frequent occurrence of groups such as SMSM and SS, as well as certain other combinations, clearly indicates a meter of $\frac{6}{8}$ rather than $\frac{3}{4}$. In certain other groups, however, such as four S's, or a combination of two S's and one S major, Besseler (in *Die Musik des Mittelalters und der Renaissance*, 161) has disregarded the principle of *via naturae*, and when the notes give the appearance of being in imperfect groups he transcribes them literally as such. The result is that the underlying meter changes from senaria imperfecta to quaternaria every time that four S's or less occur in a B-value.

The manner in which Marchetto illustrates groups in senaria imperfecta which include the S major appears among the instances of this division in Fig. 76. These groups are based essentially on the

FIG. 79A

Per,

per   un

ver-de bo - schet   to   Se -

FIG. 79B

Per,

per   un   ver-de bo - schet -   to   Se-

principle of having the long values come at the end of each of the halves that make up a measure of this division—that is, on alteration. Transcribing the piece in this way means that a single meter is preserved throughout, rather than two meters being continually and irregularly alternated as in Besseler's rendition.

Fig. 79 shows the beginning of the ballata (triplum only, which starts at the third line from the bottom) in two versions, the first after Marchetto, and the second after Besseler. A comparison shows the preferability of the first version from a musical as well as a historical viewpoint.

The text written under the music, and the added verse at the end follow:

Refrain

Per un verde boschetto seguito l'orma d'un gentil braccheto.

Strophes

Cum voce quasi humana seguito me latrando par ch' dicha,
Ond'io ai mente sana de sequitarlo non prisi fatiga,
Sperando che l'aplicha mi soglio di quel nodo cosi stretto.

PLATES LVI AND LVII. Section of a Mass: *Et in spiritum sanctum*, Frate Bartholino (Paris, Bibl. nat. ital. 568, fol. 135v and 136; fourteenth century)

The facsimile on these plates is of one of the few sacred pieces by Italian composers of the fourteenth century. Outstanding features of its notation are the several meter signs, the use of white notation, the abandonment of the dot of division, and the free use of the French dot of addition. In these respects it differs distinctly from the two previous examples. This kind of notation, which combines French with Italian elements, has already been referred to in the introductory part of this chapter as mixed notation. The necessity for the dot is obviated by the use of meter signs, and also by the careful and appropriate grouping of notes by the scribe.

The meter signs are those indicating perfection and imperfection by the whole and the broken circle for the subdivision of the B, and by two or three dots within the circle for the subdivision of the S. There are four signs of this kind in the piece, indicating an alternation of octonaria and novenaria. Two further metric changes are brought about by the use of white notes. In the first of these, on line four of Plate LVI, a change is made from novenaria to duodenaria; the white M's become sixteenth notes, as they represent coloration applied to a perfect meter (see Fig. 77b). In the other, on the next-to-last line from the bottom of Plate LVI, the division is changed by the use of white notes from quaternaria to senaria

imperfecta. An additional indication of meter—a small broken circle—has been placed at the beginning of the first of these white-
note sections as if to insure its interpretation in imperfect meter.

An interesting detail of the composition is the use of alteration
in the two M's of the lower voice above the two syllables "-mis-si-"
of "remissionem" in the fifth staff. In the upper part these same two
syllables are set with a M and a S. A similar instance of alteration,
but in both parts, occurs later on over the syllables "et ex-"
(specto).

The transcription of this piece is fairly simple; no special musical
illustrations are needed once the changes of meter indicated by the
meter signs and the white notes are recognized. In the final "Amen"
section, the bottom line of the left page continues on to the bottom
line of the facing page. The scribe has added horizontal pointers on
both music and text at the end of the page to direct the eye toward
the proper place on the opposite page.

The text, which is given below, is the latter part of the Credo of
the Mass, from "Et in spiritum sanctum" to the end; the setting
is remarkable for its rhythmical clarity and articulation.

Et in spiritum sanctum dominum, et vivificantem, qui ex patre filioque
procedit. Qui cum patre et filio simul adoratur et conglorificatur: qui
locutus est par prophetas. Et unam sanctam catholicam et apostolicam
ecclesiam. Confiteor unum baptisma in remissionem peccatorum. Et
exspecto resurrectionem mortuorum. Et vitam venturi saeculi. Amen.

PLATE LVIII AND LIX. Madrigal: *Sotto verdi fraschetti*, Ser Gher-
    ardello; Instrumental chanson: *S'amours me het*, Anon. (Paris,
    Bibl. nat. ital. 568, fol. 26v and 27; fourteenth century)

The two-voiced madrigal, *Sotto verdi fraschetti*, which also occurs in two other important manuscripts containing Italian Ars
Nova music—the Squarcialupi and Panciatichi Codices—like *Et in
spiritum sanctum* also has meter signs; but in this case they are represented in the more usual manner of lower case initials. Only two
such letters are used in this example—*i*, for senaria imperfecta, and
p, for senaria perfecta—and these alternate several times in the
course of the first part of the piece. The opening section, as is
usually the case, has no meter indication, but is obviously in octonaria; it is in the nature of an introductory melisma on the first syl-

lable of the first word of the text. The meters in the rest of the *prima pars* of the composition consist of a series of hemiolic fluctuations between the two divisions of *i* and *p*.

An interesting bar occurs in the middle of line two on folio 26v, just after the beginning of the *i* section, which begins with a dragma and ends with a note enclosed by two dots. The purpose of the dragma is to effect a hemiolic change of rhythm in this single measure only, which reads as in Fig. 80. The notes of the original are shown above the measure cited; at this same place a white S is used instead of a dragma in the Codex Squarcialupi.

FIG 80

The function of the pair of dots in Italian notation has already been described; the obvious reason for its use here is to warn against a possible alteration of the note enclosed. Alteration occurs in the measures preceding and following this measure.

A rhythmic change of the opposite kind is brought about in the next staff, where the ligature that occurs just before the first of the two L's has two dots above it, one for each note of the ligature. These are dots of addition, which change the prevailing $\frac{3}{4}$ meter to $\frac{6}{8}$. A similar rhythmic change is produced in this manner in the middle of staff five of folio 27.

The meter of the second part of the piece—the *ritornello*—beginning after the double bar through the staff in the fifth line, is not indicated; however, the context shows it to be a continuation of the senaria perfecta of the last section of the previous part. Alteration occurs a few times in the lower voice, including one passage with a scribal error—the beginning of the second ternaria after the double bar in the fourth line, where the tail should ascend rather than descend. A passage in hocket occurs shortly before the last phrase of the piece.

A few notes and ligatures have become somewhat dimmed in this manuscript, especially a B in line four of folio 26v (the eleventh note in the line), and another B in the middle of line five of folio 27, directly after the two dotted S's.

The stanzas of the *prima* and *secunda pars* are:

> Sotto verdi fraschetti molti augelly
> Tra valli chiusi con dolci versetty
> Ove que che bramata vie mi die dilecty.

The second stanza, sung to the *prima pars*, reads: [7]

> Sanza nessun pensier mandava spasso
> Subito amore si m'aperse l'arco
> Tiromi asse si che subito inbarco.

The last three staves of folio 27 contain both voice parts of another two-voiced piece, probably intended for instrumental performance, as no text is supplied beyond the French incipit, "S'amours me het." This little composition presents a very interesting combination of features of both French and Italian notation. It is essentially French, as it makes free use of perfection, imperfection, and alteration, even of imperfection *ad partem remotam* (upper part, second measure).

The meter is senaria imperfecta. The dot is employed exclusively as a dot of division, but in the French manner, as it always occurs in the middle of a measure, obviously to prevent a suggestion of hemiolic change. The use of first and second endings for the *secunda pars* is much more frequently seen in French than in Italian manuscripts, but the Italian word *"chiuso"* is used here to signal the existence of two endings. The note shapes include the specifically Italian form of the Sm, and the Italian six-lined staff is used. White notes produce fleeting hemiola.

This piece is seen to be a French virelai—corresponding to the Italian ballata—since the *clos* (*chiuso*) ending, indicating first and second endings, comes at the end of the second section of the piece. At this point the two voice parts do not leave off at the same point in proceeding to the final cadence; the upper must continue for one S longer than the lower to come out right. As with the Machaut

[7] In many Italian Ars Nova manuscripts, pieces in the form of the madrigal (which corresponds to the French ballade) have the verse of the second stanza before the beginning of the ritornello rather than at the end, as in the case of the ballata. In this instance the madrigal form is clearly indicated, as the added text at the bottom corresponds closely in poetic structure to the stanza under the music of the *prima pars*, and there is no text for further stanzas of the ritornello. It is likely that the curious sign immediately after the word "dilecty" is an indication to repeat the *prima pars* to the text below.

virelai *Liement*, it will be necessary in transcribing this piece to repeat certain notes in the second ending which occur in the first; this is illustrated in Fig. 81.

FIG. 81

PLATE LX. Keyboard arrangement (anon.): *Questa fanciulla*, Francesco Landini (Paris, Bibl. nat. n. a. fr. 6771, fol. 85; fifteenth century)

The final example of Italian notation in this chapter is an arrangement for keyboard of a ballata by Landini, from the Reina manuscript. It is a very early example of keyboard coloration, in which the anonymous arranger has altered the rhythm of the original by changing the division from senaria imperfecta to quaternaria, and by omitting the lower voice part, so that the middle part of the original becomes the "tenor" of the arrangement. The cantus of the vocal model is rather elaborately colored. (The vocal original is given in its entirety in Reese, *MMA*, 368.)[8] Unlike the vocal music of its period, this keyboard arrangement is written in score, and uses barlines instead of dots of division. The notation of the piece is clear and simple, and requires no special discussion for its transcription.

The Transcription of the Facsimiles

Italian notation was a side-current in the mainstream of the evolution of notation, branching off from Franconian notation in the direction indicated by the Petronian style of the *Fauvel* motets. It was a significant notation in its reflection of national rhythmical

[8] The original is also in Ellinwood, *Francesco Landini*, No. 147. J. Wolf, in *HdN*, II, 253, has the arrangement in part in a transliteration of old notation, and a transcription of the beginning.

feeling; in general it was simpler and more straightforward than French notation, and lacked the subtlety of syncopation at various rhythmical levels which was an important element in contemporary French style. Pure Italian notation, such as appears on Plates LIV and LV, gave way to the mixed type represented in the subsequent facsimiles, a process that was inevitable, as the French dot of addition was a device too useful to be disregarded. Once the dot of addition was accepted, however, the dot of division had to be abandoned; and with this most characteristic feature gone, Italian notation as a distinct style soon disappeared.

The principles of transcription described in this chapter are based largely on Marchetto; but it should be added that his interpretation of the S-groups *via naturae* in the divisions based on a ternary grouping of M-values was not shared by all the theorists of his period. Reference is made by Anon. III and IV to a rhythm in which the long values come at the beginning rather than at the end of such groups (♩♪♩♪.♩♪♩♪♩♪); Theodore de Campo, writing in the middle of the fourteenth century, says that the singer was free to use either of the following rhythms for a passage of five S's: ♩♪♩♪♩., or ♪♩♪♩♩. (CS, III, 185). However, in view of Marchetto's prestige—"the principal spokesman for the musicians of the Italian Trecento" (SR, 160)—it is advised that his manner of treating these note groups be followed in transcribing the facsimiles in this chapter.

8

SPECIAL NOTATIONS
OF THE LATE MEDIEVAL
PERIOD

T HE FINAL chapter of this volume is devoted to a consideration of two compositions, each of which represents a
special kind of notation that was well in advance of its
time, and that appears in only a few compositions of the
late Middle Ages. They are the earliest known examples of organ
tablature and of freely-used proportional signs, two processes of
notation that came to be widely used at a later period. The first of
these—the tablature piece—is from the early fourteenth century;
the second—the proportional example—is from the late fourteenth
or early fifteenth century, and displays a rather exceptional aspect
of the rhythmical experimentation that was being made at the end
of the medieval period. Each of the two compositions serves ex-
cellently as an introduction to the study of the special form of notation that it represents, apart from its intrinsic musical interest.

Keyboard Notation

PLATE LXI. Keyboard dance: *Estampie,* Anon. (London, Br. Mus.
Arund. 28.550, fol. 43; early fourteenth century)

The facsimile containing this example is one of four pages containing instrumental music in the socalled Robertsbridge Codex.[1]

[1] The last of the three estampies in this manuscript is reproduced in *NPM,* 38;
some of it is transcribed on p. 40, and also in the same author's *Masters of the Key-*

It is in a system of notation that later came to be called *German organ tablature*, as nearly all the German organ music of the fifteenth and sixteenth centuries is written in this manner. *Tablature* is the name given to a notation in which tones are indicated by letters or figures, or by a combination of one of these means with the symbols of mensural notation, as is the case of the organ tablature on Plate LXI. The music of this composition is written on a single staff and is in two voices, the upper of which has the same characters as Italian notation—that is, groups of B-value made up of M's, S's, and S majors, set off by dots of division; while the lower voice is written in letters denoting pitches but without time indications.[2] Occasionally a third part is added for a measure or so, usually for the purpose of cadential emphasis. Strangely enough, there is no extant manuscript in this kind of notation between the Robertsbridge Codex and the earliest German organ pieces in tablature (Ludolf Wilkin's *Tablature Book*, 1432), a period that probably exceeds a century. The facsimile page of Plate LXI contains in its first few staves the latter part of another dance, which ends at the double bar near the beginning of the third staff. The estampie to which the following discussion is devoted begins immediately after this double bar and fills the rest of the page; it is comprised of four puncta.

The upper part, which is in senaria perfecta, is fairly simple to transcribe, but it has two unusual symbols that appear to be unique to this manuscript. One is the white outlined B, which occurs at least once in every line, and which is always preceded by a black B of the same pitch. This white note has been thought by Apel and Hughes to be simply a prolongation of the previous black one; but Handschin considered it as a repetition of the previous note with

board, 22, although in different note values. A transcription of Plate LXI is in *EEH*, II, 90 (by Dom Hughes); and in "Über Estampies und Sequenz," *ZfM*, 1921, 14 (by J. Handschin). The Hughes transcription contains a number of errors; the Handschin transcription is in note values of half the length of those in Fig. 83. One of the motet arrangements in the manuscript, *Tribum quem-Merito haec-Quoniam secta*, is printed together with its vocal model in J. Wolf, *GdM*, III, 191.

[2] Apel, *Masters of the Keyboard*, 20, suggests that this manuscript is of Italian rather than English provenance because of the style of the notation of the upper part. This is possible, but does not account for the un-Italian usage of the letter notation in the lower part, and the presence of the English word *return*, written out in full at the bottom of the page.

an ornament added, probably a mordent. The other sign, which is employed somewhat less frequently, is a white circle above a note, which in every case is a B; an example is seen in the middle of line five. This may be another ornamental sign, possibly an inverted mordent.

The letter notation of the lower part lacks any signs of duration. The time value of each letter is judged by its relation to the upper part; each successive letter is usually placed carefully beneath the note of the upper part with which it is to be played. The letter *s* (for *sine*) stands for a rest; examples of this occur at the beginning of the first punctum. The letter *s* is very similar in shape to *d* in this manuscript, but a difference lies in the manner in which the curved stroke at the top is drawn; in the *d* it is brought further down on the right, touching the lower part of the letter. The sharp sign—one of which may be seen near the beginning of the first punctum—represents the note B-natural. Although there is no indication of the octave position of the letters, this is easily understood, for the lower part consists very largely of notes which double the first note of each bar in the upper part at the distance of an octave.[3]

The general arrangement on the page of the four puncta that make up this estampie involves several repeats that are indicated on the manuscript, but the meaning of these repeats is not immediately apparent. The beginning of each punctum, except the first, is marked by the expressions *Secundus punctus*, *Tertius p.*, and *Quartus p.*, written just below the staff to which they apply. The last three puncta do not have their music written out in full, however, and must be completed by a return to the first punctum at the point marked *ret* (for "return") toward the end of the third staff of the page. The music of the first punctum from this point to the end of the punctum thus serves as a refrain that is taken up by each of the subsequent puncta, and this is indicated by the word *ret* that also occurs at the end of each punctum. The notes at the end of the last three puncta are the same as those at the point of return in the first punctum; but it is almost certain that these are not intended

[3] Handschin considered that the estampies of this manuscript were originally simple monophonic dances of the type seen in Plate XLII, which were later embellished both harmonically and melodically ("vertikal und horizontal ausgeschmückt") as they appear here (Z*f*M, XII, 9).

to be played but are to guide the eye in taking up the refrain. Punctum I has *ouvert* and *clos* endings, and these are to be observed upon each return to the refrain. The piece thus represents a kind of extended rondeau form. The manner of performance described above is shown in outline in Fig. 82. (Compare the dances of Plate XLII.)

FIG. 82

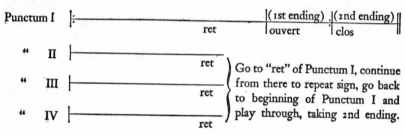

Fig. 83 shows the beginning of the first punctum.

FIG. 83

Proportional Notation

PLATE LXII. Circle canon: *Tout par compas suys composee*, Baude Cordier (Chantilly, Musée Condée 1047, fol. 12; early fifteenth century)

The circle canon of Baude Cordier, on Plate LXII, is more than a notational curiosity, although it is certainly that; in it the composer demonstrates a remarkable command of the use of the proportions in notation—that is, the diminution and augmentation of the normal note values in some sections of a composition. The piece is a sort of whimsical reversal of the trend toward rhythmical complexity which is to be seen in certain late fourteenth-century compositions: it is essentially simple in musical style, but is deliberately written in a highly complicated manner. It is one of two pieces by Cordier, notated in a spirit of fantasy, which are inserted at the beginning of the Chantilly Codex, a manuscript containing other works by this composer which are conventionally notated.[4]

This circle canon has something of the character of a puzzle canon, for the fact that it is a canon at all is conveyed indirectly through the "canon" (in the original sense of *direction* or *rule*) written between the two circular staves: *"Tout par compas suy composee en ceste rode proprement pour moy chanter plus seurement."* ("I am properly written with a compass in this round so that one may sing me more accurately.") The word *rode* (probably derived from *rota*) gives a clue to the canon form, as does the word *chacer* of the verse in the upper left corner. The symbolism of the circle emphasizes the fact that the piece is written as a perpetual canon. The texture of the piece is similar to that of the Italian *caccia*, with two upper voices in strict canon, and a supporting but independent instrumental tenor part.

The device of proportions—that is, the use of signs which bring

---

[4] The other is the "Musical Heart," a love song symbolically notated on staves arranged in the shape of a heart, which is reproduced in facsimile in Apel, *NPM*, 427, and is transcribed in *HAM*, No. 48. The "Heart" also makes use of proportions, but is not in the form of a canon. Handschin believed the Circle Canon to have been composed about the end of the fourteenth century (*MD*, 1949, 84), but Besseler places it in the second decade of the fifteenth century (*Musik in Geschichte und Gegenwart*, II, 1666).

about an augmentation or diminution of the normal value of the notes as they relate to the fundamental beat (called the *integer valor notarum*)—has early prototypes in certain of the tenors of pieces from the period of modal notation in which the cantus firmus is repeated in values half or double the length of the notes of the first statement.[5] A kind of proportional change is also seen in the effect of coloration as used in *Et in spiritum sanctum* (Plate LVI), in which three outlined notes become changed in value to equal two black ones of the same nominal value, and four outlined notes become equal to four black ones. The first recognition in a theoretical treatise of the practice of proportions appears to be by Johannes de Muris, in his *Libellus cantus mensurabilis* (CS, III, 58). By the late fifteenth century, proportional signs were in common use, and functioned to change the speed of a section of a composition. Also, as Willi Apel has noted, "proportional signs, when used simultaneously in a composition in all the parts, represent the tempo marks, nay, the metronomic marks of the 15th and 16th centuries" (NPM, 190).

In the Cordier canon, proportional changes in the notes are effected by the use of signs having the meaning of numerator and denominator, such as $\frac{2}{1}$; these signs indicate that a given note of the preceding section, represented by the denominator, is now changed in value so that it takes two such notes of the succeeding section, represented by the numerator, to make up the same value. Since the *integer valor* of the tactus of this period was the S (that is, S = the beat, or tactus), a sign $\frac{2}{1}$ means that the S is now replaced by the B as tactus, and the relationship of all the other values is changed in like manner. This is diminution, as the value of each note is now "diminished," and by the ratio of two to one, so that this degree of diminution is called *proportio dupla*.

A further degree of diminution occurs when the sign $\frac{3}{1}$ is introduced, which means that a note of the previous section is now to be represented by a note three times that value. This sign is seen in the Cordier canon on the outer staff near the top of the circle. In this

[5] See the example from the Florence Codex, Plut. 29.1, fol. 87v, quoted by Apel in *NPM*, Facs. 50, p. 255.

instance the tactus had been represented in the previous section by the M in perfect prolation (one S = three M's); but the proportional sign diminishes the values so that a S after it has the value that the M had before. Three M's after the sign, therefore, have the value of one M of the previous section. This is *proportio tripla*.

A still different degree of diminution is effected by the sign $\frac{3}{2}$, which is seen in the right side of the outer circle of the canon. In this case, the value of each S in the section before the proportional sign had been two M's—that is, the S had been in imperfect prolation. The $\frac{3}{2}$ sign means that the value of each M has diminished in the ratio of three to two, so that it requires three M's to make up the same value that previously took only two M's. Such a change is called *proportio sesquialtera* ("one-and-a-half"), and has the same effect as the use of coloration in imperfect meters.

Another set of signs was used to bring about the opposite effect, in which the proportional signs cause notes of smaller values to replace larger notes, which is called *augmentation*. For this purpose, two of the dot-and-circle signs that represented the *quatre prolacions* of the Ars Nova theorists were drawn upon. Thus the semicircle-and-dot (an example of which is seen in the "southeast" region of the outer circle) indicates that the S of the previous section, which had been the *integer valor*, is now replaced by the M, which becomes the tactus through augmentation. The sign of the full circle with dot, at the top of the outer circle, causes triple augmentation of values when used as a proportional sign; but in this particular case it does not operate as such since it is at the beginning of the cantus and hence is a regular meter sign with its usual meaning of perfect time and prolation.

Each successive proportional sign used in a piece, whether of diminution or augmentation, is to be considered in relation to the prevailing meter of the section immediately preceding it, *not* to the *integer valor*. In other words, the proportional signs are cumulative in effect. The operation of the successive proportional signs is analyzed in the outline of the circle canon that follows.

1) The cantus begins at the point in the outer circle where the mensuration sign of the circle-and-dot occurs, just above and after the clef sign at the top of the circle. (There is an upbeat—the M just before this sign

—but to avoid confusion this note should be disregarded for the time being.)

2) The circle with a horizontal line through it changes the prolation of the previous section from perfect to imperfect. After two measures, a short passage of hemiola rhythm is introduced by the two binarias that follow the B-rest. (These are colored red in the manuscript.)

3) The sign $\frac{3}{2}$ produces sesquialtera, so that each group of three M's is now equal in value to two M's of the previous section; in effect, this restores the prolation from imperfect to perfect.

4) The semicircle-and-dot sign causes augmentation of the *integer valor*, and a consequent change of the tactus from S to M.

5) The next sign, $\frac{8}{3}$, is an unusual one, but its meaning is clear: a group of eight M's now becomes the equal of three M's of the previous section, resulting in a bar with the following rhythm: .[6]

6) By reversing the figures to $\frac{3}{8}$, the previous proportion is cancelled, and the rhythm restored to what it was before the sign $\frac{8}{3}$. Coloration is applied to the only ligature in the $\frac{3}{8}$ section and to the note immediately following it.

7) The next proportional sign is $\frac{3}{1}$, which is written below the circle-and-dot sign of mensuration marking the beginning of the canon. Being a sign of triple diminution, $\frac{3}{1}$ restores the tactus, which had been in augmentation since the semicircle-and-dot, to its *integer valor*, and with perfect time and prolation, so that the melody has now returned full circle.

The last note before $\frac{3}{1}$ is the upbeat referred to at the beginning of this outline; it is a M which is equivalent in value to the S immediately after the $\frac{3}{1}$ sign. By so arranging the notes and signs at this point, Cordier has emphasized the perpetual character of the canon.

The entrance of the imitating voice is marked by the circle with a horizontal line through it that occurs at the top of the outer staff just below the C of "Cordier"; it must be preceded by the up-beat referred to in the last paragraph, of course. This symbol also

---

[6] In a recent publication, *Early 15th Century Music*, the editor, Gilbert Reaney, cites this proportional sign as being $\frac{4}{3}$ (p. xi), which is impossible, as the tactus changes during the brief passage that follows.

marks the point at which all the voices come to rest when the canon is brought to an end.

The tenor begins, as the clef sign indicates, at the circle with a horizontal line through it that establishes its mensuration. The rubric within the tenor staff indicates that when the canon is brought to a close it will end on the second note after the beginning. ("*Tenor cujus finis est 2ª nota.*") The proportional changes in the tenor are few; their operation is shown in the following outline.

1) The meter set by the mensuration sign (perfect time and imperfect prolation) continues about two-thirds through the staff. Before the first proportional sign occurs, hemiola is produced for two measures at the bottom of the circle by coloration of the L and of the B immediately following it.

2) The sign $\frac{2}{1}$ on the left side of the circle produces duple diminution (tactus $= B$).

3) The augmentation sign of semicircle-and-dot just before the end cancels out the diminution (tactus $= S$).

The dot is used in different ways in the canon; it is primarily used as a dot of division, but also as a dot of syncopation to warn against alteration, and in one case—the first note of the tenor—as a dot of addition. Although there is no sign to indicate the mode, the context shows that it is imperfect, and that this note must have the value of three B's (including the dot).

The manner in which the text is to be sung to this piece has remained an unsolved problem. The verses that are contained in the circles in three of the four corners of the page (the two on the bottom and the right one at the top) are more or less in the poetic form of the rondeau, and it was assumed by Riemann that these were intended to be sung to the music of the canon.[7] However, the musical design of the piece does not lend itself to the rondeau form. The underlaying of the text in the manuscript, which is continued in the circle of the upper left corner, was regarded by

[7] Riemann made a transcription of the canon for Aubry's *Les plus anciens monuments de la musique française,* where it appears on p. 21; a facsimile of the original manuscript page is on p. 22. For text Riemann used the first six lines of the eight-line verse in the circle of the upper right corner, disregarding the words within the circles. In Riemann *GdM,* I², there is a transcription of the canon with no text whatever (p. 352), and in note values half as long as those in Aubry.

Handschin as "normal from the point of view of the epoch," and he considered the verses in the other circles as "a kind of rubric or commentary." [8] This seems reasonable, but still leaves the enigma of what to do with the text in the repetitions of the canon. Two lines in the verse of the upper left circle indicate that the canon is to be sung through three times:

> Trois temps entiers par toy poses
> Chacer me pues joyeusement.

If one continues with the text of this verse, using three lines each time as the composer has done in his setting, there will be four lines left over if the canon is sung *"trois temps entiers."* Even assuming that this expression might mean three repetitions of the canon, there would still be one line left over.

In a recent volume containing this composition (Reaney, *Early 15th Century Music,* 11), only the text underlying the cantus has been used, and repeated with each repetition of the canon. Another possible answer to this dilemma is to consider this text as a true "canon," and the intent of the composer to have been a purely instrumental performance, in which case *chanter,* in the upper left circle, must be taken in a metaphorical sense.

The verses in the circles at the corners of the page read as follows (with a restitution of the effaced passages of the upper left corner):

> [Tout par compas] suy disposee
> Compaing je te pri chierement
> Tout par compas suy composee
> En ceste ro[de propre]ment
> Trois temps entiers par toy posee
> Chacer me pues joyeusement
> S'en chantant as vray sentement
> Tout par compas suy composee
> En ceste rode proprement
> Pour moy chanter plus seurement

> Maistre Baude Cordier se nomme
> Cilz qui composa ceste rode
> Je fais bien scavoir a tout homme
> Maistre Baude Cordier se nomme
> De Reims dont est et jusqu'a Romme

[8] "The Summer Canon and its Background," *MD,* 1949, 84.

Sa musique appert et a rode
Maistre Baude Cordier se nomme
Cilz qui composa ceste rode.

Seigneurs je vous pri chierement
Pries pour celi qui m'a fait
Je dis a tous communement
Seigneurs je vous pri chierement
Que Dieu a son definement
Li doint pardon de son meffait
Seigneurs je vous pri chierement
Pries pour celi qui m'a fait.

Par bonne amour et par dilection
J'ay fait ce rondel pour en offre
Icy peut prendre consolation
Par bonne amour et par dilection
Tout *coeur* et corps et mon affection
A son plaisir sont et li offre
Par bonne amour et par dilection
J'ay fait ce rondel pour en offre.

The beginning and ending of the canon are given in Fig. 84; the fermata applies only to the final chord on which the canon is brought to a close.

The development of musical notation from the tenth to the fifteenth century was one of several changing phases. It may be summarized in a very general way by stating that in each phase there was an adequate and expressive way available for communicating the music whose sounds it represented, and that the medieval musician always found ways of modifying those means to meet the demands made by successive changes of musical style.

The period of about five centuries that has been surveyed in this book saw the rise of neumatic writing—whose origins are wrapped in mystery—and its progress from a mnemonic system to one in which the problem of recording the exact pitch of melodies through written symbols was solved by the use of the staff. The other great achievement of medieval music—the notation of rhythm in a clear and unequivocal manner—is intimately linked to the rise of polyphony, and is one of the most absorbing episodes in the whole his-

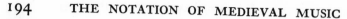

FIG. 84

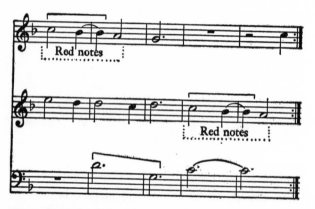

tory of music. Beginning with the limited mensurality suggested by the patterns of the rhythmic modes and ligatures, through the Franconian establishment of fundamental principles based on the assignment of unequivocal meanings to the note symbols, to the period of the Ars Nova when the notational resources were expanded to enable the composer to express a very large variety of rhythms, the story is an engrossing one. It continues in the period of the Renaissance with new developments that occur in the area of instrumental notations. The vocal notation of the fifteenth and sixteenth centuries is not without its special problems, of course, but the notation itself continues to be based fundamentally upon the principles and techniques of French notation of the Machaut period. In the early Baroque era the distinction between vocal and instrumental notation, which had existed even from the time when instrumental music first began to be notated, begins to break down, and one style of notation, which we still use today, came to serve the various media of music.

The unfolding story of notation does not end in the seventeenth century with the fixing of a general style of notation for all types of music, however, nor is it ever likely to end; for whenever a new style of music will arise with which our own system cannot cope, ways of modifying that system to meet the demands of the new style will emerge, just as surely as they did in the Middle Ages.

APPENDICES

MUSICA FICTA

THE PROBLEM of *musica ficta*—that is, the treatment of accidentals not specifically indicated by symbols—in the music of the Middle Ages is one with which the transcriber must sooner or later come to grips. Strictly speaking, it is not one of notation proper, but it must be accounted for in the final result if a transcription is made for the purpose of performance. The problem is a complex and an elusive one, and is not capable of easy solution by the application of a few simple rules.

The examples in this book contain a fair number of accidentals, particularly those compositions of the Ars Nova period. The accidentals used include the flat, natural sign, and sharp, and they are usually found a few notes before the note to which they apply. The flat is sometimes used as a key signature as well as for modifying the pitch of individual notes, and there are some instances of *partial signatures*—key signatures with an accidental (always B-flat) in one voice, but not in the other.

In addition to these written-out accidentals, others that do not appear in the music were supposed to be supplied by the performer in accordance with certain understood principles. While these unwritten accidentals comprise what is commonly known as *musica ficta*, the term was originally applied to any accidental—written or unwritten—with the exception of B-flat and B-natural, which were regarded as indigenous members of the scale.

The terms *musica ficta* and *musica falsa* appear in several treatises of the late thirteenth century, such as those of Walter Odington, Johannes de Grocheo, Johannes de Garlandia, and others. These two expressions appear to have been used synonymously, and to have referred to certain recognized alterations of the modal *musica vera*, also called *recta*, or *regularis*. These accidentals, which by the early fourteenth century included F-sharp, C-sharp, G-sharp, B-flat, and E-flat (derived from the mutations of the hexachord system, as Magister Lambert indicated), were used melodically, but they later came also to be used for harmonic purposes. Some theorists, like Anonymous II, wrote that they were used both "for necessity" and "for beauty," while others such as Philippe de Vitry and Jacob of Liége stress their necessity for instruments, "especially for organs." Some theorists warn against the overuse of such alterations.

In transcriptions of medieval music made by scholars of a few generations ago, such as Hugo Riemann, a great many editorial additions of *musica ficta* were made; but the tendency of musicologists today is to limit such additions strictly to those passages that have obvious need of them. When used in scholarly editions they are placed above the notes affected, to distinguish them from accidentals that are actually written in the manuscripts, the latter being placed before the notes in the usual manner.

As to the extent to which unwritten *musica ficta* should be applied, it appears that only a generalization can be made, namely, that much greater use of accidentals was made in the fourteenth century than in the more modal style of the thirteenth (Philippe de Vitry, for example, wrote that no motet could be performed without the use of *musica ficta*), and that they were used more in instrumental than in vocal music. It is possible that usage, like other matters of interpretation such as the use of French or Italian rhythm in Ars Nova music, was to an extent a matter of choice on the part of the performers.

As to the manner in which unwritten accidentals were applied, there are certain principles stated in many of the contemporary writings that may be summarized in the following manner.

Melodic principles:

1) The interval of the tritone, or the occurrence of this interval as the outer notes of a melodic figure, was avoided by means of B-flat or F-sharp. This principle is more applicable to secular than to sacred music —which is true of all the melodic principles here set forth—as numerous instances of tritone skips occur in Gregorian chant. In this connection, Johannes de Grocheo stated that secular music was not restricted to the modes.

2) Melodic smoothness was aimed for by reducing certain whole-steps to half-steps when they occurred in "neighboring-note" fashion. Thus a B coming between two A's was flatted, and by extension of this principle, an F coming between two G's was sharped. This was done also

with a G between two A's, and a C between two D's. This principle is more pertinent to the fourteenth than to the thirteenth century.

3) A cadence in the manner of leading tone to tonic was made semitonal by raising the lower note if it was not already a semitone. This may have been a result of the new lyrical style that was brought into music during the thirteenth century by secular song. Theorists of the period stressed the use of the *subsemitonium*, but the extent of its actual use through *musica ficta* is uncertain; a given chanson that occurs in several manuscripts may have a number of variants in the matter of leading tone accidentals.

Harmonic principles:

1) Fifths and octaves must be perfect; if the voice leading brings about diminished intervals, *musica ficta* must be employed to make them perfect. This appears to be true of even the earliest polyphonic music, and it is emphasized by Ars Nova theorists, although there seem to be cases, especially in the period of modal notation, where the tritone occurs as a "consonant" harmonic interval and where the use of *musica ficta* is doubtful; see Apel, *NPM*, 2nd ed., 253.

2) In the contrary motion of a third proceeding to a fifth, or of a sixth proceeding to an octave, the third and the sixth should be made major if they are not so already. A third going by contrary motion to a unison should be made minor. These rules apply to the Ars Nova only, and probably came into being under the influence of the increased use of the raised leading tone.

3) In the characteristic Ars Nova double leading tone cadence, both the fourth and seventh are raised, even though this is often not indicated.

The last principle stated above gives rise to some interesting situations in which the question occurs as to which should take precedence when there is a conflict between voice leading and harmonic euphony. The double leading tone cadence occurs often in the Machaut examples reproduced in this book. Sometimes the cadence comes about without the need of any accidentals, as at the end of the first word in the Sanctus of the Mass. At the final cadence of *Dame se vous n'avez aperceu*, the same cadence occurs, but the F of the contratenor must be sharped. The melodic movement of the last three notes of the contratenor is an additional reason for the use of F-sharp, and this applies also to the cadence at the end of the word "Domini" in the Sanctus. However, a more complicated situation is seen in the final cadence of the motet *Felix virgo*, a cadence which also occurs at the end of the first section of this same work. The passage in question is given in Fig. 85.

In this case it seems that *musica ficta* must be applied to the G of the tenor; but to do so would produce an awkward melodic augmented fourth. Furthermore, the tenor melody is in the nature of a cantus firmus, and has already been sung as G-natural in the equivalent place at the end of the first statement of the melody, where there is no question of a G-sharp (fol. 125, second line, second ligature). In music with such highly independent part leading as this, it is not inconceivable that the performer would yield to the horizontal drive toward G-natural.

FIG. 85

Many questions of the use of *musica ficta*, like others relating to medieval music, remain open, and cannot be approached with certainty; and in many passages an unquestionable definitive reading cannot be achieved. This appendix may serve as a rough general guide in the application of *musica ficta* to the transcribed examples, but it is primarily intended only as an introduction to the problem itself, the ramifications of which are extensive, and beyond the scope of the present volume.

ABBREVIATIONS

Adler *HMG*	Adler, G. *Handbuch der Musikgeschichte*, I, Berlin, 1930
AfM	*Archiv für Musikwissenschaft*
AM	*Acta Musicologica*
Ba	Bamberg Codex, Ed. IV6
CS	*Scriptorum de musica medii aevi*, 4 vols., ed. by Coussemaker, Paris, 1864–76
DTÖ	*Denkmäler der Tonkunst in Österreich*, 1894–1938
EEH	*Early English Harmony*, 2 vols., ed. by Wooldridge-Hughes, 1897 and 1913
Flo	Florence Codex, Plut. 29.1
GMB	*Geschichte der Musik in Beispielen*, ed. by Schering, Leipzig, 1931
GdM	Wolf, J. *Geschichte der Mensuralnotation von 1250–1460*, 3 vols. Leipzig, 1904
GS	*Scriptores ecclesiastici de musica sacra potissimum*, 3 vols., ed. by Gerbert, St. Blaise, 1784
HAM	*Historical Anthology of Music*, I, ed. by Davison-Apel, Cambridge, 1946
HdN	Wolf, J. *Handbuch der Notationskunde*, 2 vols., Leipzig, 1913–19
IMS	International Musicological Society
IPM	Suñol, Dom G. *Introduction à la paléographie musicale*, Paris, 1935
JAMS	*Journal of the American Musicological Society*
Las H	*El codex musical de Las Huelgas*, 3 vols., ed. by Anglès, Barcelona, 1931
LU	*Liber Usualis*, with Introduction and Notes in English, Tournai, 1950
Ma	Madrid Codex, 20.486

MD	*Musica Disciplina*
MMA	Reese, G. *Music in the Middle Ages,* New York, 1940
Mo	Montpellier Codex, H 196
MQ	*Musical Quarterly*
NOHM	*New Oxford History of Music,* II, ed. by Dom Hughes, Oxford, 1954
NPM	Apel, W. *The Notation of Polyphonic Music 900–1600,* Cambridge, 1944 (2nd ed.) and 1953 (4th ed.)
PM	*Paléographie musicale,* ed. by Dom A. Mocquereau and Dom J. Gajard, Tournai, Series I (vols. 1–16) 1889–1955; Series II (Vols. 1–2) 1900–1924
RG	*Revue grégorienne*
Riemann *HdM*	Riemann, H. *Handbuch der Musikgeschichte,* 5 vols., Leipzig, 1904–13
SIMG	*Sammelbände der internationalen Musikgesellschaft*
SR	*Source Readings in Music History,* ed. by Strunk, New York, 1950
W1	Wolfenbüttel Codex 677 (*olim* Helmst. 628)
W2	Wolfenbüttel Codex 1206
ZfM	*Zeitschrift für Musikwissenschaft*

BIBLIOGRAPHY

Agustoni, Dom L. "Notation neumatique et interpretation," *RG*, 1951, 173 and 219.

Anglès, H. "Gregorian Chant," *NOHM*, II, 92.

——. *La música a Catalunya fins al segle XIII*, Barcelona, 1935.

Antifonario visigotico mozarabe de la Catedral de Leon, Madrid, 1953.

Apel, W. "The Central Problem of Gregorian Chant," *JAMS*, 1956, 118.

——. *French Secular Music of the Late 14th Century*, Cambridge, 1950.

——. "From St. Martial to Notre Dame," *JAMS*, 1949, 145.

——. *Masters of the Keyboard*, Cambridge, 1947.

Aubry, P. *Cent motets du XIIIe siècle*, 3 vols. Paris, 1908.

——. "Estampies et dances royales," *Le mercure musicale*, 1906, 169.

——. "L'oeuvre mélodique des troubadours et des trouvères," *La revue musicale*, 1907, 317, 347, and 389.

——. *Les plus anciens monuments de l'art française*, Paris, 1905.

Bannister, H. *Monumenti vaticani di paleografia musicale*, Leipzig, 1913.

Baxter, J. *An Early St. Andrews Music Manuscript*, London, 1931.

Beck, J. *Le chansonnier Cangé*, Philadelphia, 1927.

——. *Le manuscrit du Roi*, Philadelphia, 1927.

——. "Die modale Interpretation der mittelalterlichen Melodien," *Caecilia*, 1907, 97.

Besseler, H. "Baude Cordier," *Musik in Geschichte und Gegenwart*, II, 1666.

——. *Die Musik des Mittelalters und der Renaissance*, Leipzig, 1931.

——. "Studien zur Musik des Mittelalters," *AfM*, 1926, 137.

Bonvin, L. "The 'Measure' in Gregorian Music," *MQ*, 1929, 16.

Bukofzer, M. Review of "The Rhythm of 12th Century Polyphony," *Notes of the MLA*, 1955, 232.

————. "Rhythm and Meter in the Notre Dame Conductus," *Bulletin of the AMS*, 1948, 63.

————. '*Sumer is icumen in*,' *a Revision*, Berkeley, 1944.

Corbin, S. "Les notations neumatiques en France à l'époque carolingienne," *Revue d'histoire de l'église de France*, 1952.

Ellinwood, L. "The Conductus," *MQ*, 1941, 192.

————. *The Works of Francesco Landini*, Cambridge, Mass., 1939.

Einstein, A. *Beispielsammlung zur Musikgeschichte*, Leipzig, 1930.

Gajard, Dom J. *La méthode de Solesmes*, Paris, 1951.

————. *The Rhythm of Plainsong*, New York, 1945.

Geraghty, Sister M. *The Genesis of Peter Wagner's Theories of Gregorian Chant Rhythm*, Diss. U. of S. C., 1953.

Gombosi, O. "Machaut's Messe Notre Dame," *MQ*, 1950, 204.

Handschin, J. "Eine alte Neumenschrift," *AM*, 1950, 74.

————. "Zu 'Eine alte Neumenschrift'," *AM*, 1953, 87.

————. "Zur Frage der melodischen Paraphrasierung im Mittelalter," *ZfM*, 1928, 516.

————. "Die mittelalterlichen Aufführungen in Zurich, Bern, und Basel," *ZfM*, 1927, 8.

————. "A Monument of English Medieval Polyphony," *The Musical Times*, 1932, 510; and 1933, 697.

————. "The Summer Canon and its Background," *MD*, 1949, 74.

————. "Über Estampie und Sequenz," *ZfM*, 1929, 14.

Hourlier, Dom J. "Le domaine de la notation messine," *RG*, 1951, 96 and 150.

Hughes, Dom A. Essays on early polyphony, in *NOHM*, II, 270, 287, 311, and 355.

————. *Medieval Polyphony in the Bodleian Library*, Oxford, 1951.

Huglo, Dom M. "La mélodie grecque du 'Gloria in excelsis' et son utilisation dans le Gloria XIV," *RG*, 1950, 35.

————. "Les noms des neumes et leur origine," *Etudes grégoriennes I*, Solesmes, 1954.

Jammers, E. "Die paleofrankische Neumenschrift," *Scriptorium*, 1953, 235.

Ludwig, F. *Guillaume de Machaut, Musikalische Werke*, Publikationen alterer Musik I¹, III¹, and IV², Leipzig, 1926–29.

——. ". . . Musik des Mittelalters bis zum Anfang des 15. Jahrhunderts," Adler *HdM I*, Berlin, 1930.

——. Review of "Geschichte der Mensuralnotation von 1250–1460," *SIMG*, 1904–05, 597.

Machabey, A. *Guillaume de Machault*, Paris, 1955.

——. *La notation musicale*, Paris, 1952.

Mocquereau, Dom A. "De la transcription sur lignes," *Riemann-Festschrift*, Leipzig, 1909.

——. *Le nombre musical grégorien ou rhythmique grégorienne*, 2 vols., Tournai, 1908–27.

Mocquereau-Gajard (trans. Dom L. Bevenot). *The Rhythmic Tradition in the Manuscripts*, Paris, 1952.

Paganuzzi, E. "Sulla notazione neumatica della monodia trobodorica," *Rivista musicale italiana*, 1955, 23.

Parrish-Ohl. *Masterpieces of Music before 1750*, New York, 1951.

Reaney G. *Early 15th Century Music*, Rome, 1955.

Rietsch, H. *Gesänge von Frauenlob, Reinmar von Zweter, und Alexander*, *DTÖ*, Bd. 40, Jg. XX², Vienna, 1953.

Rokseth, Y. *Polyphonies du XIIIᵉ siècle*, 4 vols., Paris, 1935–39.

Runge, P. *Die Sangsweisen der Colmarer Handschrift*, Leipzig, 1896.

Sachs, C. *Rhythm and Tempo*, New York, 1953.

——. "Some Remarks about Old Notation," *MQ*, 1948, 365.

Sartori, C. *La notazione italiana del Trecento*, Florence, 1938.

Schneider, M. *Geschichte der Mehrstimmigkeit*, 2 vols., Berlin, 1934–35.

Schofield, B. "The Provenance and Date of 'Sumer is icumen in'," *The Music Review*, 1948, 81.

Schrade, L. *Polyphonic Music of the 14th Century*, Monaco, 1956.

Smits van Waesberghe, J. *De musico-paedagogico et theoretico Guidone Aretino*, Florence, 1953.

——. "The Two Versions of the Gregorian Chant," *IMS*, 6th Congress, Oxford, 1955.

Spiess, L. "An Introduction to the pre-St. Martial Sources of Early Polyphony," *Speculum*, 1947, 16.

Ursprung, O. *Die katholische Kirchenmusik*, Potsdam, 1931.

Van, G. de, ed. *Missa Nostre Dame*, Rome, 1949.

Waite, W. "Discantus, Copula, Organum," *JAMS*, 1952, 77.

————. *The Rhythm of 12th Century Polyphony*, New Haven, 1954.

Westrup, J. "Medieval Song," *NOHM*, II, 220.

Whitehill-Prado. *Liber Sancti Jacobi*, 3 vols., Santiago de Compostela, 1944.

Winternitz, E. *Musical Autographs*, 2 vols., Princeton, 1955.

Wolf, J. *Musikalische Schrifttafeln*, Bückeburg, 1922–23.

————. "Die Musiklehre des Johannes de Grocheo," *SIMG*, 1899–1900, 69.

Wooldridge, H. *Oxford History of Music*, I, 1901.

ADDITIONAL BIBLIOGRAPHY

Fischer, von, E. *Studium zur italienischen Musik des Trecento und frühen Quattrocento*, Bern, 1956.

Pirrotta, N. *The Music of Fourteenth Century Italy*, Amsterdam, 1954.

Prado, Dom G. "Mozarabic Melodics," *Speculum*, 1928, 218.

Reese, G. *Fourscore Classics of Music Literature*, New York, 1957.

Rojo, Dom C. and Prado, Dom G. *El Canto Mozarabe*, Barcelona, 1929.

Wolf, J. *Der Squarcialupi Codex*, Lippstadt, 1955.

TRANSLATIONS

CHAPTER 1

PLATE I
Glory be to God on high, and on earth peace, good will towards men. We praise thee, we bless thee, we worship thee, we glorify thee, we give thanks to thee for thy great glory, O Lord God, heavenly King, God the Father almighty. O Lord, the only-begotten Son, Jesus Christ, and the Holy Ghost; O Lord God, Lamb (of God). . . .

PLATE II
Thou has freed us, O Lord, from our afflictions, and thou hast confounded those who hate us.
In God shall we be praised the whole day, and by thy name be acknowledged forever.

PLATE III
Harken unto us, O Lord, for kind is thy mercy; look upon us according to thy many mercies, O Lord.

Near the entrance and at the altar, the priests and Levites of the Lord's ministry will weep, and will say: Show mercy, O Lord, show mercy on thy people; and may thou not turn away the prayers of those calling unto thee, O Lord.

In our attire we shall be changed to ashes and haircloth; we shall fast, and weep before God, for our God through his many mercies will take away our sins.

PLATES IV–V
Here is how the first mode is known, and the second also. The third is taken thus, and this is how the fourth is tried. This is the fifth, and thus may the sixth be known. The sound of the seventh is held like this, and thus the octave.

PLATE VI
Alleluia.
O give thanks unto the Lord, for he is gracious, and his mercy endureth forever.

PLATE VII
Glory be to God on high,
　Whom the holy angels and the virtuous ones of the skies glorify;
And on earth peace,
　True peace, salvation and life of man, king of the angels,
We praise thee,
　We sing with praises to thee alone, O Lord on high.

We bless thee,
Whom they on the sea and the waters bless; to thee alone we utter praise.
We worship thee,
Whom the virtuous ones of heaven worship; to thee, holy one, trembling
we speak with praise.
We glorify thee,
Glorious is thy name forever, O king, who chose to die because of us;
O good Jesus,
We give thanks to thee. . . .

PLATE VIII
Unto us a child is born, unto us a son is given, and the government shall be
upon his shoulder, and his name shall be callled Wonderful, Counsellor (the
Mighty God, the Everlasting Father, the Prince of Peace).
O sing unto the Lord a new song, for he hath done marvellous things.

PLATE IX
Eternal rest grant unto them, O Lord: and let everlasting light shine upon
them. Thou, O God, art praised in Sion; and unto thee shall the vow be
performed in Jerusalem.
Thou that hearest the prayer, unto thee shall all flesh come.

PLATE X
How nobly you strive for heaven, O Turian.
You as host rule at the feast for the faithful guests;
Celestial praise resounds at your approach.

PLATE XI
King of heaven, Lord of the dry earth,
Of the shining sun and the wave-sounding sea;
Thy servants, venerating thee with pious accents,
Entreat thee that thou wilt order them freed from manifold ills.
I am the way, the truth, and life. Alleluia, Alleluia.
It is idle now for the powerful to oppress,
For the deprived to be wasted, for the miserable to weep.

PLATE XII
Three times three are the intervals of the connected sounds;
For now a very small tone makes the unisons equal in sound,
Now the semitone very slightly separates the melody,
Now the tone makes a division from the adjoining sound. . . .

CHAPTER 2

PLATE XIII
Of all pains, none is pleasant
Save only that of love;
This, however, is sweet and keen,
And everyone has thoughts of it;
And it can comfort so well,
And it holds so many blessings
That no one should flee from it.

PLATES XIV–XV
A sweet love and a loyal friend
I often regret and remember,
So that never, no day of my life,
Shall I forget her face, her countenance.
Love of her can no longer be felt
Because she takes her pleasure with no man,
And among all women it can never happen
That I should have good hope about mine.

PLATE XVI
For what misdeed or through what error
Have you so banished me, love,
That I receive no gift nor reward from you?
Nor can I find someone to pity me.
Poor use have I made of my service,
For I never had such a bad name as I have through you.
I never yet reproached you with my service, love,
But now do I complain,
And say that you have slain me, without reason.

PLATE XVII
My joy is all spent,
Now hear sad lament.
I repent of my sins
Which I have committed in my day.
They are, unforunately, so many;
Now, in this world, death will bring me to nothing.

My life does not last long,
Death has sworn an end to it;
No matter how I implore him
It is all in vain
When he wants to take me with him.
Alas, miserable destiny!

PLATE XVIII
Lo, I saw on the throne
A woman who was with child;
She wore a wondrous crown
That was a delight to my eyes.
She wished to be delivered,
Thus spake the very best [woman] of all.
I, at this time, chose twelve jewels
In the fastness of her crown.

Now mark how she bore,
          The lovely one,
Out of nature's fullness,
The one with whom she was burdened.
Him she saw sitting before her,
          With her wisdom,
In seven candelabras;

And saw him in yet another way,
In the form of a lamb
Upon the famed mount of Sion.

She did, therefore, what she should,
          Yea, the lovely one;
She carried the seed of the flower, an umbel.
Maid, as you became mother
Of the lamb and of the dove,
          The vine
You would have swear unto you,
I should not wonder,
That the same nourishment
Would lead to this fruit.

PLATE XIX
The world's joy does not last,
It goes away in a little while.
The longer I know it
The less value I find in it,
For it is all mingled with cares,
With sorrow and with ill favor.
And at the last, poor and bare
It leaves a man, when it begins to go;
All the bliss that's here and there
Is beset at the end with weeping.

CHAPTER 3

PLATE XX
King of heaven, Lord of the dry earth,
Of the shining sun and the wave-sounding sea. . . .

Have mercy upon me, O God.

Alleluia.
The blessed day shines on us. Come, ye peoples, and adore the Lord, for
a great light descends upon the earth today.

PLATE XXI
We rejoice, we exult, we chant the song
To the redeemer, the incarnate, the saviour of us all;
By this birth and healing power the jewel of us all.
Let each praise God, each one himself, through the eternal ages.
He who issues from Mary's womb today,
True man and king, is seen the master on earth.
So blessed because of his birth, with great rejoicing,
Praising together, exulting, we bless the Lord.

PLATE XXII
The light descends into the deep, coming into this world;
The light illuminating mankind.
The light creating the shining star enters the maiden's room,
Makes a mother of the virgin.

Through this mother deceit has been overcome,
The praiseworthy father is hailed by a chorus of timbrels.

Let every man attend, according to the fitness of the song.
In this way are fulfillled the prophetic words:
The word is made flesh; the uncorrupted virgin bears a new flower.

PLATE XXIII
May our band sing joyfully this day, on which the hero, Saint Jacob,
praises Christ in glory without end, in the court of the angels.

Let Catholics be glad together, the heavenly citizens rejoice this day.

CHAPTER 4

PLATE XXVIII
The sun was hidden behind a cloud,
But did not know of his eclipse.
When he took on human form,
The son of the highest father
Wished to wed
The word of the father on high;
He could not wed
In the flesh, because of his glory.
Rejoice in a new wedding;
It is that of faith and truth,
For he was not of corrupt flesh.

PLATE XXIX
Under the form of the true flower
Which the pure root has produced,
The pious care of our clergy
Has made a mystical flower
Beyond the understanding of the laity,
Bringing forth the hidden meaning
Of the flower from its nature.

PLATES XXX–XXXI
Protector of our times,
Defender of our country,
Prize of honor and virtue
To be emulated;
Enhancing the noble blood
Of Hector and his deeds,
Shattering the strength of the enemy;
Worthy of Nestor's years,
Excellent guerdon for the worthy.

PLATES XXXII–XXXIII
Hail, glorious mother of the saviour,
Hail, beautiful virgin, flower of chastity,
Hail, happy light, bride of splendor,
Hail, precious deliverance of sinners,

Hail, way of life, chaste, comely, pure,
Sweet, gentle, faithful, happy creature.
Mother in a marvelous way of a newly born,
Of a man, but without a man, contrary to the laws of man.
Virgin of virgins, without reproach,
Splendor that rules the light of heaven,
Health of the people, hope of the faithful,
Light of the heart, enlighten us,
And with thy son so holy and so auspicious
Re-unite us,
And to our eternal joys pray lead us,
O holy virgin Mary.

Sweet creature, virgin Mary,
Chaste, clean, pure, and without shame,
Through you hard death has ended
For those mortals who lead a righteous life.
You are the rose put forth by the thorn,
Through whom the door of life is opened,
Which was closed to good people by folly,
By Eve and Adam, who were in the fullness of life.
O, gate of salvation, you have issued forth again,
Safeguard and shield against the enemy;
You are the haven, solace, and comfort
For those whom death would have undone.
Through this song and through my tears,
Mother of the all powerful king,
I pray you with all my heart
That you may help me towards your son;
May he be my protection and have mercy upon me.

PLATE XXXIV

Hear ye all together, both the cleric and the lay,
There is no sweeter lay for us than salvation through Our Lady;
There can be no sweeter lay than the "Ave Maria";
It is the lay the angels sang when God was the bridegroom.
Eve committed us to death, the "Ave" brought us life,
Delivered us all into safe haven.

CHAPTER 5

PLATE XXXV

May praise be always ready for the cross of the Lord,
By which salvation was given to man;
Which held him who took away the sins of all
By his tortured flesh, which was sacrificed on the cross;
Which is the sign, therefore, of veneration and praise,
Because only it was truly worthy to bear the ransom of life.

O cross, shape of penitence, key of grace, branch of pardon for the sinner,
True root of the tree of justice, way of life, banner of glory,

Bridegroom of noontide, fulsome light,
You bring light to gloom, joy to knowledge.
Let a man carry this cross; let him be comforted by it.
It is fitting that the cross should bear the joys of true light.

PLATE XXXVII
Praise to thee, salvation of men, light of splendor, of brightness,
Who, in a miraculous way, carried the creator, the redeemer of all,
Thy son, who was in the shape of all of us.

Praise to thee, virgin of virgins, mother of chastity, of honor,
Bearing the flower; you who carried the Lord of heaven,
The saviour of mankind, in a marvelous way.

PLATES XXXVIII–XXXIX
God! It often makes me tremble when I see that she is moved;
It makes me all a-quiver. I often sigh for my love,
For she is wondrously fair, as fair as the rose is ruddy.

God! I was close to bliss; now I see that to cure myself
I must leave her whom I love without deceit, without desertion;
But however more I try, the more I love; 'tis a great wonder.

God! I cannot sleep at night, for then I hear I know not what
That love is counselling me, and which makes me so to
Tremble and quiver that when I sleep, love's pain awakens me.

PLATES XL–XLI
Love has cause for complaint,
Seeing himself neglected,
Because he receives less faith and constancy
Than should be given back to him;
He seeks, justifiably,
To depart at once.

To attain love,
He follows love and constancy,
And is their companion,
For he is founded upon them.
Therefore, when love is deprived of these
He wholly perishes,
And is reduced to nothing.

PLATE XLIII
Summer is a-coming in,
Loudly sing, cuckoo!
Grows the seed, and blows the mead,
And grows the wood anew.
Sing, cuckoo!
The ewe is bleating for her lamb,
The cow lows for her calf;
The bullock leaps, the buck turns bold,
Merry sing, cuckoo!
Cuckoo, cuckoo, well singest thou, cuckoo;

Never shalt thou cease now
Sing cuckoo, now, sing cuckoo,
Sing cuckoo, sing cuckoo, now!

PLATE XLIV
I have a pain in my heart that oft o'ercomes me.
Love has so cruelly wounded me with his dart
That I could not live much longer
Should my pain not be eased.
Have mercy on me, lady of gentle heart,
For I have great joy in you;
I love you faithfully, with all my heart.

I shall not repent for having loved,
For any ills that I can hardly bear.
O lady with the bright face,
It greatly pleases me to see your lovely form,
For all my thoughts are of you;
Nor can your heart be taken from mine.
And so, I pray, that you should remember me,
For I could not forget you.

Sweetly the pain of love has hold of me, sweetly,
My most sweet lady to whom I therefore belong.
Sweetly the pain of love has hold of me.
I shall serve you with all my heart,
Without falseness, and right loyally.
Sweetly the pain of love has hold of me, sweetly.

PLATE XLV
May the world, deprived of eyes,
Blind in the daytime, have respite
While in the unfolding centuries
Some ecclesiastic fights
In behalf of [his] consecrated descendants,
And the poor man shouts "Christ!"
In a word to the starving, cries now with hoarse mouth:
"Sons, turn back to your heart!"
But since they have deaf ears,
And are impious scorners
With hardened necks, and heedless,
He soon upbraids them in these words:
"Why do you, like asps,
Not deign to listen?
Even now it is clear to mute dogs.
Why do you grow fat,
Into a flock of pastured flesh?
And why do you not arm as the wolf,
You, armed with their teeth?

You shepherds, adulterers,
And true mercenaries,

Successors of Lucifer—
A false service to Christ,
The vicarious neighbor,
Having been rendered
By those of ever changing appetite,
Unoccupied with true labor."

A thief does not come except to steal, and kill, and harm.

PLATE XLVI
Haman once more proves by his death
How much it profits a man to be inflated
By a spirit of pride, to seek more
Than is fitting, and to undertake
More than is permitted,
So that he climbs what is difficult,
Like another, Icarus, for instance, who
Unknowing in the sea flood so perished,
And Phaeton did not return, having usurped
The route of the sun, but himself burned;
By his attempt he was killed.
The flight of Icarus so overly elated him
Striving to transcend [it], Haman surpasses
The theft of Phaeton; but on the mount of the falcon
He was overturned (in) the dust.
Often he is washed by the rain, he is dried by the breeze
Blowing over his remains in the depths.
Not in the same way will the last reply to the first.

Alas, tricky fortune, you who always
Until now have been a slackening
By promising on your pipe frivolity as if truth,
Now you have appeared, alas,
Graciously placing hardship afar
While you promised prosperity;
Devising immense treasure, you have
Extolled [his] name to the skies;
Now, by your turning wheel, you have plunged [him]
Naked into a doleful lake.
Just as Haman, I die through you as I learn
That you have deceived me.
As much by the rising of the higher as by the downfall of the lower
You have taught me this.

Ah, me! My soul is sorrowful.

CHAPTER 6

PLATE XLVII
All my thoughts are ceaselessly in loving and honouring you, sweet
   creature.
My eyes do not tire of seeing and admiring your lovely countenance.

I cannot prevent my heart from ever thinking of your clear face and pure
kindness.
This causes my loving ardour to be doubled, inflamed, and vivified with
desire.
I am dead if I do not see you, noble lady, for the ardour which increases
my pain in me will kill me, as I believe, for your love.
So I know not what I should do, for I hear nothing from anywhere
Which might put out my sadness or my melancholy, and I know well
that never have I had such a one, nor a greater;
For I suffer so much, and feel so much pain and fright, that I am always
weeping, and to those around me I only ask that I may neither eat nor
drink anything with savor.

Gaily I behave outwardly, but I bear joylessly and haplessly such a heavy
pain
That I am directly at the door of death, with no surcease if I get not from
love such comfort that he may take me in his care.
For when your face, the sweet countenance, I remember in my heart,
I am seized with an ardent flame, cruel and bitter, full of discomfort.
For desire torments me greatly with its stress, but my heart is strong
enough against its wounding;
So that does not discomfort me, but encourages me with hope, which gives
me promise of your sweetness.

PLATE XLVIII

Lady, if you have not seen
That I love you with all my heart, without deceit,
Try it, and then you will surely see it.
Your great beauty has blinded me,
And your sweetnesses only sadden me;
For they have so greatly moved my heart
To loving you, that I cannot conceive
That I shall ever have blessing or joy.

When I neither see nor hear my lady,
I see nothing but that which saddens me;
My heart melts within me like snow.
Never was there such pain, through my love,
For my eyes, which weep for it, are drowning me.

PLATE XLIX

Lady, from whom comes all my joy,
I cannot love nor cherish you too much,
Nor praise you as much as you deserve,
Nor serve, question, honor, nor obey;
For the gracious hope, sweet lady, that I have of seeing you
Gives me a hundred times more benefit and joy
Than I would deserve in a thousand years.

PLATES L–LI

Holy, holy, holy, Lord God of hosts; heaven and earth are full of thy glory.

Hosanna in the highest.
Blessed is he that cometh in the name of the Lord.

PLATES LII–LIII
Blessed virgin, mother of Christ,
Who brought joy to the unhappy world
By thy birth-giving,
            Sweetest one;
Thus thou didst destroy heresies
When thou hadst faith in the angel,
And bore a son,
            Purest one.
Implore thy son, most pious maid,
That he may drive away the many evils
And many torments
            Which we suffer;
For, from being the most favored people,
Most splendid light of light,
From the heights to the depths
            We have been led.
We are deprived of all good things,
We are pursued by the wicked,
Through whom we are subjected
            To the yoke of slavery.
For, as if blind, we stray,
Nor do we follow our guide,
But are diverted from paths
            Which are safe for us.
Source of grace and virtue,
Our only hope of safety, have pity on us,
For we are forsaken,
            And help us,
So that freed from guilt, and led into the right way,
And with our enemies destroyed,
            Peace with rejoicing may be with us.

Stainless mother,
Victress free from pride,
            Thou gavest birth gladly;
Keeper of the court of heaven
Who lends ear to the sorrowing,
            Star of the sea,
Who, as a mother, consoles
And prays for the fallen,
            Humbly;
Matchless fount of grace
Who rules over the angels,
            Swiftly
Prepare for us a safe journey,
And aid us valiantly,

For we are dying.
We are assailed by enemies,
And we defend ourselves weakly,
            And we do not know
Whither we can turn,
Nor through whom we can be saved
            Unless through thee.
Ah, therefore we beg
That beneath thy wings we may abide;
            O turn us back towards thee.
For thee we long, sighing and lamenting.

CHAPTER 7

PLATE LIV

I am a pilgrim who goes asking alms,
Crying: "Have pity, for the love of God."
And I go, singing with a beautiful voice,
With mild demeanor, and with blond tresses.
I have only my pilgrim's staff and bag,
And I call, and call, and no one answers me;
And when I think that all is going well,
A contrary wind comes storming at me.

PLATE LV

Through a green wood I follow the track of a noble hound.
He, being followed, seems to speak to me, barking, with an almost human
        voice;
Wherefore I, being alert, have no difficulty in following him,
Hoping that the effort might free me from that tight knot.

PLATES LVI–LVII

   And [I believe] in the Holy Ghost, the Lord, and Giver of Life, who pro-
ceedeth from the Father and the Son; Who with the Father and the Son
together is worshipped and glorified; Who spake by the Prophets: And I
believe in one Catholic and Apostolic Church: I acknowledge one Baptism
for the remission of sins: And I look for the Resurrection of the dead: And
the Life of the world to come. Amen.

PLATES LVIII–LIX

Beneath green boughs the many birds
Within closed valleys, with sweet notes,
In a pathway I sought, delighted me.
Free of care, I went walking.
At once, love drew his bow on me,
Fired darts at me, so that immediately I took off.
Time past has thus been against me,
But chance has put me on guard.

CHAPTER 8

PLATE LXII

All by compass am I arranged.
(Comrade, I pray you tenderly)
All by compass am I composed,
Fittingly in this rondel.
Three times around, put by you,
You can chase me merrily,
If you sing with true feeling.
All by compass am I arranged,
Fittingly in this rondel
So that you can sing me more se-
curely.

Master Baude Cordier is he called,
He who composed this rondel.
I want to make it known to every
man;
Master Baude Cordier is he called.
From Rheims where he dwells, to
Rome
His music is known, and beyond.
Master Baude Cordier is he called,
He who composed this rondel.

Sires, I ask you tenderly,
Pray for him who made me;
I say to all generally,
Sires, I ask you tenderly.
May God to his unworthy one
Give pardon for his misdeeds.
Sires, I ask you tenderly,
Pray for him who made me.

Through goodly love and charity
I have made this rondel to offer
Him here who can take solace in it,
Through goodly love and charity.
All my heart and body, and my af-
fection
Are for his pleasure, and to offer him
Through goodly love and charity
I have made this rondel, to offer . . .

The author wishes to express his indebtedness to colleagues at Vassar College for invaluable assistance in the translations of the texts, with particular acknowledg- ment of the time devoted by Betty Quinn. Many thanks are also due Robert Far- low of the W. W. Norton Company for his skill in overcoming the numerous technical problems that arose in the production of this book.

CORRIGENDA and ADDENDA

Page   7, lines 26 and 27: these lines should read "(*SAEcula, COELi*), or over the first of two adjacent consonants (*AeteRNum, PraeseNTet*), or to introduce the semi-consonants *J* or *I* (*Allelula, Elus*), so that the voice is to flow . . . ," etc.

Page   21, line 24: for "adest" read "et";
line 26: for "tenetur" read "tenet"; for "adest" read "et."
footnote 13: add "For a guide to important medieval treatises dealing with notation, see G. Reese, *Fourscore Classics of Music Literature.*

Page   31, footnote 19: add "For an account of the few Mozarabic melodies that scholars have been able to transcribe, see Rojo-Prado, *El Canto Mozarabe,* p. 66; also Prado, "Mozarabic Melodics."

Page   44, line 31: the rhythmic figure at the end of this line should be at the end of line 33, and vice versa.

Page   45, line 4: the second of the two rhythmic figures is upside down.

Page   51, line 14: for "*HdN*" read "*HdM.*"

Page   52, line 31: for "*HAM*" read "*HMG.*"

Page   65, line 8: for "1130, fol. 14" read "1139, fol. 41." This correction should be made also on p. x, after "Plate XXI."

Page   66, line 9: add "L. Spiess has suggested that more natural and characteristic results are obtained if the faint pitch-line is taken as F for the first four notes, with a shift to G thereafter."

Page   79, line 22: for "ground" read "group."

Page   81, line 33: after the word "manuscripts" insert the phrase "other than W²."

Page   86, footnote 7: add "Some authorities date W¹ *ca.* 1250; see *NPM,* p. 200, fn. 1."

Page   87, line 19: the word "five" should read "two";
lines 20–21: the statement "Four of these occur in succes-

sion in the middle of the line" should read "One of these occurs in the middle of the line."

Mors is a section (clausula) of a larger composition that occurs complete in W². The tenor in Plate XXVIa is seen over the word "mors" in the Alleluia Verse, *Christe resurgens, LU,* 827.

Page 110, line 12: after the word "perfection" add "or *punctus divisionis,* dot of division."

line 21: after "four B's" add "of which the first began a perfection."

Page 113, line 32: the sentence beginning on this line should read: "The major S-rest stands for a note whose value is two-thirds of a B, while the minor S-rest stands for a note with one-third B value."

Page 114, line 7: for "fol. 112" read "fol. 11." This correction should be made also on p. xi, after "Plate XXXV."

Page 115, line 8: add "(The faded B at the beginning of line five of the triplum must not be overlooked.)"

Page 120, line 3: for "fol. 378ᵛ and 379" read "fol. 44ᵛ and 45." This correction should be made also on p. xi, after "Plates XXXVIII and XXXIX."

Page 121, line 7: for "triplum" read "quadruplum."

Page 126, lines 10–11: The dance to which this statement refers can be transcribed without disregarding the descending tail; the reason for advising its omission was to preserve the general phrase symmetry that prevails in the dances. Aubry disregards the tail in his transcription. (See p. 126, footnote 12.)

Page 141, line 33: add here "This can only be done by consulting Wooldridge's complete representation of the original form of the canon in *OHM,* as Fig. 55 goes only to the second incise of the second line in the facsimile."

Page 151, line 21: "third beat" should read "second beat."

Page 155, lines 16–17: this sentence should be disregarded, as the vertical sign following the second L is not a rest, but an indication of the termination of the second ending. (See the last sentence on this page, and the first sentence of the next page.)

Page 156, line 7: "honourer" should read "hounourer";
line 9: "Qui" should read "Que."

Page 159, line 7: add this sentence: ("There are several MS errors in Plates L–LI, as the student will discover for himself.")

Page 160, line 9: the sign "$\frac{2}{3}$" should read "$\frac{3}{2}$".

footnote 10, line 3: the clause "but it has since disappeared" should read "and its whereabouts were unknown for a while afterward; the MS is now in a private American collection."

Page 171, line 5: "stems" should read "flags."

Page 173, line 26, after "Ars Nova": add "(with the exception of MS Rossi 215 of the Vatican Library.)"

Page 174, footnote 5: "Further description and commentary are found in J. Wolf, *Der Squarcialupi Codex;* N. Pirrotta, *The Music of 14th Century Italy;* and K. Fischer, *Studien zur italienischen Musik des Trecento und frühen Quattrocento.*"

Page 179, line 24, after "the previous part": add "The ritornello may also be transcribed in quaternaria, in which case the emendation on lines 26 and 27 is not necessary. This method produces syncopation across the bar, but makes for better consonances in some places."

Page 186, after Fig. 83: add "The curious rest at the beginning may be the composer's way of indicating the arsic nature of the first chord."

Add also "It has been suggested by E. Lerner that the pair of S's that occurs towards the end of line three of the facsimile (and also, in a similar cadential position, in lines 7, 9, and 10) might be rendered as two dotted quarters, rather than the half and quarter seen in Fig. 83."

Page 192, lines 4–13: The meaning given to the phrase "trois temps entiers"—that the canon is to be sung through three times— is incorrect. Had this been the case, the word "foys" rather than "temps" would have been used. The real meaning here is to indicate the distance of the voice entry in canon, "trois temps entiers," or "three full tempora" (*i.e.,* three full bars). Consequently, in the translation on p. 219, the following might be substituted for lines 5 and 6, col. 1.

"After full three breves
You can merrily pursue me."

Page 199, line 18: the figure "253" should read "252."

Page 204, line 36: "alterer" should read "älterer."

INDEX